ISRAEL, A BEACHHEAD IN THE MIDDLE EAST

OTHER BOOKS BY STEPHEN GOWANS

Washington's Long War on Syria (Baraka Books, 2017)

Patriots, Traitors, and Empires. The Story of Korea's Struggle for Freedom (Baraka Books, 2018)

Stephen Gowans

ISRAEL, A BEACHHEAD IN THE MIDDLE EAST

From European Colony to US Power Projection Platform

Baraka
Books

Montréal

© Baraka Books

ISBN 978-1-77186-183-0 pbk; 978-1-77186-193-9 epub; 978-1-77186-194-6 pdf; 978-1-77186-195-3 mobi/pocket

Cover photo: iStock
Book Design by Folio infographie
Editing and proofreading: Barbara Rudnicka, Robin Philpot

Legal Deposit, 2nd quarter 2019

Bibliothèque et Archives nationales du Québec
Library and Archives Canada

Published by Baraka Books of Montreal
6977, rue Lacroix
Montréal, Québec H4E 2V4
Telephone: 514 808-8504
info@barakabooks.com

Printed and bound in Quebec

Trade Distribution & Returns
Canada and the United States
Independent Publishers Group
1-800-888-4741 (IPG1);
orders@ipgbook.com

We acknowledge the support from the Société de développement des entreprises culturelles (SODEC) and the Government of Quebec tax credit for book publishing administered by SODEC.

CONTENTS

INTRODUCTION

> *"The United States has vital strategic interests in the Middle East, and it is imperative that we have a reliable ally whom we can trust, one who shares our goals and values. Israel is the only state in the Middle East that fits that bill."*
>
> Jesse Helms, Chairman of the Senate
> Committee on Foreign Relations, 1995-2001

> *Israel is the West's outpost in the Middle East.*
>
> Benjamin Netanyahu, 1993.[1]

Since the French Revolution, the political Left has embraced the view that human nature is benevolent and capable of progress toward perfection, that the roots of humanity's problems are to be found in its social institutions and not in individuals, and that embodied in the future is the promise of prosperity and relief from dehumanizing toil, freedom from superstition, religion and mythology, and growing social, political and economic equality.

The political Right, by contrast, prefers the status quo or a return to a presumed glorious past, favors hierarchy over equality, promotes religion and mythology over reason, and embraces the conviction that human beings are afflicted by inherent and immutable weaknesses, and that the potential for human progress is, therefore, limited.

For the Jews, two signal events in the history of the political Left were significant: the French Revolution and the Russian Revolution. The French

Revolution, committed to the ideals of human progress, reason and expanded (but by no means universal) equality, emancipated the Jews in France. The Jacobin Maximilien Robespierre insisted on the repeal of all discriminatory laws against the Jewish community. "How can you blame the Jews for the persecutions they have suffered in certain countries?" he asked. "These are, on the contrary, national crimes that we must expiate by restoring to them the imprescriptible rights of man of which no human authority can deprive them...Let us give them back their happiness...and their virtue by restoring their dignity as men and citizens."[2]

The Russian Revolution, which overthrew the Tsarist monarchy—an institution that had treated the Jews as sub-humans, and engineered countless anti-Jewish riots (pogroms)—emancipated the Jews of the Russian Empire. The Tsar's secret police had used anti-Semitism as a weapon against the advancing political Left, relying on the Black Hundreds, an ultranationalist organization—Nazis *avant la lettre*—to shore up flagging support of the Romanov monarchy. Lenin, the Bolshevik leader, commented: "If in a country as cultured as England...it was necessary to behead one crowned brigand in order to teach [subsequent] kings to be 'constitutional' monarchs, then in Russia it is necessary to behead at least one hundred Romanovs to teach their successors not to organize Black Hundred murders and Jewish pogroms."[3]

Jews were vastly over-represented in the movement for equality inaugurated by the French Revolution and extended by the Bolsheviks. They were drawn to the political Left's commitment to freedom from discrimination and its vision of a future of social, political and economic equality.

Political Zionism, a movement to reconstruct 'the glorious past' of Jewish nationhood in Palestine, is a movement of the political Right. Zionism, today, is concretely expressed in the state of Israel, the recreation of an antique Jewish state on land that Old Testament mythology defines as promised to the Jews by their deity.

The father of political Zionism, Theodore Herzl, a non-religious nineteenth century Austrian Jew, was clearly a partisan of the political Right. He saw anti-Semitism, not as a social institution that could be changed, but as a largely incorrigible part of the nature of non-Jews that was resistant to change. In his view, and in the view of Zionists today, anti-Semitism is inhered in human nature—permanent and ineradicable. The only solution to the presumed immutability of anti-Semitism, according to Herzl and his Zionist followers, is Jewish separation—a viewpoint that antici-pates black separatist solutions to the supposed fixity of anti-Black preju-dice and persecution. Accepting Zionism as a legitimate solution to anti-Semitism is tantamount to trying to solve the problem of anti-black racism in the United States by depopulating a section of the African con-tinent by force to make way for the mass migration of US citizens of African origin.

Herzl rejected political equality in favor of aristocracy, was a social Darwinian who believed the triumph of the strong over the weak was desirable, and, like reactionaries before and after him, embraced a return to a 'glorious past'—in his case, to the Jewish state of antiquity.

Herzl sought the backing of colonial powers for his palingenetic pro-ject, offering Zionism as a solution to the challenge posed by the political Left in Europe in exchange for their sponsorship of his plan to colonize Palestine. The Austrian journalist promised that, rather than pursuing revolution in Europe, Jews would settle in the land of the Arabs, a process of exporting Europe's problems to the hinterland. By turning restless pro-letarians into landowners, as the philosopher G. W. F. Hegel had once termed the outcome, the danger of revolution in Europe would be eclipsed through a spatial solution—though at the expense of the natives who would be dispossessed. Labor Zionism, the dominant Herzl-inspired Zionist movement in Palestine until the 1970s, even lent a façade of Leftist legitimacy to the project, promoting agricultural communes and invok-ing Marxist rhetoric. Eventually, Labor Zionism collapsed, incapable of resolving its contradictions. Socialism, with its commitment to universal equality, does not mix with Zionism, with its commitment to Jewish particularism.[4]

Herzl also promised the rulers of imperial Europe that a Jewish state under their sponsorship would protect their interests in the Middle East; it would be an outpost of civilization in what he called a sea of barbarism. The state apparatus of Herzl's political Zionism would become a power projection platform for whatever part of Europe's political Right would sponsor it. The initial sponsor, in the second decade of the twentieth cen-tury, was imperial Britain. Imperial France followed in the sixth decade, providing Israel with the foundation of a nuclear arsenal. Since 1967, the United States, the greatest imperialist power in history, has used Israel in exactly the manner Herzl intended a future Jewish state in Palestine to be used—as a battering ram to knock down all resistance to the domination of the Orient by the Occident.

Not surprisingly, given the origins of its founding ideology, Israel's role in the world has been to advance the interests of the political Right, or, to put it another way, to frustrate the advance of the political Left.

At home, the self-appointed Jewish state—not all Jews support Israel and some take great exception to its speaking for Jews *en bloc*—favors a hierarchy of rights that places Jews, no matter their place of birth, ahead of Arab natives, and promotes mythology over reason, treating the Old Testament as an historical record of actual events. It denies that anti-Semitism is a social institution, and strives energetically to uncover anti-Semitism wherever it can, including where it doesn't exist, while at the same time embracing unambiguous anti-Semites, who share a common abhorrence of the political Left. If hatred and persecution of Jews is a remediable feature of human nature, then the argument for Zionism collapses. Zionists—many of them choosing to live prosperous, comfortable lives outside of Israel in the United States as members of the most successful ethno-religious minority in US history—insist their access to a safe-haven they feel no compulsion to live in must be maintained by the continued dispossession of the Palestinians. If Kant's categorical imperative is that we must treat others as ends in themselves, and not means to our ends, then Zionists have clearly run afoul of the philosopher's maxim.

Abroad, Israel's support for colonial movements has been second to none. The Jewish colonial settler state was an energetic supporter of white supremacist Rhodesia, as well as apartheid South Africa, a state also founded by a self-designated 'chosen people' of European origin, the Afrikaners, similarly imbued with a vision based in religious mythology of a divine right to occupy the land of 'a lesser people.' Israel's current imperialist sponsor, the United States of America, is no less a part of the settler colonial tradition, and of a national mythology of providential guidance. Indeed, one of Israel's pre-eminent historians, Benny Morris, defends his country's dispossession of the Arab natives whose land was expropriated in 1948 to create Israel by reference to the United States. "Even the great American democracy could not have been created without the annihilation of the Indians," he explains.[5] Aisha Fara, a Palestinian, has a message for Morris, and Americans who back his right-wing state: "I want the American pigs to hear: We are not Red Indians!"[6]

On top of supporting the world's right-wing movements, Israel has vigorously opposed the Arab world's major movements of the political Left, all of which have opposed Israel. Israel worked unceasingly to crush secular Arab nationalism, and to undermine the communists who supported it.

The self-appointed Jewish state went to war with Gamal Abdel Nasser, the most popular Arab since the Prophet Mohammed— "an educated revolutionary" who had imbibed "the teachings on equality and freedom of the Koran, Voltaire, and Gandhi, Lenin, Nkurmah, and Trotsky."[7] Nasser undertook a program of agrarian reform in Egypt, the Arab world's most populous country, championed women's rights, supported national liberation movements elsewhere in Africa and West Asia, tried to free Egypt from its economic dependency on the West, pursued the pan-Arab project of bringing the Arab world together into a United Arab States, and inspired such luminaries of the Third World political Left as Nelson Mandela, Fidel Castro and Hugo Chavez.

Antipathetic to all Nasser represented, the state inspired by Herzl went to war with Arab nationalist Egypt twice. The first time was in 1956, in a war known in the Western world as the Suez Crisis, and in the Third World as the Tripartite Aggression—a war of aggression carried out by a triumvirate of Britain, France and Israel. The second time Israel attacked Nasser was in the June 1967 Six Day War, or, from the perspective of the Palestinians, the *Naksa* (Arabic for setback) War, when Israel aggressively and illegally expanded its borders by conquest, absorbing Egypt's Sinai and Gaza Strip, Jordan's West Bank and East Jerusalem, and Syria's Golan Heights. The war, which Israel won handily, was a humiliation for Nasser and a major setback for secular Arab nationalism and the Leftist project it pursued.

Secular Arab nationalism, while greatly weakened in 1967, was not exterminated by its Israeli foe. In 1969, a young Arab colonel, Muammar Gaddafi, seized power in Libya from King Idris I, a monarch imposed on Libyans by the West. While Arabs had worshipped Nasser, perhaps none worshipped him more than Gaddafi. In the immediate aftermath of the Libyan's *coup d'état* against Idris, Gaddafi proposed that he turn power over to Nasser, whose lieutenant he would become.

Secular Arab nationalists in Iraq and Syria ruled under the banner of the Arab Ba'ath Socialist Party. The party was formed from the merger of the Arab Ba'ath (or rebirth) Party and the Arab Socialist Party. The Arab Ba'ath Socialist leader in Iraq, Saddam, aspired to lead his oil-rich country as the Prussia of the Arab world, a reference to the prominent German state which, in 1871, united other German states under its leadership to form a predecessor to today's Germany. Under Saddam's 'Prussian' project, Iraq would act as the lead state among more than a dozen Arab states that had been created by Britain and France to keep the Arabs divided, forging pan-Arab unity. In doing so, the Arabs would overcome the political divisions London and Paris had deliberately imposed on the Arab world to keep it weak. The Iraqi leader had the personal qualities necessary to lead an Iraq that was, on the one hand, fractured by internal schisms hard-baked into it by imperial Britain and, on the other, menaced by the determination of the United States to undermine its Arab socialism (a non-Marxist socialism adapted to the strong conservative Islamic roots of the Arab world). As the Persian Gulf monarchs, quislings to a man, facilitated the flow of the Arab world's oil wealth to the West, Saddam used his country's great petroleum bounty to build what a US State Department adviser called a Golden Age.[8] Importantly, it was a Golden Age for Iraqis, and not in the usual course of affairs a Golden Age for Western investors.

Israel did what it could to contribute to the demise of the Saddam-led secular Arab nationalist project. Its speciality was undermining Saddam's efforts to build an independent arms industry. No country, the Iraqi leader explained, could be truly independent, if it had to rely on other countries for the means to defend itself. Mossad, the Israeli intelligence agency, assassinated the scientists and engineers Baghdad recruited to staff the Iraqi defense industry's R&D arm, and in 1981, while Iraq was distracted by war with Iran, Israel bombed a nuclear reactor at the Iraqi town of Osirak. The reactor was to be the source of fissile material to fuel Iraq's planned military nuclear program, a program that, had it been successful, would have made Iraq virtually invulnerable to the aggressive designs of Washington. The destruction of the reactor spelled the end of Iraq's nuclear program, and cleared the way for US and British forces to control Iraqi airspace throughout the 1990s and invade the oil-rich country in 2003. Thus, Israel played an important and today largely unrecognized role in facilitating the US conquest of Iraq and the destruction of Baghdad as a center of Arab socialism and national assertiveness. The first act of

Paul Bremer, the pro-consul Washington imposed on the conquered Arab state, was to outlaw secular Arab nationalism. The socialist basis of the state was quickly dismantled and the economy restored to private hands and opened to US investors.

Today, secular nationalism, as the ideological foundation of an Arab state, hangs on in Syria alone, 'the Den of Arabism,' or the place in which Arab nationalism (in the view of Syrians) was born. Until the British and French carved it up in the wake of World War I, Syria was a single geographical unit comprising Palestine, Jordan, Lebanon and modern-day Syria. Damascus has an irredentist view of historical Syria, regarding it as a country over which it has an incontestable historical claim. This accounts, in part, for why the Syrian military long maintained a presence in Lebanon. France created Lebanon as an artificial country, severed from Syria, from which the Quai d'Orsay's Christian Maronite ally, whose historical territory was Mount Lebanon, could rule over a Muslim majority. It also accounts, in part, for why the Syrian state has been the unparalleled Arab enemy of Israel. Syria looks at the territory on which Zionists have erected their state in much the same way North Korea looks at South Korea: as stolen territory under occupation by a state that is an instrument of the West. Syria's irredentism also accounts, in part, for Israel's resolute opposition to the country's Arab nationalist leadership.

Israel has waged a long war on the Den of Arabism. To keep its Arab foe weak, the Mossad has assassinated engineers and scientists engaged in research and development for the Syrian military. In 2007, Israeli warplanes destroyed a Syrian nuclear reactor to prevent Syria from breaking Israel's regional monopoly on nuclear arms. Israel provided cash, weapons, ammunition and medical support to jihadists waging a war to overthrow the Assad government in Syria, joining the Saudi monarchy, with which Tel Aviv has a semi-covert partnership, in the project of undermining Arab nationalism in the Levantine state.

Israel has also proved to be a good friend to right-wing Islamists, including the Muslim Brotherhood, the anti-communists who battled the Soviet Union in Afghanistan, as well as al Qaeda and ISIS, offshoots of the organization. The self-appointed Jewish state supported Hamas, which originated from the matrix of the Muslim Brotherhood, as a counterweight to the secular Palestinian Liberation Organization, or PLO, an organization founded by Nasser. Emblematic of Israel's relationship with right-wing Islamism, Michael Oren, a former Israeli ambassador to the United States, told *The Wall Street Journal's* Yaroslav Trofimov in 2016 that if Israel had "to choose between ISIS and [Syria's] Assad, we'll take ISIS."[9]

At the heart of the endless wars in the Middle East lies a single question: Who will control Arab and Persian oil and the routes to and from it—the inhabitants of the region, or Western governments and their local agents acting on behalf of Western investors? As an outpost of the West in the Middle East, the answer of Israel is clear: Western investors. This is the story of how Zionists, seeking to escape anti-Semitism in Europe, rented themselves out to Western powers as mercenaries in a never-ending war to deny Arabs and Iranians their land, markets, labor, and above all, their oil.

CHAPTER ONE

Anti-Semitism

*"Every nation in whose midst Jews live
is either covertly or openly anti-Semitic."*

Theodore Herzl, 1896[1]

From what ideology springs a state that prefers ISIS to secular anti-colonialists, that was among the most vigorous supporters of apartheid South Africa (to the point of offering to sell the country's white supremacist leaders nuclear arms), and that agrees to do the United States' dirty work anywhere in the world?

Zionism antedates Herzl. Indeed, the Austrian journalist's view of Zionism, known today as political Zionism, arose late in Zionism's development. Most Zionists have been either non-Jews, or, like Herzl, Jews who abandoned Judaism as a religion or never practiced it. Max Nordau, one of Herzl's lieutenants, was an atheist.

Early Zionists were Christians, not Jews, and the reality that Zionism has pervaded Christian thought accounts for why the project of returning Jews to Palestine was acceptable to imperialists, many of whom were steeped in Christian Zionism.

Christian—and imperialist—calls for Jews to return to Palestine were made as early as 1799. Visiting Palestine, the French emperor, Napoleon Bonaparte, issued perhaps the first Zionist proclamation, urging Jews to reclaim the Holy Land.[2]

"Until the late nineteenth century, most plans for a Jewish entity in Palestine were Christian," observed Shalom Goldman, a US professor of Hebrew and Biblical Studies. In his 2009 study of Christian and Jewish perspectives on the idea of the Promised Land, *Zeal for Zion*, Shalom writes, "These plans were predicated on the perception that geographical Palestine was the ancient homeland that 'belonged' to Jews. This perception, rooted in a biblical worldview, influenced wide sectors of Christendom,"[3] including, importantly, European and US statesmen.

In 1825, the second US president, John Adams, expressed his hope that the Jews would return to Judea as "an independent nation" with an "independent government, and no longer persecuted, they would soon wear away some of the asperities and peculiarities of their character."[4]

Anticipating left-wing Labor Zionism, Moses Hess wrote a classic early text of political Zionist thought, *Rome and Jerusalem: The Last National Question*. Overshadowed by Herzl's *The Jewish State*, Hess's book set forth a plan for the creation of a socialist Jewish state in Palestine, sponsored by France. Hess would not be the first socialist to propose the establishment of a utopian community whose creation presupposed the dispossession of a native population in the hinterland. Charles Joseph Fourier and Henri de Saint-Simon concocted plans for utopian communities built along socialist lines. Their followers proposed to build socialist communities on land brutally taken from the natives of Algeria.[5]

Viewing favorably the creation of a Jewish state in Palestine as an enterprise that would confer a geopolitical advantage on Britain, the British statesman, Lord Shaftesbury, in 1876 wrote:

> Does not policy… exhort England to foster the nationality of the Jews and aid them, as opportunity may offer, to return as a leavening power to their old country? England is the great trading and maritime power of the world. To England, then, naturally belongs the role of favoring the settlement of the Jews in Palestine. The nationality of the Jews exists: the spirit is there and has been there for 3,000 years, but the external form, the crowning bond of union is still wanting. A nation must have a country. The old land, the old people. This is not an artificial experiment: it is nature, it is history.[6]

In 1891, William Blackstone, a US Christian, petitioned US president Benjamin Harrison to promote the immigration of Russian Jews to Palestine. The petition read:

Why not give Palestine back to them again? According to God's distribution of nations it is their home—an inalienable possession from which they were expelled by force. Under their cultivation it was a remarkably fruitful land, sustaining millions of Israelites, who industriously tilled its hillsides and valleys. They were agriculturists and producers as well as a nation of great commercial importance—the center of civilization and religion.... We believe this is an appropriate time for all nations, and especially the Christian nations of Europe, to show kindness to Israel. A million exiles, by their terrible suffering are piteously appealing to our sympathy, justice, and humanity. Let us now restore to them the land of which they were so cruelly despoiled by our Roman ancestors.[7]

Blackstone sought to facilitate the return of the Jews to Palestine, in order to fulfill what he believed was a necessary precondition for the return of the Christian Messiah. "We might fill a book with comments upon how Israel shall be restored, but all we have desired to do was to show that it is an incontrovertible fact of prophecy, and that it is intimately connected with our Lord's appearing, and this we trust will have satisfactorily accomplished."[8]

Statesmen who favored the creation of a Jewish state in Palestine were pious Christians who, like Blackstone, believed that a precondition of Christ's Second Coming was the return of the Jews to the Holy Land. Arthur Koestler, the Hungarian-British author and journalist, noted that the Western statesmen who supported political Zionism "were Bible lovers. They were profoundly attracted by the Old Testament echoes which the Zionist movement carried."[9]

For example, British foreign secretary Lord Arthur James Balfour—one of the most consequential figures in the creation of Israel and dispossession of Palestine's native Arabs—was a devout Christian who believed that British support for a Jewish homeland in Palestine, promulgated in the eponymous Balfour Declaration, was the fulfillment of biblical prophesy which brought closer the return of Christ.[10]

US president Woodrow Wilson was no less a pious follower of Christ, perhaps "the most Christian president the U.S. has ever had," and also an ardent Zionist. The "son and grandson of Presbyterian ministers," Wilson "prayed on his knees twice a day and read the Bible every night."[11] Wilson favored a Jewish Palestine and supported Balfour's declaration.[12] The devout Christian appointed the first Jew to the Supreme Court, Louis Brandeis. Brandeis led the Zionist movement in the United

States, at a time few Jews adhered to it, but many Christians sympathized with it.

Importantly, as J. L. Talmon, a Jewish anti-Marxist observed, "Zionism would never have had a chance of success if centuries of Christian teaching and worship, liturgy and legend had not conditioned the Western nations to respond almost instinctively to the words 'Zion' and 'Israel,' and thus to see in the Zionist ideal not a romantic chimera or an imperialistic design to wrest a country from its actual inhabitants, but the consummation of an eternal promise and hope."[13]

It could be said that non-Jews established the conditions that made the political Zionism of Herzl possible. Christian eschatology made the idea of a Jewish return to the Promised Land acceptable to the Christian political elite of Europe and America. Nationalism, originating in European thought, mixed with anti-Semitism, defined Jews as a people. It followed from this that a people needed a territory on which to found a state. The reality that Jews were Europeans offered the tantalizing prospect of exporting an Occidental community to the Orient as a Western imperialist outpost capable of protecting and advancing European economic, political and military interests.

Anti-Semitism, as a tool of the political Right, found an early expression in the conservative reaction against the French Revolution. The uprising against French feudalism, reviled throughout Europe by established authority, was seen as a project secretly orchestrated by the Jews. The idea of revolution, or more broadly, of challenges to the established order by the political Left as a conspiracy of the Jews, has a hoary history. The identification of Jewry with Bolshevism and with Bolshevism's French revolutionary predecessors, was not Hitler's invention. "It was the common property of a whole literature from Henry Ford to Otto Hauser,"[14] noted the Italian philosopher Domenico Losurdo, and reached back earlier still. Hitler was only the culmination of a long tradition, the end point, not the beginning.

Martin Luther, the sixteenth century German theologian, a principal figure of the Protestant Reformation and father of the Lutheran Church, saw peasant uprisings against the feudal order as a Jewish conspiracy.

Joseph de Maistre, Louis Gabriel Ambroise, Vicomte de Bonald, and Sir Edmund Burke, eighteenth century giants of the political Right, located the origins of the French Revolution in a Jewish conspiracy.[15] This view was seconded by the nineteenth century German philosopher Friedrich Nietzsche, a favorite of the political Right. Jews, Nietzsche insisted, agitated the people and incited revolutions.[16]

Anti-Jewish riots were incited by right-wing Tsarist forces following the 1905 revolution in Russia—a revolution that challenged the Russian monarchy and threatened to topple it. It was a dress rehearsal for the revolutions of 1917, including the March revolution which toppled the Tsar and the October revolution that brought the Bolsheviks to power. "Jews in Russia," wrote Losurdo, "tended to be identified with the subversive intellectuals plotting revolutions or conspiracies in the shadows,"[17] and were blamed by the political Right for both the 1905 and 1917 revolutions. Conservative Russians "laid the blame for their country's troubles on materialist ideas and on the Jews, who were accused of inventing and manipulating these ideas for their own benefit," according to the historian Arno J. Mayer.[18] But it was not only Russian conservatives who saw a Jewish hand in the Tsar's overthrow. So too did US industrialist Henry Ford, and British statesman and future prime minister Winston Churchill, both of whom were concerned with a phenomenon that would equally agitate the mind of Adolph Hitler—the 'international Jew.'[19]

Following the Bolshevik Revolution, a civil war broke out in Russia, in which the political Right once again set upon its favored target, the Jews. So too were Jews targeted by right-wing forces after the collapse of the Austro-Hungarian Empire at the end of the First World War. In both cases, Jews were reviled and attacked "for allegedly being in the vanguard of social and political radicalism and being inconstant in their national loyalties,"[20] Mayer observed.

In France, right-wing fascist movements *avant la lettre* declared a 'holy war' on the French republic, the creation of the left-wing French Revolution, and advocated a return to a presumed glorious past, before Jacobin ideas of equality had taken hold. They threatened to drown Parliament in the Seine, and saw Jews operating in the shadows as the architects of the movement toward universal equality.[21]

It was Lenin, a non-Jew, inspired by the thinking of "the Jew, Karl Marx," as Hitler would call him, who extended the concept of humanity to include all races. More than the question of reform versus revolution, Leninism is distinguished from orthodox Marxism by its universalization of the concept of equality. Leninism is a theory of universal emancipation that speaks to all people, regardless of national borders and differences in race and gender. Lenin linked the struggle of the Western working class to be recognized as equal and fully human (and therefore to be free from servitude) with the struggle of 'inferior' races and women for the same. In other words, he identified the struggles against white supremacy, male supremacy, and bourgeois supremacy, as, not separate and unrelated movements, but as inter-related and indissolubly connected. All of these struggles were different aspects of the fight to overcome the supremacy of white, male, property-owners, or more broadly, to overcome inequality. The Italian Marxist leader and thinker, Antonio Gramsci, argued that Leninism is the expression of the universal concept of equality inherent in liberalism but not actualized by it. The march of Marxism-Leninism, then, is the march toward the realization of the process of emancipation that liberalism leaves unfinished.[22]

Benjamin Beit-Hallahmi, an Israeli psychologist who has written critically on Zionism and Israel, observed that it was universal equality that led Jews to radicalism. Jews have been highly attracted to left-wing movements, especially Lenin's communist movement.[23] Because Jews have been treated so pervasively through time and space as aliens, many have quite naturally embraced movements that seek to build a world in which all people are accepted as fully human and equal and all institutions of supremacy, including those based on class, religion, ethnicity, and gender, among others, are overcome. The parallel in the Middle East is the strong attraction of marginal groups, the Alawites and Kurds, for example, to such movements as Arab Ba'ath Socialism and communism, which promote ethno-religious equality. The Islamist nationalism of Iran, can also be seen in this light, as a movement attractive to Shias, because it envisions a world of sectarian equality in which the persecution of the Shia Muslim minority by the Sunni Muslim majority is overcome. Jews, categorized as members of an alien nation, and therefore discriminated against, quite naturally gravitated to movements that aimed to abolish ethno-religious origin as a basis for discrimination. For Jews, as well as for all other marginalized or subordinate groups, the political Left, especially that part of it committed to universal equality, was seen as an instrument of emancipation.

Jews have been very strongly over-represented among revolutionaries. Indeed, the history of radical socialism pullulates with secular Jewish figures, not all of them Marxist-Leninists to be sure, but all committed to universal equality. The list includes: Kurt Eisner, the premier of the Bavarian Socialist Republic at the end of WWI; Gustav Landauer, Eisner's education minister; the Polish-German Marxist Rosa Luxemburg, a founder of the German Communist Party; Bela Kun, leader of a short-lived Soviet republic in Hungary at the end of WWI; George Lukacs, the republic's education minister, and later an illustrious Marxist scholar; Matyas Rakosi, the leader of communist Hungary after 1948; the American anarchists Emma Goldman and Noam Chomsky; and members of Lenin's inner circle, including Trotsky, Zinoviev, Kamenev, and Radek.[24]

According to Herzl, half of the members of revolutionary parties in Russia prior to 1917 were Jews.[25] "Between 1930 and the end of the Second World War, Jews made up almost half of the membership of the Communist Party of the United States,"[26] wrote Beit-Hallahmi. He added: "The majority of American whites who took part in the civil rights struggle of the early 1960s were Jewish. They made up two-thirds of the Freedom Riders in the [US] South in 1961, and between one-half and two-thirds of the volunteers in the Mississippi Summer of 1964. Even in communist parties in the Arab countries of Egypt and Iraq, Jews were founders and leaders. Jews are still overrepresented in radical left-wing groups all over the world."[27]

Jews gravitated to the most radical left-wing movements because they were often rejected by those moderate parts of the political Left that were more acceptable to the established order. Anti-Semitism could be found here and there in the socialist movement, but it was virtually absent among communists. Owing to their secularism and commitment to international solidarity and universal equality, communists were intolerant of anti-Semitism and welcomed Jews, as they welcomed all people, nations and ethnic groups.[28]

Because most Jews had abandoned Judaism, and, as a consequence, had a secular outlook, they also fit quite comfortably into secular, atheist communist parties. What's more, because they had been defined by the larger societies in which they lived as aliens, they were unlikely to have strong national attachments to the ethnic majority of the countries in which they lived, and accepted communist internationalism easily, seeing themselves less as citizens of ethnic-nation-states and more as citizens of the world.[29]

The attraction of Jews to communist internationalism was the root of Hitler's anti-Semitism and origin of the concept of Judeo-Bolshevism—the idea that Bolshevism was a Jewish conspiracy. For Hitler, nation and the great German Volk, were everything. But his views were out of vogue with the German proletariat. From Hitler's point of view, German workers, under the influence of Jewish socialists, saw the nation as a bourgeois creation intended to facilitate the exploitation and control of workers. Germany's proletarians weren't identifying with Germany as a people imbued with a manifest destiny, but instead, saw the German nation as divided along class lines. Rather than lining up to fight the race war—the war of nations for survival in a great social Darwinian struggle among peoples—they were lining up to fight the class war. Who else but the Jews, without commitments to the ethnic majorities of the nation states in which they lived, could be behind this? And wasn't Karl Marx, the great champion of the class war, a Jew?

The US industrialist Henry Ford, founder of the Ford Motor company, was an early champion of the Judeo-Bolshevik theory, and an inspiration for Hitler and other Nazi leaders. Ford founded a newspaper, *The Dearborn Independent*, to propagate his ideas about 'the international Jew' and to mobilize opposition to revolutionary movements as instruments of a Jewish conspiracy. Ford assembled his major newspaper articles into a volume titled *The International Jew*, locating the source of Marxist-Leninist internationalism in the absent ethnic-national affiliations of rootless Jewry. SS leader Heinrich Himmler credited his understanding of the 'the Jewish danger' to his reading of Ford's book. Ford's rallying cry against the 'Judeo-Bolshevik' danger was published in the Third Reich with much fanfare.[30] Hitler admired Ford, and conferred on him the Grand Cross of the German Eagle, an accolade bestowed on prominent foreigners who supported Nazism.

In 1920, a document was published in London and Paris claiming to offer hard proof of a Jewish conspiracy to overthrow capitalism, abolish Christianity, and establish an international state—in other words, to undertake a vaguely Marxist-Leninist-style project. The book was entitled *The Jewish Peril*, and was a translation from Russian of *The Protocols of the Learned Elders of Zion*, purportedly a record of secret *fin de siècle* meetings of Jews and Freemasons.[31]

The Protocols had been published in Russia in 1903 in newspapers and two years later in book form. Sergei Nilus, an official of the Tsarist government, was said to have discovered them. Nobody paid much attention to the Protocols until the Bolshevik Revolution of late 1917. People on the political Right, long accustomed to using anti-Semitism as a weapon against the political Left, started to point out similarities between the conspiracy described in the Protocols and the alleged aims of the new Bolshevik government. Jews were vastly over-represented among communists, and the Bolshevik program seemed suspiciously close to the Protocols' planned overthrow of capitalism. This was enough to label Bolshevism a Jewish conspiracy to destroy Western civilization and overturn the established order.[32]

In this view, the Bolsheviks were seen neither as Russians or purveyors of a left-wing ideology, but as secret agents of a Jewish plot to take over the world. British officials regarded Lenin and his followers as agents of a clandestine Jewish scheme. The British novelist John Buchan, who headed the agency that controlled public information services for Britain's WWI government, wrote a novel, *The Thirty-Nine Steps*, which reinforced the British government view that Jews lurked in the shadows manipulating international affairs. "Away behind all the governments and the armies there was a big subterranean movement going on," he wrote, "engineered by very dangerous people...[T]he Jew was behind it, and the Jew hated Russia worse than hell...[T]his is the return match for the pogroms. The Jew is everywhere... with an eye like a rattlesnake.... [H]e is the man who is ruling the world just now."[33]

Mark Sykes, the British diplomat whose name lives in infamy in the Arab world as co-author, along with his French counterpart, François Georges-Picot, of a secret pact to carve up Arab West Asia, never abandoned his childhood belief in a shadowy cabal of Jews who moved in mysterious ways to control world affairs. One of Syke's professors claimed Sykes saw Jews in everything.[34]

Belief in a Jewish world conspiracy was no less present in France. The top French official in Syria, Robert de Caix, saw in Bolshevism "the revolutionary and prophetic spirit which is so often found among Jews." France's Catholic missionaries were alarmed. Bolshevism, in their view, was merely a front for a Jewish world conspiracy to destroy Christianity.[35]

US officials also saw confirmation of their beliefs in the Protocols. Alan Dulles, a fervent anti-communist who, along with his brother, John Foster Dulles, would plot anti-Soviet strategy as leaders respectively of the post World War II CIA and US State Department, was a US diplomat in Europe when *The Jewish Peril* was published. Dulles found the alleged Jewish conspiracy so compelling that he sent "a coded report about the secret 'Jewish' plot back to his superiors in Washington."[36]

"It was in this context," wrote David Fromkin, whose book, *A Peace to End All Peace*, recalls the role of the Great Powers in shaping the post-World War I Middle East, that the Bolshevik "Revolution was seen by British officials as the latest manifestation of a bigger conspiracy. Jews were prominent among the Bolshevik leaders; so the Bolshevik seizure of power was viewed by many within the British government as... Jewish-directed."[37] Indeed, British intelligence believed that Bolshevism was an instrument of a cabal of Jewish financiers with no national allegiances who were machinating to bring about a world government under their leadership[38] —a view fully shared by Hitler!

In the summer of 1921, a correspondent for *The Times*, based in Constantinople, Philip Graves, revealed that the Protocols were a forgery, invented by none other than the source of countless other anti-Semitic slurs—the Tsarist secret police.[39] Fromkin wrote that, "While in the clear light of history this conspiracy theory seems absurd to the point of lunacy, it was believed either in whole or in part by large numbers of otherwise sane, well-balanced, and reasonably well-informed British officials."[40] It was also believed by Hitler. His views were hardly unique, and, on the contrary, meshed quite comfortably with the thought of his contemporaries of the political Right—Winston Churchill, officials of Whitehall and the Quai D'Orsay, Alan Dulles, Henry Ford, Mark Sykes, and others. Hence, the identification of Jewry with Bolshevism was not Hitler's invention; it was, rather, the common property of the Western establishment.[41] Indeed, the association of Jews with radical movements of the Left, as we have seen, has a long lineage, extending back to Luther. Herzl, himself, acknowledged this, pointing out that the Jews "are blamed for socialism, like everything else."[42] Hitler, inheriting this idea, and carrying it forward, defined Jews as the carriers of a Marxist 'plague,' which threatened all of Western civilization, and which therefore needed to be exterminated. As the presumed carriers of the 'plague,' Jews transfixed him.

Interestingly, the anti-Semitism that developed in reaction to the Bolshevik Revolution, characterized the Jews as alien to the West, and part of the East. Bolshevism was defined by the political Right as a doctrine arising from the realm of barbarism. Syllogistically, it followed that if Bolshevism was both a barbaric doctrine and a conspiracy of the Jews, then Jews must be a barbaric people. The Nazis used the adjective Eastern, as in 'Eastern Bolshevism,' to identify communism as a doctrine alien to the Western world, and to associate it with Jewry by identifying Moscow as the 'Semitic-Hebrew headquarters of the Near East.' By contrast, a Jewish state in Palestine has always been envisaged by Zionists, from Herzl to the Israeli prime minister Benjamin Netanyahu, as an outpost of Western civilization in the East and as a Western state. The Arabs, by contrast, are located in the realm of barbarism, as the Jews were when anti-Semitism was a useful tool of the political Right for combating a radical Leftist challenge to the established order.[43]

On February 8, 1920, Winston Churchill, at the time British Secretary of State for Air in the Lloyd George government, wrote an article in the *Illustrated Sunday Herald*, titled "Zionism versus Bolshevism: A Struggle for the Soul of the Jewish People." Therein Churchill set out a theory of the Judeo-Bolshevik menace, which the Nazis would borrow from the right-wing doctrines of the time, and feature prominently in their ideology. For the future British prime minister, some Jews were good, and some were bad. Churchill identified the bad Jews as "the international Jew," the bane of every conservative and reactionary from Burke to Hitler. All other Jews—those who preoccupied themselves with banking and industry, or migrating to Palestine rather than seeking, from their European homes, to bring about a world of universal equality—were good.

The international Jew, argued Churchill, is a member of "a sinister confederacy" which incites rebellions against the established order. The confederacy is not new, but stretches back to Karl Marx, and includes Trotsky, Radek, Zinoviev, Bela Kun, Rosa Luxemburg, and Emma

Goldman. According to the future British prime minister, the international Jew guides "a worldwide conspiracy for the overthrow of civilization and for the reconstitution of society on the basis of... impossible equality." Echoing his reactionary predecessors, Churchill added that the international Jew had played a definitely recognizable part in the French Revolution, a blow against aristocracy and landed privilege, which Churchill, the Duke of Marlborough, denounced as "a tragedy." The International Jew, continued the British aristocrat, "has been the mainspring of every subversive movement" and "the predominance of Jews" in the Soviet government was "astonishing." Churchill conceded that there were many non-Jews in revolutionary movements, but that "the part played by" Jews "in proportion to their numbers in the population" was significant.

The language and argument Churchill used would have fit quite comfortably in *Mein Kampf*, which Hitler would publish four years later. In his autobiography, the Nazi leader spent much time musing about the predominance of Jews in radical movements of the political Left, and invoking established reactionary theories about the hidden hand of the Jews lurking behind every rebellion. He also undertook an examination of the question of whether Jews constitute a race, or a religious community, concluding that they form a race, about which more later. Churchill agreed, accepting as a matter of fact, that Jews were a race separate from the people in whose lands they dwelled. This implied that the British comprised the people of Britain—the English, the Scots, the Welsh—but not British Jews, who were an alien race.

Churchill's purpose in defining Jews as a distinct race at the center of a conspiracy to overthrow Western civilization is clear. He was attempting to discredit the Bolsheviks by portraying them as aliens in pursuit of a hidden, sinister agenda, rather than as an instrument of a disaffected Russian population. The context is important. Churchill was writing soon after the Bolsheviks came to power. A 'Red Scare' was sweeping the West. In cabinet rooms throughout North America and Western Europe, politicians worried that Red revolution was about to knock at their doors. Defining Bolshevism—a movement for universal equality—as an instrument of a Jewish conspiracy, was a way of discrediting the interconnected struggles for equality that had come to the fore at the end of World War I—the struggles for female suffrage, for Ireland's freedom and for decolonization more broadly, and for an end to exploitation. By defining Jews as an alien race and the struggle for universal equality as Jewish-led, Churchill's intent (and we can include Hitler in this too) was to cast the struggle for equality as originating, not in the aspirations of subordinate groups to be accepted as fully human, but in the sinister machinations of a foreign cabal.

Arguments of this sort die hard, and have a tendency to recrudesce in an altered form. From 2011 forward, Western journalists aped an argument put forward by politicized Sunni Islam, that the Arab Ba'ath Socialist doctrine of the Syrian government was not an authentic ideology of anti-colonialism and social reform but an instrument of an Alawite minority to rule Syria's Sunni majority.

In Syria, class and sect were highly correlated. As a consequence, minority sects, such as those of the Alawites, were disproportionally drawn to a party that championed a society free from discriminations of sect and class. Conservative Sunnis took a page from Churchill's (and Hitler's) book. If the two European reactionaries could point out the predominance of Jews in the communist movement to advance the argument that revolutionary socialism was in fact a Jewish conspiracy for world domination, so too could conservative Sunnis point out the predominance of Alawites in the Arab Ba'ath Socialist party to advance the argument that secular Arab socialism was in fact an Alawite conspiracy to dominate Syria's Sunni majority.

Churchill juxtaposed the international Jew and its subset, the "terrorist Jew" (by which he meant the leading figures of the Bolshevik Revolution), with a group he considered altogether more commendable: the nationalist Jew, or Zionist, who was taking advantage of the opportunity secured by the British government to build "a home and a center of national life" and a "Jewish State under the protection of the British Crown" on "the banks of the Jordan" in "harmony with the truest interests of the British Empire." Zionism, Churchill argued, "directs the energies and the hopes of Jews in every land towards a simpler, a truer, and a far more attainable goal" than does the Bolshevik quest for all the desiderata of the political Left: progress over tradition, equality over hierarchy, rationalism over religion. Clearly, Churchill saw in Zionism the possibility of a bulwark against communism.

Churchill closed his article with an appeal that anticipated George W. Bush's demand in the wake of the attacks on New York and Washington of September 11, 2001, that people and states choose a side: "Either you're with us or against us," Bush announced. Muslims in the United States were pressured to condemn the attacks, attributed to Arab political Islamists, for fear of being accused of disloyalty. Similarly, in the wake of the Bolshevik Revolution, in a climate of the Red Scare, Churchill demanded that Jews choose sides: either they were with the West, or with the "terrorist Jews." The future prime minister wrote, "It is particularly important in these circumstances that the national Jews in every country who are loyal to the land of their adoption should come forward on every occasion, as many of them in England have already done, and take a prominent part in every measure for combating the Bolshevik conspiracy. In this way they will be able to vindicate the honor of the Jewish name and make it clear to all the world that the Bolshevik movement is not a Jewish movement, but is repudiated vehemently by the great mass of the Jewish race."

All the same, concluded Churchill, "a negative resistance to Bolshevism" was not enough; Jews needed to do more. They should build "up with the utmost possible rapidity a Jewish national center in Palestine." That is, Jews, the carriers of the Marxist contagion, should get out of Europe as rapidly as possible, and devote their energies to their "own tribe" rather than trying to bring about a world of 'impossible" equality in Russia, Britain, France and Germany.

"Jewish radicals"— the Leftists Hitler deplored for undermining the attachment of German workers to the Volk, the 'conspirators' the anti-revolutionary theorists attributed momentous revolutions to, and the 'terrorists' Churchill denounced for their devotion to equality—stood apart from the national Jew. As Beit-Hallahmi observed, they "refused to limit their concerns to their own tribe. Theirs was a grander, purer dream. Salvation not just for Jews, but for the whole of humanity, and that would eliminate the ills of the Jewish condition once and for all."[44]

CHAPTER TWO

Zionism

*"The movement...cannot even be carried out without the
friendly intervention of interested Governments, who would
derive considerable benefits from it."*

Theodor Herzl, 1896[1]

Herzl wrote two books expositing his views on political Zionism. The first, *The Jewish State*, published in 1896, presents an outline of a plan for the development of a state for his co-religionists in the East. The second, *Old New Land*, published in 1902, imagines a Jewish state in Palestine. The second book is written in the form of a utopian novel in the vein of William Morris's *News from Nowhere* and Edward Bellamy's *Looking Backward*. Herzl's novel, however, was fundamentally different in an important way. Whereas the utopian novels of Morris and Bellamy imagined a glorious socialist future, Herzl envisaged a return to an imagined glorious past. In his novel, Herzl's political Zionist movement obtains a charter from the Turkish government, under whose dominion Palestine then fell, to establish a colony in Palestine. Jews migrate from Europe *en masse*, bringing Western civilization to Palestine. Western technique and know-how redeem a barren and neglected land, fallen into decrepitude under the backwardness of its Arab inhabitants. Everyone is happy: the Jews, who escape the blight of European anti-Semitism; Europe's gentiles, who are relieved of the presence of a 'hated' alien race; and Europe's rulers, who are finally rid of the Jews who orchestrated every rebellion against them.

Anti-Semitism is the alpha and omega of the Zionist movement. The movement holds that hatred of Jews and their persecution is inevitable; it is part of the human condition, and cannot be changed. The ideas of the political Left, that human progress toward perfection is possible, and that anti-Semitism can be overcome, are, in the Zionist creed, naïve dreams. The solution to anti-Semitism is not the radical Leninist vision of universal equality, but the Zionist project of relocating the *shtetl* to Palestine.

Herzl clearly rejected the view that anti-Semitism was a remediable problem. "Were we to wait till average humanity had become... charitably inclined... we would wait beyond our day, beyond the days of our children, or our grandchildren and our great-grandchildren,"[2] he wrote. True, he conceded, "there was a period of enlightenment" when the French Revolution emancipated the Jews, but "that enlightenment," he added, "reached in reality only the choicest spirits."[3] A "change in the current feeling" of ubiquitous anti-Semitism cannot be hoped for.[4] Clearly, Herzl's view that anti-Semitism comes from within individuals, and does not come from the social order and is not learned, places him firmly in the tradition of the political Right.

Anti-Semitism, which Herzl dubbed the "Jewish question," exists "wherever Jews live in perceptible numbers. Where it does not exist, it is carried by Jews in the course of their migrations,"[5] Herzl believed. Persecution drives Jews to new lands, and in those new lands their presence reproduces the persecution of the lands they left behind. Wherever Jews settle, they suffer. "This is the case in every country," argued Herzl *"and will remain so"* (emphasis added) "even in the most highly civilized."[6] That, then, is the Jewish problem: permanent and irremediable anti-Semitism.

Anti-Semitism, Herzl insisted, "is impossible to escape." And anyone who says otherwise is a "soft-hearted" visionary, who believes that "the ultimate perfection of humanity" is "possible." Herzl rejected as naïve the political Left view that humans can embrace equality. Humans are inherently corrupt and will forever remain so. Anyone "who would found this hope for improved conditions on the ultimate perfection of humanity, would indeed be painting a Utopia!"[7]

Zionism, then, is a profoundly pessimistic doctrine which holds that mankind is evil and corrupt by nature, not by circumstance, and that social institutions are products of an immutable and tenebrous human nature. The ideas of the Enlightenment, of universal equality and amity, are but soft-hearted utopian ideals. "Universal brotherhood," the goal of the Marxist movement, was "not even a beautiful dream,"[8] Herzl wrote, but an illusion. The hard, cold, reality was that a war of all against all was permanent and at the root of the human condition.

Herzl's conservative views are further revealed in his preference for what Hitler would later celebrate as "the aristocratic principle."[9] "I am a staunch supporter of monarchical institutions," wrote the Zionist, "because these allow of a consistent policy, and represent the interests of a historically famous family born and educated to rule, whose desires are bound up with the preservation of the state."[10] "Unlimited democracy," in his view, was to be avoided because it "produces that objectionable class of men, professional politicians." Democracy would allow rabble rousers to sway the "masses" who would "be led away by heterodox opinions," making it "impossible to formulate a wise internal or external policy."[11] No, the masses were unfit to govern. "Politics," Herzl insisted, "must take shape in the upper strata and work downwards."[12]

Hitler had similar views. Like Herzl, he mistrusted the masses, who he saw as lacking in "powers of comprehension"[13] and who he thought were all too easily swayed by the rhetoric of politicians.[14] To the Nazi leader, the "broad masses of the people are… but a vacillating crowd of human children who are constantly wavering between one idea and another" and whose "thought and conduct are ruled by sentiment rather than sober reasoning."[15] Condemning democracy, Hitler wrote: "Nowadays when the voting papers of the masses are the deciding factor, the decision lies in the hands of the numerically strongest group… the crowd of simpletons and the credulous."[16] For Hitler, democracy replaces rule by the wise with rule by "the dunderheaded multitude,"[17] and therefore must be rejected.

In line with his preference for hierarchy, Herzl outlined in *Old New Land* a society that is marked by sharp social cleavages. Servants, depicted as "negroes,"[18] attend to the domestic needs of the novel's main characters. And the poor exist, because poverty, Herzl informs us, is part of human nature, and cannot be changed,[19] a highly conservative view, comporting with the equally pessimistic Zionist belief in permanent and incorrigible anti-Semitism.

At the core of Zionism is the question of how to acquire territory on which to settle Europe's Jews. In Herzl's day, various projects had already arisen, in Argentina and Palestine, of a gradual influx of Jews. Jews in small numbers had migrated to these lands and established colonies. Territorial Zionists, the advocates of this project, hoped to gradually build an ever larger community, that, one day, would constitute a majority of the territory's population. The plan, Herzl augured, was bound to end in disaster. There would come "the inevitable moment when the native population" would feel "itself threatened," and force "the Government to stop further influx of Jews."[20] Of course, he was right. This is exactly what happened in Palestine, where during the years between the First and Second World Wars, as Jews flowed into British-ruled Palestine, the native population grew increasingly alarmed and restive, and importuned British authorities to halt the influx of Jews to whom London had promised the Arabs' land as a homeland. The Arabs hated the immigrant Jews, not because they were Jews, but because they were usurpers. The natives of Palestine foresaw the loss of their country as the inevitable outcome of Jewish migration to Palestine. The British promise of a home for the Jews in the Holy Land, however, fell short of what Herzl insisted was vital to his project: assured political supremacy.[21] The Balfour Declaration, the document that formalized the British promise, was not the fruition of Herzl's project; it did not confer political supremacy over Palestine upon nationalist Jews. This, the Zionists would have to take for themselves by force, which they did in 1948, after the United Nations proposed a year earlier that Palestine be partitioned into Jewish and Arab states.

The land question, in Herzl's thinking, needed to be "a political world-question to be discussed and controlled by the civilized nations of the world in council."[22] One or more Great Powers, which, at the time, had almost entirely divided the world among themselves, would need to be enlisted as sponsors of the project. But they would not grant the new Maccabees territory on which to restore the Jewish state of antiquity without expecting to receive an advantage in return. "The movement" Herzl argued, needs "the friendly intervention of interested Governments," and that in turn meant showing that they would "derive considerable benefits from it."[23]

There is no doubt that Herzl regarded the Zionist project as colonialism. He compared Jews who would migrate *en masse* to Palestine, with the "Puritans, persecuted for their religious beliefs, [who had] colonized North America." He likened Jews settling in Palestine to Christian Europeans who had settled in South Africa, India and Australia.[24] Indeed, in his utopian novel, Herzl envisaged the 'old-new land' coming to life under the stewardship of an organization called "The New Society for the Colonization of Palestine." Herzl imagined Jewish colonizers invested by the Turkish government with a charter giving them "autonomous rights to the regions which" they "were to colonize."[25] In *The Jewish State*, Herzl acknowledged readily that Zionism aims "to solve the Jewish problem through colonization on a large scale."[26]

Herzl's European colonial ideology is never more evident than in a discussion on Africa he imagines between two characters in his novel. The vast continent is described as an enormous area "available for the surplus population of Europe," providing a "healthy outlet" for the otherwise revolutionary energies of Europe's "proletarian masses."[27] But not only is Africa conceived as a solution to the dangers of revolution in Europe, it is also presented as a way to rid the United States of what Herzl calls its "negro problem."[28] The Zionist pioneer regarded the black populations of the Americas as equivalent to the Jewish population of Europe. Both were persecuted. And both could escape their persecution by returning to the soil from which their ancestors sprang.

> There is [another] problem of racial misfortune unsolved. The depths of that problem, in all [its] horror, only a Jew can fathom. I mean the negro problem. … Think of the hair-raising horrors of the slave trade. Human beings, because their skins are black, are stolen, carried off, and sold. Their descendants grow up in alien surroundings despised and hated because their skin is differently pigmented.[29]

The solution to this horror—the horror of anti-Hamitism—paralleled the Zionist solution to anti-Semitism: "restoration of the Negroes" to Africa.[30]

Marcus Garvey, a Jamaican of African origin who lived in the United States, championed a view which comported with the theory Herzl sketched in *Old New Land*. Garvey believed that white Americans would never accept black Americans as equals. The solution to what he believed would be the permanent, inevitable subordination and persecution of blacks, lay, he advocated, in separation and a return to Africa.[31] Garvey's movement enjoyed little success, mainly because few black Americans were interested in migrating to the continent from which their ancestors came. Black Americans of the political Left, in contrast to Garvey, proposed that blacks fight for racial equality and integration at home. This, they did, with the assistance of their white comrades, including a prominent cohort of 'internationalist' Jews. Garvey, not surprisingly, favored the separatist doctrine of the 'nationalist' Jew to the integrationist doctrine of the 'internationalist' Jew, and on 'the Jewish question' supported "the determination of the Jew to recover Palestine."[32]

〜

It is often said that Zionists justified their colonization of Palestine with the argument that the territory was "a land without people for a people without land." This is nonsense. Herzl did not regard Palestine as a devoid of inhabitants. In *Old New Land*, his alter-ego Friedrich Loewenberg, travels to Jaffa and Jerusalem and clearly sees that the land is teeming with poor "Turks, dirty Arabs and timid Jews."

Loewenberg encounters Palestine as "backward," "forsaken," "decrepit," "neglected," "miserable," "tomblike," "malodorous," "dirty" and "hopeless." Jerusalem, to which he travels on a "miserable railway," is portrayed as a once-great city reduced to ruins under the tutelage of the Arabs. The landscape through which he passes is "a picture of desolation." The lowlands are "mostly sand and swamp." The "lean fields look as if burnt over."[33] "The inhabitants of the blackish Arab villages" look "like brigands. Naked children" play "in the dirty alleys. The hills of Judea are deforested. "The bare slopes and the bleak, rock valleys" show "few traces of present or former cultivation."[34] As for the Arabs themselves, they're described as people who live in "clay hovels unfit for stables"[35] in "wretched" villages[36] that contain "filthy nests,"[37] where their "children lay naked and neglected in the streets, and" grow "up like dumb beasts."[38] Loewenberg laments: "If this is our land…it has declined like our people."[39]

Herzl contrasts the Arab Palestine of poverty, filth, decay and neglect with the Palestine of "Jewish settlements," the actual project of the "Lovers of Zion," territorial Zionists of the day, who promoted Jewish immigration to Palestine as farmers. After his depressing visit to poverty-stricken and decaying Jerusalem, Loewenberg "drove out to the colonies," Jewish villages that "lay like oases in the desolate countryside." "Many industrious hands must have worked here to restore fertility to the soil," observed Herzl. The fields were "well-cultivated," the vineyards "stately" and the orange groves "luxuriant."

Herzl, thus, did not view the colonization of Palestine as a project to fill an empty land, but as a *mission civilisatrice*, a program of conferring the benefits of Western civilization on what he saw as the backward and inferior people of the Middle East. European Jews would be the "heralds of technical civilization in the Orient."[40] One of the novel's Arab characters, Reschid Bey, understands "the beneficent character of Jewish immigration."[41] "Were not the older inhabitants of Palestine ruined by the Jewish immigration?" Bey is asked. "What a question!" the Arab exclaims. "It was a great blessing for all of us."[42]

"You're queer fellows, you Moslems," remarks a visitor to Herzl's imagined Jewish utopia. "Don't you regard these Jews as intruders?" Perish the thought, rejoins Bey. "Would you call a man a robber who takes nothing from you, but brings you something instead? The Jews have enriched us. Why should we be angry with them? They dwell among us like brothers."[43]

Herzl clearly held the Arabs in contempt. He invoked one obloquy after another to portray them as a backward, dirty, noisome, and indolent, little more than "dumb beasts," who had allowed the imagined glorious Palestine of the past to fall into ruin and neglect. In his view, they were a people unfit to rule the land. His revulsion at their alleged filth and fetidness is an anti-Semitism of another stripe, not one of odium directed at the Jews but at their Semitic cousins, the Arabs. For how different are Herzl's descriptions of the Arabs of Palestine from those of Hitler of the Jews of Vienna? "Cleanliness… had its own peculiar meaning for these people," Hitler wrote in reference to the Jews.

> That they were water-shy was obvious on looking at them and, unfortunately, very often also when not looking at them at all. The odor of those people in caftans often used to make me feel ill. Beyond that there were the unkempt clothes and the ignoble exterior. All these details were certainly not attractive; but the revolting feature was that beneath their unclean exterior one suddenly perceived the moral mildew of the chosen race.[44]

Benny Morris's view of the Arabs suggests something of the same racist revulsion expressed by Herzl, and of Hitler against the Jews. "Something like a cage has to be built for them," Morris told an interviewer. "There is a wild animal there that has to be locked up in one way or another… they are barbarians. The Arab world as it is today is barbarian."[45]

"We are a people—one people,"[46] Herzl proclaimed, not a religious community alone, but something more: a nation. Jewish nationalism concedes the very point anti-Semites make: that Jews are aliens, foreigners who must be rejected, not accepted, assimilated or treated as equals. Many Jews objected strenuously to Jewish nationalism, arguing that they were equal citizens of the countries in which they lived, much as Americans of African origin might argue that they are equal citizens of the United States, not part of an alien nation whose homeland lies across the ocean to which a return must be made as quickly as possible. Many feared that nationalizing or racializing Jews, as Herzl, Churchill and Hitler did, would cast suspicion upon their loyalty and mark them as untrustworthy outsiders.

In *Mein Kampf*, Hitler wrote about how his "ideas about anti-Semitism [had] changed… in the course of time."[47] He started out believing that Jews constituted a religious community. He ended up believing they were a race. The catalyst for his conversion was Zionism. Hitler wrote that before becoming acquainted with Jewish nationalism:

> In the Jew I still saw only a man who was of a different religion, and therefore, on grounds of human tolerance I was against the idea that he should be attacked because he had a different faith. And so I considered that the tone adopted by the anti-Semitic press in Vienna was unworthy of the cultural traditions of a great people. The memory of certain events which happened in the Middle Ages came into my mind, and I felt that I should not like to see them repeated.[48]

What changed? Hitler's encounters with unassimilated Jews brought him face to face with people who looked and spoke differently from other people he knew. Assimilated Jews, on the other hand, would have been, from Hitler's perspective, indistinguishable from non-Jews. "Is this a German?"[49] he asked, referring to the religious Jews he encountered. Any "indecision" he may "have felt about" the question of whether Jews were Germans "was finally removed by the activities of a certain section of Jews themselves. A great movement called Zionism arose among them. Its aim was to assert the national character of Judaism."[50] That, Hitler asserted, was the deciding factor that led him to conclude that Jews were a race.

But Hitler's argument ran into a problem. In the first decades of the twentieth century, the time Hitler was writing, most Jews rejected Zionism, as most Jews have since in deeds (choosing to live outside of Israel), if not in words. Indeed, Hitler acknowledged that Zionism was a movement of a small minority. But if most Jews rejected the idea that they belonged to a distinct nation, on what grounds could Hitler say that the Jews were a distinct race? Most Jews didn't think of themselves in racial terms. To circumvent the problem, Hitler simply did what he so often did when he argued himself into a corner: he abolished the corner. In this case, he claimed that the Jews had crafted a "purposely misleading" outward appearance to create the impression they were like everyone else, but covertly recognized each other as members of a single race.[51] "Is not their existence founded on one great lie," he asked, "namely, that they are a religious community when in reality they are a race?"[52]

Interestingly, Herzl anticipated Hitler's argument, and, more interestingly, accepted it. For both Herzl and Hitler, the Jews constituted one people, distinct from the people in whose company they dwelt. "It might... be objected that I am giving a handle to anti-Semitism when I say we are a people—one people; that I am hindering the assimilation of Jews,"[53] Herzl wrote. But this wasn't the case, he countered. Anti-Semitism, he argued, was inherent in the souls of men. As such, it didn't matter whether he called Jews a nation or a religious community. Either way, anti-Semitism would continue to flourish; it was an inescapable part of being a non-Jew. Gentiles had no choice but to be anti-Semites. In modern parlance, Herzl might say that hatred of Jews is part of the gentiles' genetic code, and that no amount of social engineering is ever going to change it. So, assimilation could hardly be frustrated by Herzl calling Jews a distinct people, since anti-Semitism, permanent and irremediable, ensured that Jews would never be truly assimilated.

Herzl's pessimism on the prospects of overcoming anti-Semitism is of a piece with his pessimism about humanity in general. Like Hitler, Herzl believed in a Hobbesian world of permanent struggle, of a war of all against all, where the strong devour the weak, and life (for the weak) is nasty, brutish and short. What's more, in Herzl's view, this was almost certainly the permanent condition of humanity. "Might precedes right," Herzl theorized, "and for an indefinite period it will probably remain so."[54]

Borrowing from social Darwinism, Herzl believed that the strong devouring the weak should be welcomed. It was the means by which nature 'culled the herd' and kept the human race strong. "Whatever is unfit to survive can, will, and must be destroyed," declared the Zionist sage.[55] Herzl's thinking was not out of place with the social Darwinian preoccupations of the political Right. In 1869, Charles Dilke, a British aristocrat, wrote in his pro-imperialist oeuvre *Greater Britain* that, "The gradual extinction of the inferior races is not only a law of nature, but a blessing to mankind."[56] Genocide, remarked the author Sven Lindqvist, "now emerged as a source of pride."[57] Evidence that Herzl's social Darwinist thinking continues to pervade Zionism is offered in this 2018 tweet from Israeli prime minister, Benjamin Netanyahu: "The weak crumble, are slaughtered and are erased from history while the strong, for good or for ill, survive."[58] Herzl—as well as Hitler, and a cast of other right-wing luminaries—couldn't have said it better.

The distinguishing feature of political Zionism—what set it apart from the territorial Zionism of gradual infiltration of European Jews into Palestine—was the program it set for itself of enlisting one or more Great Powers to grant nationalist Jews political supremacy over some territory, preferably the Levantine territory that the natives knew as south Syria on which a Jewish state had once existed. Herzl and his followers recognized that the project would be stillborn unless at least one imperialist power of Europe could be persuaded that cooperation with the Zionist project would yield benefits. If Jews were the instigators of the socialist danger, or were blamed for socialism, then an obvious benefit of the mass migration of Europe's Jews to a Western colony in Asia would be the removal of the Marxist menace.

Europe's Jews, Herzl wrote, had "become the deadly enemies of" European society.[59] The uneducated among them had "become a revolutionary proletariat, the subordinate officers of the revolutionary party."[60] Educated Jews were "fast becoming Socialists."[61] Zionism held out the promise of a Europe that would be "would be rid of" a "Jewish proletariat"⁶² that threatened to upend the social order. Mass migration of Jews to Palestine would cleanse the continent of the instigators of every rebellion since the French Revolution. "The penniless young intelligentsia, for whom there were no opportunities in the anti-Semitic countries and who there sank to the level of a hopeless, *revolutionary-minded proletariat*," [emphasis added] would become "a great blessing for Palestine" to which they would bring "the latest methods of applied science."⁶³ We "are everywhere at grips with revolutionaries," warned Herzl. Zionism would "detach young Jewish intellectuals and workers from socialism and nihilism."⁶⁴

Equally important for Europe's crowned rulers and presidents, Herzl pledged that Zionists would safeguard Great Power interests in the Orient. Zionism would become an agent of Western imperialism. The Jewish state, Herzl vowed, would "form a portion of the rampart of Europe against Asia, an outpost of civilization as opposed to barbarism."⁶⁵ And since 'civilization' equated to 'colonial control' and 'barbarism' equalled 'the natives,' Herzl offered to put European Jewry at the service of asserting European colonial rule over West Asian Arabs. Additionally, appealing to Christians, Herzl proposed that a Jewish state implanted in the Holy Land would act as "a guard of honor" protecting "the sanctuaries of Christendom,"⁶⁶ presumably from the Muslim 'hordes.'

There would be benefits all around. Europe's ruling classes would be more secure, with the problem of Jewish-instigated challenges from the political Left solved by geography. What's more, a people steeped in Western civilization would man an outpost of civilization in the heart of barbarism, protecting Western interests. For Europe's canaille, there would be relief from the presence of an alien nation in their land, which had called forth their anti-Semitic irritation. And for Jews, a harbor would be founded against the indignities and dangers of anti-Semitism. Even the natives, whose country would be invaded, would benefit, despite their dispossession. They would reap the advantages of Western civilization. Herzl's program, then, was Panglossian—the best of all possible worlds.

CHAPTER THREE

Nakba

> *"Seeing the Israelis as former or present victims is totally unfounded in reality. [They] have never been the victims and they apparently don't understand what being a victim means. On the other hand, they know quite well what it means to be oppressors, because that is what they have been all their lives. An Israeli-born officer who is thirty-five years old has not been a victim under any circumstances. The only reality he knows is that of being dominant, in control, on top of other people."*
>
> Benjamin Beit-Hallahmi, 1987[1]

The aim of political Zionism, as formulated at its first congress at Basel, Switzerland in 1897, was to "create for the Jewish people a home in Palestine secured by public law."[2] There is an apocryphal story that following the congress two representatives of the rabbis of Vienna travelled to Palestine to investigate Herzl's idea of establishing a Jewish state in Palestine. The rabbis returned with the following negative assessment: "The bride is beautiful, but she is married to another man."[3] According to an equally apocryphal story, Golda Meir, who held a number of political posts in Israel, replied: "I thank God every night that the bridegroom was so weak, that the bride could be taken away from him."[4] These two stories summarize the problem at the core of Zionism: the land on which Zionists aspired to settle and build a state belonged to someone else. As it turned out, the someone else, the Arabs, were weak, and easily overwhelmed. That was the key to Zionism's success.

In pursuit of this dream, Herzl approached a number of European heads of state and government officials, seeking their assistance in acquiring Palestine. These included the Ottoman Sultan, the Italian monarch, the German Kaiser, and the British colonial secretary, Joseph Chamberlain. To each of these statesmen, Herzl promised various benefits. To the Sultan he promised Jewish capital. The Kaiser was tempted with the prospect of a Jewish state at the crossroads of Asia and Africa that would serve as an outpost of German imperial power. The British were offered the same.[5]

At the core of Herzl's strategy was the relegation of the Palestinians to a nullity. They were neither to be consulted, engaged, nor given the slightest thought or consideration. Their wishes, interests, and lives were immaterial. All that mattered was securing the sponsorship of one of "a few chosen nations" that based its "own prosperity and primacy on despoliation and domination of the rest of humanity," as Lenin described the Great Powers.[6] Political Zionism was an ideology seeking a partnership with an Empire, any empire that would sponsor the theft of Palestine in exchange for services rendered. Herzl envisaged his Jewish state as a mercenary state, bound to an imperial master. The currency in which it would be paid would be the land of the Palestinian Arabs. At the core of Zionism, then, existed a rotten guidepost: The Arabs of Palestine don't matter. Imperialists do.

It was Chaim Weizmann, a Polish professor of chemistry who moved to Britain, who led the successful campaign of the Zionist movement to secure the backing of the British Empire for the establishment of a Jewish homeland in Arab Palestine. Weizmann became president of the World Zionist Organization in 1920, and the first president of Israel in 1948, serving until his death in 1952.

The fruit of Weizmann's efforts was the Balfour Declaration of November 2, 1917. Balfour, the Christian Zionist foreign secretary, had written a letter to Lord Rothschild, a representative of the Jewish community in England, expressing the British government's support for the creation of a Jewish homeland in Palestine. Balfour wrote:

Dear Lord Rothschild,

I have much pleasure in conveying to you, on behalf of His Majesty's Government, the following declaration of sympathy with Jewish Zionist aspirations which has been submitted to, and approved by, the Cabinet.

"His Majesty's Government view with favour the establishment in Palestine of a national home for the Jewish people, and will use their best endeavours to facilitate the achievement of this object, it being clearly understood that nothing shall be done which may prejudice the civil and religious rights of existing non-Jewish communities in Palestine, or the rights and political status enjoyed by the Jews in any country."

I should be grateful if you would bring this declaration to the knowledge of the Zionist Federation.[7]

At the time, Palestine was under the jurisdiction of the disintegrating Ottoman Empire, not Britain, though, with the Ottoman Empire's imminent defeat in the Great War, the British and French would soon carve up the West Asian territory of their wartime enemy. South Syria (today's Palestine and Jordan) and Iraq were parcelled out to John Bull, while Marianne absorbed north Syria (today's Syria and Lebanon.) Despite the conspiracy of the colonial Brobdingnags to feast on the Arabs' land, the land belonged by right to its inhabitants. Against this reality, Koestler said of the Balfour Declaration that, "In this document one nation [Britain] solemnly promised to a second nation [the Jews] the country of a third [the Palestinians]."[8]

"Jews were thus recognized for the first time, by an international body, as a nationality, and Zionism was recognized as its legitimate expression. Giving Zionism such privileges, when Jews were less than 10 percent of the population of Palestine (and most of these were not even Zionists) clearly violated the natural rights of the natives," observed Beit-Hallahmi.[9]

In 1917, when Balfour granted the Zionist movement the recognition of an imperialist power it so fervently sought, few Jews in Britain regarded their co-religionists as members of a nation, or even as an nation in embryo, as Herzl termed it, nor wished to be considered a member of a Jewish nation.

Zionism had little support among British, French and American Jews. The Quai d'Orsay treated Zionism with contempt, partly because it commanded little support among France's Jews.[10] French Jews favored the French Revolution and saw in Zionism a reaction against what the French Revolution stood for: emancipation and equality.[11] At the turn of the twentieth century, less than one percent of the United States' one million Jews belonged to a Zionist organization. By 1917, 95 percent continued to eschew

Zionism.[12] Most US Jews were as interested in Zionism and migration to Palestine as black Americans were in Garveyism and relocation to Africa. As a movement, Zionism had managed to attract the support of a paltry one percent of the world's Jews.[13]

The Conjoint Committee, an organization representing Britain's Jews, opposed political Zionism from its very beginning.[14] For this reason, it is not so strange that opposition to the Balfour Declaration came from within the Jewish community. Edwin Montagu, the Jewish secretary of state for India, was an implacable opponent of the declaration. As David Fromkin wrote:

> [Montagu] along with his cousin Herbert Samuel, and Rufus Isaacs (Lord Reading) had broken new ground for their co-religionists; they had been the first Jews to sit in a British Cabinet. [Disraeli, a British prime minister, was of Jewish ancestry, but baptized as a Christian.] The second son of a successful financier who had been ennobled, Montagu saw Zionism as a threat to the position in British society that he and his family had so recently, and with so much exertion, attained. Judaism, he argued, was a religion, not a nationality, and to say otherwise was to say that he was less than 100 percent British.[15]

Herzl himself acknowledged this view in *Old New Land*. Prior to his conversion to Zionism, Herzl's alter-ego Freidrich Loewenberg dismisses the suggestion that Palestine is his fatherland. "I have no connection with Palestine," Loewenberg says. "I have never been there. It does not interest me. My ancestors left eighteen hundred years ago. What should I seek there? I think only anti-Semites can call Palestine our fatherland."[16]

Montagu had discerned that the act of defining Jews as a nation would make Jews living outside a Jewish state foreigners by definition.[17] "If all Jews in the world form one nationality," observed Beit-Hallahmi, "then every Jew in the Diaspora is a dual national, whether he or she likes it or not. Even if an individual Jew defines himself or herself as a loyal citizen of his or her nation, by Zionist definition he or she is still a foreigner." Zionism, then, concedes the anti-Semitic view that Jews are aliens.[18]

London's principal motivation for promising to support the establishment of a Jewish homeland in Palestine was to rally the world's Jews to the British side in the First World War. Imbued with the view that Jews exercised great subterranean influence over world affairs, members of the cabinet—who as we've seen were greatly influenced by the Protocols— believed that the declaration would encourage Jewish financiers in the

United States to pressure the US president Woodrow Wilson to bring his country into the war on the British side. They also thought that Russia's socialist movement, teeming with Jews in its higher echelons, would persuade the Russian prime minister, Aleksandr Kerensky, to keep his country in the war, resisting demands that Russia withdraw from the conflict. (Britain was determined to stop the Russians from arriving at a separate peace with Germany. If that happened, the German high command would shift its resources from the Eastern front to the Western front, imperiling the British war effort.[19])

Ze'ev Jabotinsky, the founder of Revisionist or right-wing Zionism, was a fervent opponent of Wiezmann.[20] Jabotinsky opposed the partition of Palestine, and sought a Jewish state that contained both Palestine and Jordan, covering both banks of the Jordan River. He led the Irgun (Military Organization), a Jewish militia that broke away from the main militia, known as the Haganah, Hebrew for 'Defense.'

Jabotinsky had a decidedly colonial view of Zionism, and made no secret of the fact that Zionism is a colonizing enterprise. He saw Zionism, not in Christian Zionist terms, as the return of the Jews to the Holy Land, but as a project of creating in the Arab world an outpost of Western civilization. He perceived the necessity of an alliance with a Great Power, whose metropolis the Jewish state would be attached to as a beachhead. Moreover, since, in Jabotinsky's view, the Arab natives would hardly voluntarily submit to the transformation of their land into the land of an alien people acting on behalf of a foreign hegemon, the Jewish state would need to be allied with a Western empire *against* the Arabs.[21]

Jabotinsky famously conceived the idea of "the iron wall," which, in contemporary vernacular, might be characterized as 'hard power.' The Revisionist leader dismissed Herzl's view that the Arabs would welcome their colonization as a Quixotic fantasy, which it surely was, and advocated overwhelming force, an iron wall of bayonets, as the only realistic way in which the Arabs could be forced to submit to their dispossession. Only when the Arabs "have given up all hope of getting rid of alien settlers," he predicted, would they accede to their colonization.[22] Jabotinsky's doctrine, then, was one of fomenting hopelessness in the Palestinian community. The revisionist tenet that violence was the lone route to breaking "Arab resistance to the onward march of Zionism" eventually became Zionist orthodoxy, in actions, if not words.[23]

David Ben-Gurion, Israel's first leader, was an avowed socialist, who immigrated to Palestine from his native Poland in 1906. The Jewish social-ist movement believed that the only relevant conflict in Palestine was between Arab landowners and Arab peasants, and that the interests of the latter were linked to those of the Jewish working class against the for-mer. As members of subordinate classes, Jewish workers and Arab peas-ants had an affinity based on class that bridged their cultural differences— or so labor Zionists believed. Privately, Ben-Gurion regarded the analysis as naïve, and recognized that Arab opposition to the Zionist enterprise was unavoidable. Perceiving an inherent antagonism between Zionist aims and Arab interests, he rejected the idea of an anti-imperialist alli-ance of Jews and Arabs against the British, despite the reality that such thinking was congenial to the socialist ideology Ben-Gurion had presum-ably embraced. Instead, Ben-Gurion sought an alliance with the British against the Arabs.[24]

In 1936, the Arab community in Palestine launched a great revolt that would last three years— an *intifada* (shaking off) *avant la lettre*. The goals of the revolt were two-fold: to throw off the chains of British colonialism and to put a stop to Zionist efforts to transform Palestine into the Land of Israel. Ben-Gurion used the occasion of the conflict to openly express his theretofore private reservations about Herzl's doctrine of the Arab natives gladly accepting the theft of their country. "We and they want the same thing. We both want Palestine." That—and not class conflict between the propertied classes and workers—was "the fundamental conflict." Converging on Jabotinsky's view, Ben-Gurion acknowledged "that only war, not diplomacy, would resolve the conflict." And echoing Jabotinsky's 'iron wall of bayonets' idea, Ben-Gurion now argued that "only after total despair on the part of the Arabs… may the Arabs possibly acquiesce in a Jewish" Land of Israel. [25]

The outcome of the great Arab revolt, which the British successfully quelled, was the appointment of a Royal Commission, led by Lord Peel. Peel concluded that the only solution to the mutual hostility of the two communities was to partition Palestine into Jewish and Arab states. The Jewish community was divided over whether to accept this proposal. One part, led by Weizmann and Ben-Gurion, looked upon the commission's recommendation with favor: It heralded the birth of a Jewish state in Palestine; true, not encompassing all of its territory, but it was a start. Ben-Gurion accepted the partition plan, seeing a Jewish state in restricted borders as a base from which the Zionists could eventually expand their hegemony in Palestine. The Revisionists, by contrast, rejected the partition recommendation altogether; it frustrated their plan of immediately establishing a Jewish state in all of Palestine.[26] The Arabs, for their part, were justifiably opposed. The country, after all, belonged to them. Who were the British to grant part of it to recent immigrants whose arrival on their territory was carried out without their consent?

In 1939, with Britain on the brink of war with Germany, the British made a *volte-face*. Seeking to favorably influence the Muslim world against the Axis powers, and to mollify Palestinian opposition to the Zionist presence in the Holy Land, the Foreign Office issued a White Paper, in which Britain's former support for Zionism and a Jewish state in Palestine was reversed. Jewish immigration to Palestine would be curtailed, and Jews would remain a permanent minority in the country. This, of course, dashed Zionist hopes of the British creating a Jewish state in Palestine. If the British could no longer be relied upon, then the Zionists would take matters into their own hands.[27]

In August 1945, the Zionists decided to launch an armed struggle to drive the British, now an obstacle to the planned transformation of Palestine into the Land of Israel, out of the country. Military operations began in October. The Haganah, the main settler paramilitary organization, was joined by two Revisionist military groups: the Irgun, which was to be led by a future Israeli prime minister, Menachem Begin, and the Fighters for the Freedom of Israel, known by the British as the Stern Gang, after its founder Avraham Stern. The Fighters for the Freedom of Israel included among its leaders another future Israeli prime minister, Yitzhak Shamir.

After two years of fighting, the British, already greatly weakened by the Second World War, their empire collapsing under the weight of national liberation struggles, decided to throw in the towel. With its intractable conflicts, Palestine had become more trouble than it was worth, an intolerable drain on a severely diminished British treasury. London looked to the infant United Nations as a *deus ex machina*.

On November 29, 1947, the United Nations General Assembly approved Resolution 181, calling for the partition of Palestine into separate Jewish and Arab states, linked by an economic union, with Jerusalem set aside as an international territory outside the jurisdiction of either state. Palestine would be divided into eight parts. Three parts would constitute the Jewish state, while the Arab state would be comprised of three other parts, plus a fourth, Jaffa, which would be an Arab exclave within the territory of the Jewish state. Jerusalem—envisaged as a *corpus separatum*, or international city—was the eighth part.[28]

The Jewish population had grown rapidly from World War I under the stewardship of the British colonial administration from approximately 10 percent of the population to about one-third. Yet, while Jewish settlers remained in the minority and were outnumbered two to one by the indigenous Arabs, the resolution granted the Jewish state 56 percent of the Palestinians' country, while the Arabs, with two-thirds of the population, were given only 42 percent. The balance, two percent, represented Jerusalem.[29]

Some people continue to see the partition resolution—and its descendant, the two-state solution—as fair and practical, but it was neither of these things. Laying aside the inequitable apportionment of a greater territory for a Jewish state to a smaller Jewish population, there are larger issues to confront.

The first is the denial of Palestinian sovereignty. There is no question that the indigenous population was adamantly opposed to the expropriation of its land. While it made up the majority of Palestine's inhabitants, its wishes were completely ignored by the United Nations. This was predictable. At the time the world body was dominated by First World powers steeped in the colonial tradition. Many of the countries that voted for the resolution were settler colonial states themselves: Britain, France and Belgium, and the British settler offshoots, the United States, Canada, Australia, New Zealand, and South Africa. There was no chance that a similar resolution would have passed from the 1960s onwards, when the balance of power in the United Nations General Assembly shifted from the First World to the Third World. Countries with colonial pasts unwaveringly considered Zionism a legitimate political ideology, while countries victimized by colonialism regarded it as a form of colonialism.[30]

The second issue, following from the first, is that the partition resolution called for the creation of an unacceptable institution: a colonial settler state. Colonial settler states have been overcome one by one by the determined resistance of the political Left—in Algeria, Rhodesia, South Africa, and elsewhere—to the deserved applause of the majority of humanity. The demise of each settler colonial state is a sign post in the progress of humanity. The question of whether the Jewish state envisioned by the partition resolution, or Israel today, is a colonial settler state isn't even controversial. Neither Herzl, Ben-Gurion nor Jabotinsky were in any doubt that a Jewish state built by settlers on the land of another people was unequivocally settler colonialism.

As to the practicality of Resolution 181, it is as indefensible as the partition plan's alleged equity. A practical settlement to the conflict would have been one that all sides accepted. But neither side accepted the resolution. The indigenous population rejected it for the obvious reason that it denied them sovereignty over 58 percent of their territory and handed it to a minority population of recent immigrants. No people on earth would have accepted this proposal for themselves; why the Palestinians were expected to accept it, boggles the mind. Ben-Gurion accepted the resolution in words, but only as a tactical manoeuvre, recognizing that an embryo Jewish state could be incubated into the Land of Israel through military conquest. The Revisionists rejected the planned partition, because it fell short of fulfilling Zionist aspirations for a Jewish state in all of south Syria.

For the settlers, the demographics of the partition plan were all wrong. The Jewish state would contain 500,000 Jews but almost as many Arabs. There would be 440,000 Arabs living in the territory Resolution 181 envisioned for the Jewish state. Jews, then, would constitute only a bare majority. A bare majority could quickly become a minority, depending on immigration and the birth rates of the two communities. Moreover, how could 500,000 Jews rule almost as many Arabs, considering that the Arabs rejected Jewish rule? The plan was completely unworkable. The only way to create a viable Jewish state would be to engineer a radical reduction in the number of Arabs living within its frontiers while at the same time expanding its borders to absorb as many of the 10,000 Jewish settlers the resolution had assigned to the Arab state.

The resolution's proclamation immediately touched off fighting between the native Arabs and the immigrant Jewish settlers. The settlers were determined to drive as many natives as possible out of the territory assigned by the UN to a Jewish state, while capturing territory assigned by the UN to an Arab state. When the dust settled, a Jewish state, named Israel, was proclaimed, comprising 78 percent of Palestinian territory, not the 56 percent envisaged by the resolution. Meanwhile, 700,000 Arab natives had been exiled from their homes and the settlers refused their repatriation, keen to protect the outcome of their demographic engineering.

Today, Israelis insist their state grew out of a UN resolution that Arabs rejected and Jewish settlers accepted. While the Arab natives certainly rejected the resolution, the settlers rejected most of it as well, accepting only one small part of it—the call for the creation of a Jewish state. They rejected all the other parts, including the call for the creation of an Arab state within specified borders; the prohibition against expropriating Arab land within the Jewish state; the designation of Jaffa as an Arab exclave; the creation of an international Jerusalem; and the creation of an economic union between two states.[31]

British rule of Palestine came to an end on May 15, 1948. On May 14, Ben-Gurion proclaimed the State of Israel, sparking what has become known as the 1948 Arab-Israeli War. It was the first in a series of settler-native wars—armed conflicts between the army of the Jewish colonial settler state and various Arab armies and Arab irregulars.

The Arab belligerents in 1948—Egypt, Jordan, Iraq, Lebanon, and Syria—dispatched some 20,000 troops to help their compatriots resist settler efforts to transform Palestine into the Land of Israel. Only three of these states— Egypt, Jordan, and Iraq—had armies of consequence, and only one, Jordan, had an army that was prepared for war. All three states were British clients, governed by kings who served at the pleasure of London. All were armed by John Bull, and Jordan's army, was under the direct command of 21 British officers who took their orders from London. This was significant, since Britain favored the settlers, and could—and did—restrict the flow of weapons and ammunition to their client states. It's not by accident that the core Arab armies did not intervene in Palestine until *after* British forces exited Palestine, even though settler forces began operations to drive the Arab natives out of Palestine five months earlier. When the British-controlled Arab armies did finally intervene, the settlers had largely ethnically-cleansed Palestine, and their entry into the affray was a near farce.

The Arab forces had no central command and no coordination. It has been remarked that one of the reasons five Arab armies were defeated by one Israeli army was because there were five Arab armies.

Worse, there were inter-Arab rivalries that further weakened the combined Arab forces. Jordan and Iraq, led by British-installed kings, brothers of the Hashemite dynasty, were eager to see the defeat of the Egyptian army of King Farouk. Farouk was a rival for influence in the Arab world, and the Hashemites desired his defeat. Jordan and Iraq, then, had no intention of doing anything to help their rival's military forces.[32]

On top of these problems, was the general weakness of the Arab armies. The Egyptian forces were under equipped and poorly led. They had no maps, no tents, and insufficient logistical support. Their officers were generally incompetent, having attained their rank through political connections. When orders were issued to soldiers in the field, they were often contradictory.[33] The Iraqi army was even worse; it was sent into battle without ammunition.[34]

Finally, there was betrayal. Abdullah, the king of Jordan, had secretly worked out an arrangement with the settlers to annex the West Bank to his kingdom.[35] Glubb Pasha, the British officer who commanded Abdullah's army, deliberately restrained his forces, ordering them not to enter territory assigned by the UN to a Jewish state, though Israeli forces had seized territory assigned to an Arab state.[36]

It would have been difficult enough for the Arab armies to prevail under these trying circumstances, but the fact that they were outnumbered made victory all but impossible. Under-manned, lacking coordination, incompetently-led, ill-equipped, largely untrained, betrayed from within by Abdullah, and sabotaged by their British masters, 20,000 Arab soldiers were no match for the 60,000 unified and determined settlers under arms, many of whom were highly trained soldiers, having served in the British Army during the Second World War.

The Israelis have misnamed the First Settler-Native War as The War of Independence, as if it were a national liberation struggle of an oppressed people against a colonial power, Britain. On the contrary, it was a colonial war fought by Jewish settlers whose victory was aided in the background by the British. It was a war of dispossession, not a war of restitution.

The First Settler-Native War was a total defeat for the Arab natives of Palestine. They called it the *Nakba*, Arabic for 'catastrophe.' It was also a total defeat for the larger Arab world. The Arabs were humiliated. Colonial Britain and colonial France had carved up Arab West Asia into a series of artificial countries, and imposed rulers on its inhabitants. The British sponsored a settler colonialist project in the Arab homeland, and helped bring it to fruition. London and Paris treated the Arabs with contempt. They ignored Arab aspirations, disdained Arab views, and attached no value to Arab lives. To colonial Europe, the Arabs were a nullity.

Churchill's view of the Arab natives of Palestine was emblematic. The British reactionary referred to Palestinians as "barbaric hordes who ate little but camel dung,"[37] recalling Herzl's depiction of Arabs as dirty, malodorous, slothful, and beast-like. Churchill saw the dispossession of Palestine's Arabs as a matter of insignificance, likening it to the near exterminations of the indigenous peoples of North America and Australia. Rather than great crimes, he saw the dispossession of the weak as a desirable social Darwinian outcome. "I do not admit that a wrong has been done to these people," he said, "by the fact that a stronger race, a higher-grade race, a more worldly wise race to put it that way, has come in and taken their place."[38] Hitler couldn't have said it better. For his part, Balfour regarded the settlement of Jews in Palestine as "of far profounder import than the desires and prejudices of the 700,000 Arabs who now inhabit that ancient land."[39]

In 1948, control of the Suez Canal, Arab oil, and keeping the Soviet Union out of West Asia, were the Middle East priorities of the United States, Britain and France. Ruled by quislings answerable to London and Paris, the Arabs now lived with a settler colonial state at the very center of their homeland, whose envisaged role, from Herzl forward, was to keep the Arabs down. Local forces of independence and national assertiveness were to be prevented from laying their hands on the Suez Canal, redirecting their oil wealth to internal development, and allying with the Soviets. The Israelis were given the task of ensuring that these threats to Western power were not allowed to flourish.

In 1951, Gershom Schocken, editor of the Israeli newspaper *Haaretz*, touted Israel as a strategic asset for Western powers, particularly the

United States and Britain. Schocken saw Israel's military prowess in suppressing the natives, fully demonstrated in the First Settler-Native War, as an asset Israel could offer Western powers with imperial interests in West Asia.

Israel has proven its military prowess in the 1948 war against the Arab countries, and so a certain strengthening of Israel is a convenient way for the Western powers to create a political equilibrium in the Middle East. According to this conception, Israel is destined for the role of a watchdog. There is no reason to fear that it will follow an aggressive policy against the Arab countries, if that will run clearly counter to the wishes of the United States or Britain. But if the Western powers will prefer, once, for whatever reason, to close their eyes, you can rely on it that Israel will be capable of sufficiently punishing one or more of the neighboring countries, whose lack of courtesy towards the West has gone beyond the permissible limits.[40]

US and British oil companies wanted access to Persian Gulf oil on terms favorable to making generous profits. Britain and France wanted to preserve their monopoly over the Suez Canal. Arabs who thought the region's oil wealth should be used to improve the lives of impoverished Arabs, rather than enriching the lives of wealthy Western oil company shareholders, would have to be eliminated. Israel could help. It wanted to help.

CHAPTER FOUR

Imperialism

> *"The United States today is, by its own reckoning, the over-whelmingly dominant power of the globe in nearly all spheres, with the determination to impose its will by one means or another. The phenomenon is called by many 'hegemony,' or imperial power...[N]ew forms of imperialism were introduced in the modern era, especially in the Middle East, starting with the pliant rulers selected by the British to dominate the newly 'independent' governments of most states; these rulers were expected to be responsive to Western needs and preferences, even in the absence of support from their people."*
>
> Graham E. Fuller, former vice chairman
> of the US National Intelligence Council at the CIA.[1]

Imperialism is the process of one country dominating another, directly or indirectly. Empire is the outcome. The ultimate purpose of dominating another country is to secure from it opportunities for wealth accumulation for the community within the dominant country that exercises decisive political sway. Today, the community that exercises decisive political influence in the United States is made up of the owners of major privately owned financial, industrial and commercial enterprises—big business. In their 2014 study of over 1,700 US policy issues, the political scientists Martin Gilens and Benjamin I. Page demonstrated that "economic elites and organized groups representing business interests have substantial impacts on government policy, while average citizens and mass-based interest groups have little or no independent influence."[2] In other words, the United States is not a democracy, where influence is distributed uniformly, but a plutocracy, where political power is concentrated in the hands of a numerically insignificant elite of wealthy investors and shareholders who, by virtue of their outsized wealth, are able to dominate US public policy. This elite uses its economic resources to: lobby governments; fund think tanks to promote policies congenial to its interests; influence public opinion by buying mass media; place its members in cabinet positions and high political office; and offer lucrative job opportunities to politicians who advance big business interests while in office. Through these mechanisms big business is able to obtrude its profit-making imperatives on government policy. It is almost axiomatic that a country dominated by big business will have a foreign policy that defends and promotes the interests of big business.

The ultimate purpose of dominating another country is to secure from it opportunities for the owners of big business to accumulate wealth. The dominated country may provide direct opportunities for wealth accumulation, or may only be a stepping stone to securing profit-making opportunities in a third country, without offering any attractive opportunities of its own. For example, a country offering no immediate investment or trade opportunities may still become the target of an imperialist power because it is favorably placed geographically. Perhaps it bounds important shipping lanes and therefore is prized as a site for a naval base, from which the movement of goods can be protected from rival imperialist powers that might choke off the flow to gain leverage. Or perhaps the aim is to position military power at a shipping choke point to gain advantage over an imperialist rival. Or maybe the territory is strategically located militarily, in proximity to enticing targets that could be absorbed into the dominating power's orbit through military coercion. Perhaps the dominated country is close to an imperialist competitor and is therefore attractive as an outpost for encircling a rival. There are scores of possible reasons why an imperialist power might seek to dominate a country that offers no immediate or direct economic benefit, but the reasons for dominating the country are ultimately traceable to a perceived economic advantage that can be secured for the dominating country's major investors.

Colonialism is a form of direct political domination that is much out of favor, and imperialism as currently practiced almost invariably takes the form of indirect domination. There are multiple forms of indirect domination, but they can be broadly categorized as political or economic. Political forms of indirect domination are exercised through local proxies who hold political office and have *de jure* sovereignty but are constrained in their decision-making by the leverage the metropolitan power is able to bring to bear. Proxies may be rulers who are unacceptable to the local population and therefore depend for survival on the security guarantees provided by the imperialist power in whose orbit they revolve. They trade off security guarantees in exchange for making decisions that favor the imperialist power's interests. This is a strong form of indirect political domination. Weaker forms involve co-option arrangements in which promising individuals, groomed by the US state to fill important posts in their country's government, are educated at high-profile US universities, where they imbibe imperialist values and make important connections to metropolitan decision-makers, are placed in jobs in organizations that look after investor interests, such as the World Bank or Goldman Sachs, and then return home to occupy high offices of state in their own country.

Economic forms of indirect domination flow from economic dependency on the imperial center. Indirect domination through economic dependency is a form of blackmail, where the dominated country's almost complete economic dependence on a metropolitan power, forces it to make whatever concessions are demanded in order to avoid starvation. The dependence of a country on another for arms, can also leave it vulnerable to indirect domination. Unless it accommodates the interests of its arms supplier, it may not be able to defend itself.

Zbigniew Brzezinski, a theorist of US imperialism and US president Jimmy Carter's national security adviser, identified two major imperialist imperatives.[3]

First, an imperialist country must guarantee its satellites' security. It must also ensure that its satellites remain dependent on the security it provides. The provision of protection to satellites gives the imperialist power leverage. A satellite that is dependent on US protection, must comply with Washington's directives, or face danger. Another reason to guarantee a satellite's security is that if it is able to protect itself, it may also become strong enough to challenge the United States' primacy. A Japan and Germany that undertook programs of major military expansion to guarantee their own security would be in a position to contest US 'leadership.'

Second, an imperialist power must prevent countries outside of its orbit from coalescing. In Brzezinski's words, the barbarians must be prevented from coming together. As we'll see, this imperative is highly relevant to the role Israel plays in US imperialist strategy.

In the modern era, the Turks were the first to dominate the Middle East. Turkey's Ottoman Empire stretched over three continents: Europe, Asia and Africa. In 1799, Napoleon challenged the Ottoman's primacy in the Middle East, occupying Egypt. The country would later fall under the domination of Britain, but would remain a nominal possession of Turkey. Egypt wouldn't secure its independence until Nasser overthrew King Farouk, a figurehead behind whom the British exercised power.

Britain's interest in the Middle East was multi-fold, but mostly it was related to India. The shortest naval route from London to India is through the Suez Canal. The canal traverses Egypt, connecting the Mediterranean to the Red Sea. The shipping route follows the Gulf of Aden to the Arabian Sea and thence to India. Ships plying this route pass between Sudan and Saudi Arabia and then pass by Aden and Oman. Britain controlled Sudan, Aden and Oman, and had an alliance with the Hashemite dynasty of the Hijaz, the western part of what would later become Saudi Arabia. It is home to the Muslim holy cities of Mecca and Medina, the birthplace and burial place, respectively, of the Prophet Muhammad.

London had its eye on Palestine and Jordan, as extensions of the band of territory the Empire controlled from the southern tip of Africa to Egypt in the north. Palestine and Jordan, known at the time by the natives as south Syria, abutted the Hijaz. British domination of Mecca and Medina could give the Empire influence over the world's Muslim population.

Britain wasn't the only imperial power keen on dominating the Arab world. France too was vying for control of this vast region, which stretches from the Atlantic Ocean to the Persian Gulf. The two imperialist behemoths had created fourteen countries out of the Arab world: Syria, Iraq, Lebanon, Jordan, Palestine, Kuwait, Saudi Arabia, Bahrain, Qatar, the United Arab Emirates, Oman, Yemen, Egypt, and Sudan. They placed these countries—mainly artificial creations conjured in imperial map rooms, and many of them simply borders around oil wells—under the control of local proxies, or collaborators. Most of the collaborators were autocrats—kings, emirs, and sultans, who would run day-to-day affairs on behalf of London and Paris, sparing their imperial masters the expense of direct rule. Beholden to the Great Powers who protected them, and unacceptable to the people they ruled, they could be relied on to do the bidding of Whitehall and the Quai d'Orsay.

By the end of the First World War the Middle East had become important to the British for a reason other than protecting its route to India: oil. Oil was becoming an important commodity, not only as a lubricant for machinery, but as a fuel for locomotion. Navies were switching from coal to oil, and military supremacy (and therefore economic advantage) would depend on an empire having a reliable source of petroleum. At the same time, the region's promise as a rich source of oil was becoming evident. Oil had been discovered in Iran in 1908. One year later, the Anglo-Persian Oil Company, know today as BP, was founded. Six years later, the British government bought 51 percent of the company. It needed a reliable source of oil for the Royal Navy. In 1927 oil was discovered in Iraq. Discoveries followed in Saudi Arabia and Kuwait in 1938.

The Middle East's oil fields, and the shipping routes connecting them to Western Europe, namely the Suez Canal and the Strait of Hormuz, become valuable assets. There were two reasons for this: First, they held out the promise of immense profits. Second, control of these assets would give an empire leverage over countries that had no domestic sources of petroleum and would need to rely on oil from the Middle East to fuel their industrial economies. That leverage could be used to command economic concessions, and therefore even more profits. Suddenly, then, the following countries hove into view as important territories for an imperialist power to control: Iran, Iraq, Kuwait and Saudi Arabia. These were important sites for establishing oil wells; additionally: Bahrain, Qatar, the United Arab Emirates, Oman, Yemen, Somalia, Djibouti, Eritrea, Sudan and Egypt; these countries surrounded the shipping routes linking the region's oil wells to the markets in which the oil would be sold. Unless these territories were kept under direct or indirect control, they could be used by forces of local independence and national assertiveness, or hostile imperialist rivals, to disrupt the flow of oil and the tranquil digestion of oil profits. A world power that could dominate these countries directly or indirectly would command opportunities of wealth accumulation for its dominant economic class of Pantagruelian proportions. These would be obtained both directly, through the sale of oil, and indirectly, through economic concessions exacted by the leverage obtained by controlling Middle East oil.

It is important to understand two things about the United States. First, it has always been an imperialist power, ever expanding to secure new economic opportunities for its dominant economic class. Second, it is, and has always been, one of the world's top producers of oil, and has never been dependent on Middle Eastern oil to satisfy the bulk of its energy requirements. Dominating the Middle East, then, has never been a necessity of US energy security, and has always been an outcome of a compulsion that has chased US investors over the entire surface of the globe, to nestle everywhere, settle everywhere, and establish connections everywhere: the compulsion of profit-making.

From the earliest days of the republic, US leaders—wealthy land speculators and slave-owners almost to a man—aggressively promoted western settlement and expansion to the west. Thomas Jefferson described the United States in imperial terms as an 'empire of liberty.' Jefferson's empire was built on the plunder of coerced African labor and the stolen land of the indigenous population—hardly an institution of liberty, unless we designate African slaves and native Americans as non-persons. Indeed, 'empire of liberty' is an oxymoron, since empire implies subordination and the negation of sovereignty. This was an imperialism based on dispossession and theft, driven forward by the exploitation of non-white populations, and producing a republic that would span a continent.[4]

If the United States is not an empire—as many people would insist it is not—how do we explain how thirteen British colonies situated along the Atlantic coast of North America became a political unit of continental expanse before the end of the nineteenth century? This was accomplished by the conquest of land that belonged to other people, as indeed was the establishment of the original thirteen colonies. "Ultimately," wrote historian Alan Taylor, "the Americans succeeded and exceeded the British as the predominant colonizers of North America."[5]

Manifest destiny, the doctrine that the European settlers who called themselves Americans had a divinely given destiny to conquer North America, was complemented by the Monroe Doctrine, which defined the whole of the Western hemisphere as a sphere of influence for the United States. By the turn of the twentieth century, US business interests had propelled the Stars and Stripes even farther afield, into Hawaii, Samoa, Puerto Rico and the Philippines. The US military undertook regular interventions in Central America to secure new investment opportunities for US investors and to protect old ones that fell under the challenge of local forces of independence resolved to use their land, labor and resources for their own benefit.

In the first half of the twentieth century, US business interests had to compete for profit-making opportunities with investors from a number of other countries, backed by their own governments. German, Japanese, British and French businesses vied with US firms for control of world markets. But a period of war, crisis and revolution centered in Eurasia, from 1914 to 1945, knocked these countries out one by one, until the United States, isolated from the great conflagration by two great oceans, and reaping enormous profits through arms sales to many of the belligerents, emerged as a global Leviathan. With only five percent of the world population, it controlled 50 percent of the planet's wealth. Before the end of the Second World War, US strategists recognized that they had an opportunity to build an empire of unprecedented scale and scope, unmatched in human history.

The Middle East, with its bountiful supplies of oil, would become an important part of the new US world empire. Recognizing that Saudi Arabia was "a stupendous source of strategic power, and one of the greatest material prizes in world history"[6]—as a US State Department analysis concluded—US president Franklin Delano Roosevelt declared "the defense of Saudi Arabia [to be] vital to the defense of the United States."[7]

Washington was signalling an imperial claim to the largest part of Arabia, the vast desert peninsula that comprises today's Saudi Arabia, Yemen, Oman, Qatar, Kuwait, Bahrain and the United Arab Emirates. Roosevelt's claim to Saudi Arabia as a *de facto* US protectorate, was the first of many 'Monroe Doctrines' of the Middle East that would follow, in which, like a dog marking its territory, US leaders marked the Middle East as their domain. In this case, Roosevelt planted the US flag in Saudi Arabia, claiming its material prize and source of strategic power for big business in the United States. Returning from the Yalta summit, at which he conferred with Stalin and Churchill, Roosevelt met the Saudi monarch, Ibn Saud, aboard a US warship anchored in the Suez Canal. The two worked out a deal. Saud would grant US investors privileged access to the great material prize of Saudi oil; in exchange, Washington would guarantee the security of the Saudi royal family against foreign invasion and internal challenge.[8]

This, in many ways, resembled the kind of arrangement a mafia don might work out with someone whose cooperation is needed to make a money-making enterprise run smoothly. "Give us what I want and I'll ensure you don't get hurt," Roosevelt, in effect, told Ibn Saud. There was an implicit threat lurking in his words. If I can prevent you from being harmed, I can also hurt you, but don't want to, because it will be easier if you just comply. But if I have to hurt you, I will. This basic arrangement— the United States guaranteeing the House of Saud wouldn't be overthrown, or toppled by invaders, in return for Saudi kings directing the flow of the kingdom's oil wealth to US investors—carries on to this day, and the United States has had to make good several times on its pledge to protect Saudi rulers, from both external threats and internal subversion.

The external threats have come from Arab nationalist states, whose view that Saudi oil belongs to the Arab nation as a whole and ought to be used for the Arabs rather than US business people and their Saudi collaborators has raised alarm in Riyadh. The preternaturally popular Nasser agitated the Saudi monarchy with the slogan 'Arab oil for the Arabs.' The Arab Ba'ath Socialists of Syria, and the Arab Ba'ath Socialists of Iraq, before they were expunged and outlawed by the 2003 US invasion of their country, had a dim view of the Saudi royal family as the steward of a resource they believed was the patrimony of the Arab people, not of Arabian aristocrats and US investors. The United States has done much to undermine, weaken and destroy Arab nationalism, and Israel has been at the center of that effort, a subject that will be taken up at length later on. The beneficiaries of the continuing Roosevelt-Ibn Saud deal, of course, have been the House of Saud, whose position has been safeguarded at the apex of the Arabian pyramid, and US investors, to whom the wealth of the country flows. The losers have been the local population.

Saudi Arabia has a large internal security apparatus, separate from the military, consisting of a National Guard of 225,000 full-time personnel, whose mission is to suppress internal revolts, and a Praetorian Guard of 33,000 members, which protects the Saudi royal family. The National Guard alone has more members than all five branches of the Saudi military combined. The internal security apparatus is trained and equipped by the United States and its satellites. General Dynamics Land Systems, based in Canada, has struck a deal with Riyadh to provide the National Guard with almost $15 billion worth of light armored vehicles to be used to suppress civil unrest. The reality that the Saudi monarchy needs such a large, and generously equipped, internal army indicates that its rule is unacceptable to large parts of the Saudi population. This is a predicable consequence of the monarchy collaborating with Washington to share out the country's oil wealth between itself and the US business community, at the expense of Saudi subjects and the larger Arab community. In 2018, US president Donald Trump told supporters at a political rally that he had reminded Saudi Arabia's king, Salman bin Abdulaziz Al Saud, that "We're protecting you. You might not be there for two weeks without us."[9]

It was not that the United States needed access to Arabia's large reserves of oil to meet US domestic energy requirements that made Saudi Arabia a huge material prize and stupendous strategic asset for the United States. The United States had its own vast reserves of oil and was handily meeting its domestic energy requirements internally and would continue to do so until the 1970s. In 1973, the United States produced more oil than any other country in the world, including Saudi Arabia.[10] But the story was different for other major industrialized countries, none of which (with the exception of Britain and North Sea oil) was blessed with a rich internal source of petroleum. Germany, France, Italy, and Japan were almost entirely dependent on foreign sources. Preferential US access to the vast mines of black gold lying beneath the Saudi dessert would mean that US oil corporations would have a commodious supply of oil to sell to a hungry market of industrial economies in Western Europe and Japan. And that, in turn, meant a Himalaya of profits for US investors.

It also meant strategic advantage for the United States. One of the ways the United States would fold its former imperialist rivals into a post-war US-led global economic order—a global empire—was by guaranteeing the security of their ruling classes against external aggression (from the

Soviet Union) and internal challenges (from the political Left). As we've seen, by yielding to the United States' ultimate responsibility for their self-defense, Britain, West Germany, Italy and Japan implicitly agreed to forego the building of large militaries that could be used to challenge US 'leadership.' Military dependency, then, became a way of holding potential rivals in check.

Oil dependency would serve the same purpose. By controlling Saudi oil, and bringing its extraction, refinement, transportation and marketing under the control of corporate America, Washington could keep potential competitors dependent on the United States to deliver the oil they would need to keep their economies running at a high level. As A. A. Berle, an adviser to Roosevelt, would tell the president, controlling the Middle East's oil resources meant "substantial control of the world."[11] Washington helped foster Western Europe's dependency on the United States by conditioning post-War Marshall Plan aid on conversion of Western European economies from domestically-produced coal to US-supplied oil.[12]

In the decades to follow, Washington would repeatedly declare West Asia to be a US sphere of influence in which the Soviet Union must not interfere. Whatever interest the Soviets had in the region was based on considerations entirely different from those that impelled the United States to seek hegemony over it politics and resources. The USSR was able to meet its own energy requirements as well as those of its Eastern European satellites through its own enormous reserves of natural gas and oil. There was no need to intervene in West Asia to meet Warsaw Bloc energy needs. What's more, with a planned, publicly-owned economy based on need, the Soviets had no compulsion to compete for access to Middle Eastern oil to bring it to hungry foreign markets for a profit. While the Soviets did form troubled alliances with two oil-rich Arab states, Iraq and Libya, and two with little oil, Egypt and Syria, there was a poor economic fit between the USSR and the Arab world. From the point of view of economic exchange, the Arab world offered the Soviet Union very little. Arab states could trade their oil for goods and services from Western Europe and Japan, mediated by US oil companies, but the Soviet Union already had oil in abundance. The Soviet's economic relationship with the Arab states was, then, like its relationship with other Third World states, non-complementary, and mainly a drain on the Soviet economy, with Moscow subsidizing its Third World clients. While the nature of the US economy and circumstances drove Washington to seek domination of the Middle East, similar compulsions were absent for the Soviet Union.

Until 1970, the United States imported very little oil. As domestic demand increased, US oil production kept pace. By 1970, however, the oil demand and supply curves started to diverge. Oil consumption continued to grow, and domestic oil production declined. The United States now became dependent on foreign sources of oil to meet that part of its energy requirement that couldn't be fulfilled by domestic production. The United States relied primarily on Canada, Mexico and Venezuela—countries of the Americas—to top up its energy requirements. In 2012, 62 percent of oil consumed in the United States was produced within North America. Only 13 percent came from the Persian Gulf, and only a fraction of the 13 percent was from Saudi Arabia.[13] Today, the United States is self-sufficient in energy, reclaiming a position it last held in 1973. In August 2018, the United States became the top producer of oil in the world, surpassing Saudi Arabia and Russia.[14] Forecasts anticipated that the United States would become a net energy exporter by 2022,[15] but by October 2018, the country was exporting more oil and gas than it was importing.[16] By contrast, "for Western Europe and Japan, as well as the developing industrial powers of eastern Asia, the Gulf is all-important. Whoever controls it will maintain critical global leverage for decades to come," observed Robert Dreyfus, a journalist and author who has written extensively on Arab oil.[17]

That Washington seeks to keep its satellites dependent on energy resources under its control is evident in the struggle that has persisted since the 1980s between the United States and Western Europe over the construction of pipelines to bring Russian natural gas to the region. In the 1980s, Washington objected strenuously to Western Europe importing natural gas from the Soviet Union. US leaders charged that NATO countries would become dependent on the USSR for their energy. Left unsaid was that they would also become less dependent on oil imports from the US-controlled Persian Gulf, a state of affairs that would give the Soviets a new revenue stream and eat into US oil company profits. US president Ronald Reagan used sanctions to try to stop the Soviet pipeline project.[18]

The struggle carries on today. In 2011, a pipeline called Nord Stream came online with a capacity to deliver billions of cubic meters of Russian natural gas to Germany. A second pipeline, Nord Stream 2, scheduled to go online in 2019, would double the capacity.[19] US president Donald Trump criticized Germany, saying the pipeline should never have been allowed to have been built, and vowing to impose sanctions to stop it. Germany's purchase of Russian natural gas, Trump charged, would make the US satellite "captive to Russia" and enrich Moscow.[20] The reality, of course, was that the pipeline would make Germany less captive to the United States. Nord Stream 2 would allow Germany to reduce its imports of Persian Gulf oil, thus eroding US oil company profits. Successive US administrations, reported *The Wall Street Journal*, "have pushed Europe, and Germany in particular, to create the infrastructure required to receive shipments of liquefied natural gas from the U.S.—a potential source of large revenues" for US big business, as an alternative to buying from Russia. But liquefied gas "from the U.S. needs to be shipped over the Atlantic and would be considerably more expensive than Russian gas delivered via pipelines. A senior EU official working on energy regulation said Russian gas would be at least 20 percent cheaper." All the same, Washington wants Europe to "agree to some sort of racket and pay extortionate prices," as one EU official put it,[21] in order to maintain Germany's energy dependency on the United States.

Keeping Europe and East Asia dependent on corporate America for energy security is "one of the main reasons the United States has been so interested in Middle Eastern oil," observes the US foreign policy critic Noam Chomsky. "We didn't need the oil for ourselves;" until the early 1970s "North America led the world in oil production. But we do want to keep our hands on this lever of world power, and make sure that the profits flow primarily to the US. That's one reason why we have" a special relationship with Israel. It's "part of a global intervention system aimed at the Middle East to make sure indigenous forces there don't succumb to" nationalism,[22] guided by the slogan of 'Arab oil for the Arabs.'

CHAPTER FIVE

Division

> *"I believe the documentary evidence clearly illustrates*
> *America's grand design for the Middle East: America looks*
> *forward to a permanent Israel... and to a weak and divided*
> *Arab world based on personal rivalries and led by military*
> *dictatorships and traditional monarchies."*

Leila Khaled, 1973[1]

The basic arrangement Washington worked out with Ibn Saud was that he would grant US oil companies access to Saudi oil on very favorable terms. In exchange, the Americans would guarantee his security and see to it that he and his family became very wealthy. It was a cozy arrangement, but far from the only one that was possible.

Most of the inhabitants of the Saudi kingdom were cut out of the deal, as were Arabs as a whole. The basic capitalist logic that underlies the relationship of US private enterprise to the Middle East is that if the region's oil wealth is a pie then US oil industry shareholders should get as much of it as possible and the region's inhabitants as little as possible. The greater the share of oil wealth that flows to the local population, the smaller US shareholders' returns—an undesirable situation the US government works diligently to prevent. The collaborators the British and French had installed as rulers in the Middle East were happy with this arrangement, as long as they were well looked after by Washington. As far as the kings, emirs, and sultans of the Persian Gulf were concerned, their subjects could live mean and difficult lives forever. US security guarantees would see to it that troublemakers were held in check. What mattered was whether Uncle Sam would allow them a sufficient income to build palatial residences and underwrite sumptuous lifestyles. Since Washington proved to be quite happy to indulge the Arab world's quislings, the Middle East's imposed leaders reigned over impoverished subjects, looking the other way as US big business plundered the region's oil wealth.

Of course, there was much opposition to an arrangement that was clearly unfavorable to the local population. Three movements arose to replace the Arab collaborators with governments that would be responsive to the needs of the local population, rather than to Western investors. The movements promised to redirect the region's oil wealth to internal development, rather than satisfying the profit-making imperatives of rich Western business owners. The movements were Arab nationalism (or Arabism), Islamic nationalism (or Islamism), and communism.

Two of the movements, Arabism and Islamism, were indigenous, and the most successful, while communism, originating in the Bolshevik Revolution, lacked local resonance and struggled to gain traction. It did, however, become an important prop for Arabism.

Arabism used ethnolinguistic identity to mobilize the region's inhabitants to support the project of overthrowing local collaborators who ruled on behalf of the West. Islamism pursued the same goal, but used appeals to the Arab world's shared religious experience in Islam to galvanize opposition to indirect rule by non-Muslim powers.

Arabism was more strongly a movement of the political Left than was Islamism. It took belief in equality further along the road to universalism. For example, Arabism spawned Arab socialism, which promoted women's rights, sought to overcome discrimination based on religion and sect, and implemented programs to reduce economic inequality. It also emphasized economic planning and public ownership of the commanding heights of the economy, and, partly under Soviet influence, Arab socialist governments adopted an essentially Soviet economic model.

While there was some affinity between Arabism and communism, Arabists distrusted local communists, seeing them as agents of Moscow and rivals for the leadership of the Arab world. In the Arabist view, a communist Arab world would be an Arab world dominated by the USSR, and hence, a negation of Arabism's principal aim of Arab independence. The pumice stone of experience, however, quickly ground away all Arabist illusions about charting a course between the Scylla of Washington and the Charybdis of Moscow. Of the two 'monsters,' it was Moscow alone that was congenial to the aims of Arabism, and Arabists eventually settled into an uneasy relationship with Moscow. They never, however, established viable working relationships with the local Arab Communist parties, except short-term, and then often only as a way of accommodating Moscow.

Islamism, on the other hand, is more socially and economically conservative than Arabism, tilting to the political Right. Significantly, while the shared Leftist values of Arabists and communists, particularly their commitments to secularism, socialism and women's rights, allowed Arab socialist governments and the Soviet Union to work together, cooperation between communists and Islamists was infrequent. Islamism, with its emphasis on religion over reason, tradition over progress, support for profit-making and antipathy to communist atheism, kept the two movements apart. Instead, Islamism became a favored ally of convenience for Western powers seeking to undermine Arabism and communism.

Communism in the Arab world gained its greatest traction in Iraq, where the Communist Party became the main political support for Abd Al-Karim Qasim, who governed the country from 1958 to 1963. Qasim regarded the Arabist program as timid and unrealistic, more an exercise in rhetoric than concrete action. He favored a robust socialism and practical steps toward Arab independence, and believed that the Arabists' goals were only achievable with Soviet support, [2] a position the Arabists would eventually arrive at themselves.

While also present as a major political force in Egypt and Syria, the communists were never as strong as the Arabists, who used their control of the state to suppress them, often with the help and approval of the United States. The Arabists' objection to the communists originated, not in a clash of broad political values, but in the communists' rejection of the Arabists' ultimate goal of creating a pan-Arab state. Qasim in Iraq, for example, implemented many policies the Arabists applauded, but was opposed, and eventually overthrown, by the Arabists, because they saw him as too strongly devoted to Iraqi causes at the expense of larger Arab nationalist goals.[3]

That the opposition to Western domination of the Arab world was split among three movements was a great boon to the United States and its

Western satellites. The movements shared the same overall goal of denying the West control of the region, and removing quisling governments
in favor of those that were responsive to local needs. The threat posed by
Arabists, communists, and Islamists to Washington's command of Arab
oil is evident in the following chronology of events:

- One of Nasser's slogans was "Arab oil for the Arabs."[4] Nasser rallied
  millions of Arabs to this cause.
- In 1972, at the instigation of Saddam, Iraq nationalized its oil and signed
  a fifteen-year friendship and cooperation treaty with the Soviet Union.
  "Radio Baghdad began beaming the revolutionary message of 'Arab oil
  for the Arabs.'"[5]
- In February 1990, Saddam launched a broadside against US control of
  the Persian Gulf, and advocated Arab control of Arab oil.[6]
- In 2006, Libyan leader Muammar Gaddafi, a devoted follower of
  Nasser, announced that, "Oil companies are controlled by foreigners
  who have made millions from them. Now, Libyans must take their place
  to profit from this money."[7]
- Syria sees itself as the "Den of Arabism," birthplace of a movement
  whose goal is to return the Arab world and its resources to the control
  of its inhabitants.
- Under Arabist leaders, Egypt, Iraq, Libya, and Syria were all client states
  of the Soviet Union.
- In June, 1996, Osama bin Laden told British foreign correspondent
  Robert Fisk that Washington had turned Saudi Arabia into an American
  colony and drained its oil wealth. Despite producing more oil than any
  other country in the world, Saudis were burdened by taxes and inadequate public services. The kingdom's oil wealth was used to buy
  weapons from US arms manufacturers that it didn't need, rather than
  being invested in the welfare of the Saudi population. For these reasons,
  he explained, the United States was "the main enemy" and Muslims
  should resist Western occupation of their countries, as Europeans had
  resisted occupation of their countries by foreign fascist forces during
  the Second World War.[8]

While Arabists, communists and Islamists opposed US domination of
the Arab world, and hated the Arab quislings who ruled on the West's

behalf, the three movements disagreed on a sufficiently large number of questions that they were unable to form a united front against their common enemy. But on top of this, the British, French, and Americans, experts at deepening divisions, sowing discord, and exacerbating rivalries, pulled out all the stops to "keep the barbarians from coming together," as Brzezinski had defined one of the imperatives of empire-maintenance.

Washington recruited the Islamists to fight the Arabists, a process that began with joint US-Muslim Brotherhood efforts to overthrow Nasser in the 1950s and 1960s, and continued with the US training, arming, and financing of Islamist guerrillas to destabilize the Den of Arabism in the twenty-first century.

Uncle Sam also backed Islamists against the communists, infamously in Afghanistan, where US-backed 'freedom fighters,' including Osama bin Laden, destabilized a modernizing Marxist-Leninist government backed by the Soviet Union. The Soviet's decade-long involvement in the Afghan quagmire—the USSR's Vietnam War—did much to bleed Soviet communism, and likely contributed to its exsanguination. The Soviets did not have unlimited resources, and the demands of conducting a war in Afghanistan against US proxies, while simultaneously trying to keep pace with a US arms build-up, certainly limited the support the Soviets were able to provide their Arab clients, and likely contributed to the Soviet Union's demise.

Additionally, the United States sought alliances with the Arabists to weaken the communists, and the Arabists were often happy to oblige. Saddam, for example, colluded with the CIA to exterminate members of the Iraqi Communist Party in order to put the Arabists on top in Iraq. Nasser too was forever jailing local communists, whose party he outlawed. And the only concrete Arabist effort of building a pan-Arab state—the short-lived 1958 merger of Egypt and Syria as the United Arab Republic— was in reality an Arabist manoeuvre to prevent the communists from taking power in Syria. As soon as the merger was completed, Nasser ordered the purge of communists who were high-ranking officials in the Syrian state, and the party's members arrested. It was, in effect, a successful repeat of an earlier failed US-British plot, organized by Kermit Roosevelt—who would become infamous for orchestrating the overthrow of Iran's nationalist prime minister, Mohammad Mossadegh—to block a possible communist ascendancy in Damascus. With the communist 'danger' eliminated,

Syria's Arabists withdrew from the union, despite their professed devotion to pan-Arabism.

Following along these lines, Israel provided support to Hamas, an organization that originated in the Muslim Brotherhood. The Zionists' aim was to split the organized Palestinian opposition between Arabists and Islamists. Hamas dispatched young Palestinians to fight the communists in Afghanistan, diverting opposition from the settler colonial Jewish state to the followers of Marxism-Leninism, much to Israel's delight. Hamas also broke with Iran and Syria, over the two states' war with Sunni Islamists, who in 2011 rekindled their longstanding jihad against the Arabists of Damascus, a jihad dating from the 1960s. Israel was pleased. With Washington's major opponents at daggers drawn, maintaining control of Arab oil as a great material prize and stupendous strategic asset turned out to be far less challenging than it might have been had Arab forces of independence not been politically divided and consumed by rivalry. The greatest enemies of Arab liberation have often been the Arabs themselves.

Pan-Arabism is an unlikely but enormously dangerous threat, not only to US control of the Middle East's lucrative and strategically important oil reserves, but to Western power on a global scale. The Arabs constitute the second largest pan-ethnic group, or nation, in the world. Only the Han Chinese are more populous. A single Arab nation-state, if one were to be formed, would cover a vast territory stretching from the Atlantic Ocean to the Persian Gulf and would comprise 400 million people. Territorially and in population, it would be larger than the United States. It would also control vast reserves of oil, gas and other resources, which it could harness for its own internal economic and military development. A pan-Arab state, a United Arab States, if you will, would threaten Western claims to geo-political and economic supremacy.

Western powers recognized that Arab nationalism posed a dual threat to their empires. First, the coalescence of the Arab world into a single state could block Great Power exploitation of the Arab homeland. Not only would a pan-Arab state control an important strategic resource, oil, it would also control trade routes between Europe and South and East Asia. Second, a pan-Arab state would be large enough to compete with other global powers on the world stage. As early as 1907, British prime minister Henry Campbell-Bannerman sounded the alarm. Bannerman wrote:

> There are people who control spacious territories teeming with manifest and hidden resources. They dominate the intersections of world routes. Their lands were the cradles of human civilizations and religions. These people have one faith, one language, one history and the same aspirations. No natural barriers can isolate these people from one another.... [I]f, per chance, this nation were to be unified into one state, it would then take the fate of the world into its hands and would separate Europe from the rest of the world.[9]

Having identified a problem of great significance to the continued domination of the world by the West, Bannerman proposed a solution.

Taking these considerations seriously, a foreign body should be planted in the heart of this nation to prevent the convergence of its wings in such a way that it could exhaust its powers in never-ending wars. It could also serve as a springboard for the West to gain its coveted objects.[10]

> Bannerman's solution was to establish an outpost at the Arab world's center—a foreign body, to serve as a beachhead for the West to gain its coveted objects, as he put it—an obvious anticipation of Israel. But in broader terms, his solution was to create conditions that would foster never-ending wars.

One way to engender ceaseless internal rivalry and conflict is to politicize existing divisions. The Great Powers did this by carving the Arab world into multiple political units. Today, there are twenty-two Arab states, stretching from Western Sahara in the West to Oman in the East, most created by Britain, France, and Italy to satisfy the interests of their economic elites. The division of a single ethno-linguistic body into multiple states is reminiscent of the variegation of the German nation into over two dozen states, most of which, following a Pan-Germanic impulse, were unified as the German Empire in 1871. The rise of Germany as a great industrial power presupposed the unification of the multiple German principalities. The largest German state, Prussia, was instrumental in unifying most of the divided German nation. Sati' Al-Husri, an early twentieth-century theorist of Arab nationalism, saw Iraq as the German equivalent of Prussia, the pivotal Arab state that would unify the divided Arab world into a single political unit. Husri's ideas were influential in Iraq among Saddam's generation, who called themselves 'the Prussians of the Middle East' and sought to live up to the name.[11]

Carving the Arab world into separate states would do little to weaken Arab nationalist proclivities, if Arabs identified with the Arab nation as a whole. The key was to fracture the Arab community into multiple states and then foster patriotic identification with each individual state. Instead of seeing themselves as Arabs, members of the community were encouraged to see themselves as Egyptians, Iraqis, Syrians and Jordanians. "The British," observed Said Aburish, a Palestinian journalist who wrote a series of biographies of key Arab figures of the twentieth century, "had invested considerable money and effort creating individual Arab identities to defeat the larger Arab one. They wanted Iraqis to be Iraqi, the Syrians Syrian, and so on."[12]

Nasser's 1956 constitution for the first time ever described Egypt, a country that existed for centuries, as part of the Arab nation.[13] Syria's constitution of 1973 defined Syria as "part of the Arab homeland," its people as "part of the Arab nation," and the Syrian people's task as working and struggling "to achieve the Arab nation's comprehensive unity." Emphasis on Syria's identification with the larger Arab nation is no less evident in the country's 2012 constitution. The revised foundational law acknowledged that the "Syrian Arab Republic is proud of its Arab identity" and "that its people are an integral part of the Arab nation." Moreover, the constitution committed the state to the "pan-Arab project" and "to support Arab cooperation in order to promote integration and achieve the unity of the Arab nation."

By contrast, the Basic Law (constitution) of the informal US colony Saudi Arabia makes no reference to pan-Arabism. Rather, it defines the "Kingdom of Saudi Arabia" as "a sovereign Arab Islamic State" whose "constitution is Almighty God's Book, *The Holy Qur'an*, and the Sunna (Traditions) of the Prophet." There is no reference to Saudi Arabia being part of a larger Arab nation.

The 1925 Constitution of the Kingdom of Iraq, a state under the *de facto* control of the British Crown, made no reference to Iraq as an Arab country. This changed, when in 1970, Iraq's Arabists, who had liberated their country from Britain's indirect rule by overthrowing the British-installed king, created constitution that defined the country as "part of the Arab Nation." The state's "basic objective" was defined as "the realization of one Arab State." The goal was to foster pan-Arab identity: to have Iraqis think of themselves as Arabs, rather than as Iraqis.

Efforts to induce Iraqis to identify with the Arab nation as a whole were overturned in the US-imposed 2005 constitution. The revised basic law—the country's current legal foundation—makes no reference to Iraq belonging to an Arab nation. Instead, the emphasis is on particularism rather than Arab universalism. Iraqis are referred to as "the people of Mesopotamia," and Iraq as "a country of many nationalities, religions and sects." The stress is no longer on fostering Arab identity and overcoming divisions based on religion, sect, and externally-imposed artificial state boundaries. Instead, parochial identities and divisions within the country (among nationalities, religions and sects) are brought to the fore, while ethno-linguistic affinity is effaced as an overarching identity.

Division with Iraq is emblematic of another Great Power ploy to occasion endless war within the Arab nation: on top of creating many Arab states, imperialists have also created politicized divisions within them. Iraq is fractured politically between Arabs and Kurds, on the one hand, and Sunni Muslims and Shia Muslims, on the other. The monarchical system designed for Iraq by the 1921 Cairo Peace Conference not only ensured that by politicizing the country's cleavages that bad governance would ensue, but intended that the country be badly run in order to keep 'the barbarians' from coming together.[14] The divisions in the country were used by the British to keep the country weak.[15] London, seeking to perpetuate its dominion over the local Arab population, maintained separate lines of communication with Iraq's three major communities: the Kurds, the Sunnis, and the Shia. Each community was played off against the other. To add to Iraq's political fracturing, the British mandated that the minister of finance be a Jew. (One can imagine the religious division that would ensue if the US Constitution required that the post of secretary of the treasury could only be filled by a Jew.)

Playing the same divide-and-rule game, the United States imposed a constitution on Iraq following its 2003 conquest of that country that politicized Iraq's ethno-sectarian divisions, making them the basis for political power. The act was tantamount to a foreign power sweeping into the United States and rewriting its constitution to replace the currently existing Democratic and Republican parties with parties based on skin color (the Black party, the White party, the Hispanic party) and religion (the Christian Evangelical party, the Roman Catholic party, the Jewish party and the Muslim party.) To protect the fissiparous nature of Iraqi politics from unifiers, such as Saddam, Washington built into the Iraqi constitution a ban on centripetal Arabism, under the guise of de-Ba'athification. Any Iraqi promoting unity—one of the key goals of the Arab Ba'ath Socialist Party—was banned from the political arena, in favor of politicians representing ethnic or religious communities.

A third way the Great Powers stoked endless conflict in the Arab world was by sponsoring ethnic and religious minorities, whose members, afraid of disappearing under the weight of the majority's demographic preponderance, could be relied on to oppose the liberation movements of the majority. For example, Western powers made alliances with the Kurds, a non-Arab people distributed over four Middle Eastern states: Turkey, Syria, Iraq and Iran. The British, in their time, as indirect rulers of Iraq, and the United States, today, as the British successor, built up the Kurds in Iraq, where they constitute a substantial part of the population, to weaken the central government. In Syria, the Kurds became the US 'tip of the spear,' the main ground troops used to deny the Den of Arabism almost one-third of its territory in the second decade of the twenty-first century. In the view of US officials, Kurds were to be used as "mercenaries and security contractors"[16] against the Arabists.

France created Lebanon out of territory grafted from Greater Syria, a coherent geographical unit whose inhabitants sought a single Greater Syrian state at the end of World War I. Instead, the British and French dismembered Syria, splitting it into four separate countries. Lebanon was created as a state of the Maronite Christians, a minority that, through constitutional fiat, is accorded executive power in Lebanon, and therefore political rule over the country's Muslim majority. Non-Maronites, 80 percent of the population, are barred from holding high political office, including that of president.[17]

Great Powers have also allied with religious minorities to politicize existing divisions within the Arab world. France, for example, recruited Alawites, followers of a heterodox Shia sect who are often regarded by Sunni Muslims as heretics, into Syria's colonial police force. The Alawites, already greatly despised by the Sunni majority, and relegated to the bottom ranks of Syrian society, became even greater objects of enmity as agents of the hated French colonial overlords. The Alawites later became great devotees of Arabism, for its emphasis on overcoming the religious and social prejudices which had kept them down, and in this respect, were like Jewish devotees of communism, attracted to a doctrine of equality that promised relief from oppression.

Jewish settlers represented yet another minority within the Arab heartland with which the Great Powers had allied, specifically for the purposes of keeping the Arabs down. Moshe Dayan, an Israeli chief of defense staff, minister of defense, and minister of foreign affairs, is reputed to have said that the "Jewish people has a mission, especially its Israeli branch. In this part of the world, it has to be a rock, an extension of the West, against which the waves of... Arab nationalism will be broken."[18] In pursuit of that goal, Israel has encouraged non-Arab and non-Muslim minorities in the Middle East—among them the Lebanese Maronites, the Druze, and the Kurds—to seek political independence in cooperation with Israel.[19]

Kurds, Maronites, and Zionist Jews—these are the ethno-religious minorities that imperialist powers and their subalterns have used against the Arabs. Divided, and distracted by endless war, ruled by quislings who answer to Washington, Arabs have failed to unify and form a United Arab State, capable of claiming the great material prize of Arab oil for their own development. Today, the prospects of Arab unity look bleak, and as we shall see, Israel's great service to its Western patrons has been to create the conditions that substantiate this pessimistic outlook. But it wasn't always so. In the early 1950s there stepped onto the world stage a liberator who Arabs, from the Atlantic to the Gulf, revered as a new Saladin, the Muslim military leader who drove the Crusaders out of the Arab heartland. While he's largely forgotten today, Gamal Abdel Nasser, an Egyptian army colonel inspired by the most cherished values of the political Left, in his day consternated Western statesmen. A "Mussolini of the Nile" they thundered. A new Hitler! Although reviled in the West, Nasser was more popular than any Arab since the Prophet Muhammad. Arabs hung on his every word. They overthrew quisling governments in his name, and then invited him to lead them. His name became an eponym for Arab nationalism. Arabists called themselves Nasserites and followed a doctrine they called Nasserism.

In her autobiography, the Palestinian revolutionary Leila Khaled wrote of Nasser that he awakened "the Arab giant which roared with fury at the

West. Mass adulation for Nasser became an Arab phenomenon; Nasserism became a world-wide doctrine.... Diplomats from the Third World made pilgrimages to Cairo to declare their solidarity with the Arabs ... the Arab world applauded; the oppressed saw a spark of hope. Europe and America stood in awe while Nasser became the brown giant of the Third World."[20] When the great hope of the Third World died, countless Arabs were overwhelmed with grief. Millions attended his funeral.

The Eisenhower administration recruited the Muslim Brotherhood, the original Islamists, and assigned to it the task of overthrowing Nasser, setting a precedent for how Washington would deal with Arabists, including Bashar al-Assad, the last of the Arabist leaders. Israel schemed against Nasser, taunted him, waged war against him, not once, but twice, and on the second occasion, destroyed him. Nasser, remarked Said Aburish, was "the most popular failure in history."[21] And it was Israel that helped make him so.

CHAPTER SIX

Nasserism

"We know what you expect from us. We shall have to be the guards of the Suez Canal. We shall have to be the sentinels of your way to India via the Near East. We are ready to fulfil this difficult military service, but it is essential to allow us to become a power in order to enable us to do our task."

Zionist leader Max Nordau to British foreign Secretary Sir Arthur Balfour and British prime minister David Lloyd George, 1919.[1]

From 1882 until the 1950s, the British occupied Egypt and exercised a tyranny over its inhabitants, ruling through their proxies, the Egyptian monarchy and feudal landlords. The British inaugurated their rule over Egypt by visiting upon Alexandria, the Egyptian port city on the Mediterranean, a nineteenth century version of the 'shock and awe' campaign the United States would use 119 years later to inaugurate its tyranny over Iraq. "The British navy shelled Alexandria from sunrise to sunset," wrote the author Sven Lindqvist, until "the city was transformed into a sea of fire." British prime minister William Gladstone justified the cremation of Alexandria by pointing to the international community's prerogative "to intervene in the affairs of other states in the name of peace, humanity, and progress,"[2] prefiguring the argument US president George W. Bush and his crony, British prime minister Tony Blair, would use to justify their 2003 invasion of Iraq.

In 1922, Britain granted Egypt nominal independence, but maintained its military occupation. A veiled colonialism, hiding rule from London, thus continued to oppress the country. London premised its military presence in Egypt, and denial of authentic Egyptian sovereignty, on its self-assigned right to protect the Suez Canal as the route to its empire in South Asia.

India, a great material prize for Britain, was the equivalent of the Middle East for Washington today. And just as the United States regards the Middle East as a vital interest, entitling Washington to negate the sovereignty of the region's inhabitants, so too did Britain consider its trade routes with India vital interests that trumped the sovereignty of the Egyptians.[3]

Nasser's generation loathed the British presence in Egypt, regarding British soldiers as aliens and infidels who backed the local landlords. All that afflicted Egypt was due, in their minds, to the British, their colonialism, and their indirect rule through the retrograde institution of feudalism. Inspired by revolutionary thinkers, from Voltaire to Lenin, Nasser resolved to oppose all oppressions in Egypt. This included the direct oppression of the monarchy and feudal landlords, and the indirect oppression of their patrons, the British.[4]

World War II forced Britain to redirect troops from its colonies unthreatened by rivals to theaters of active combat. To compensate for the loss of British troops in Egypt, London ordered Farouk, the Egyptian king, to increase the number of his subjects under arms from 11,500 to 60,000.

The Egyptian officer corps was comprised of the sons of landlords. This was an expedient of protecting feudal privilege. Since the class-loyalty of officers drawn from aristocratic ranks was all but assured, control of the military was deliberately placed in the hands of the aristocracy. But the aristocracy was too small to support the increase demanded by the British. As a consequence, the officer academy was opened to the middle class. Middle-class officers, however, did not support the monarchy and aristocratic privilege, or the British overlords who stood behind these archaisms. And so it happened that from the Egyptian officer academy emerged a group of middle-class officers, led by Nasser, who developed a conspiracy to overthrow the monarchy, abolish feudalism, and drive the British out of Egypt. It was called the Free Officers Movement. On July 23, 1952, the

Nasser-led conspiracy carried out a *coup d'état,* known as the July 23 Revolution.[5]

The Free Officers promulgated a six-point program for an independent Egypt. It included:

- An end to colonialism and the Egyptian traitors who supported it.
- The abolition of feudalism.
- The end of plutocracy.
- Social equality.
- Creation of a powerful military.
- A healthy democratic atmosphere.[6]

Almost immediately, the new government abolished feudalism. An agrarian reform law was enacted, which limited land ownership to two hundred acres and distributed land to landless farmers. Feudal landlords, less than two percent of the population, owned two-thirds of the land and exploited over four million peasants as tenant laborers.[7] The new government seized the abolished monarchy's properties, and used the proceeds to build schools, hospitals and economic infrastructure.[8] Egypt's major Islamist organization, the Muslim Brotherhood, the only major internal opposition to Nasser throughout the Arabist's almost two-decades rule, opposed the land reform program as 'un-Islamic.'

Nasser also negotiated the exit of the British military, completed in 1956.

After abolishing feudalism and Britain's colonial presence, Nasser focused on the fifth point of the Revolution's six-point program—building a powerful military, one able to defend Egypt's newly won independence. One of the keys to accomplishing this objective was to buy arms for the ill-equipped Egyptian army. This led the Egyptian leader to approach major powers to sell him military gear. He was also interested in securing from them financing for the Aswan High Dam, a major infrastructure project at the heart of the new government's plans for Egypt's economic development.[9]

Nasser turned first to the United States. The Americans were willing to do a deal, but required a pledge of obedience first. Specifically, Washington wanted Egypt to sign on to a US-led anti-communist crusade. Nasser refused, and the United States, consequently, refused to sell him arms or underwrite his dam project.

The dam—to be built at Aswan on the Nile River—was Nasser's key to modernizing the Egyptian economy. It would produce hydro-electricity, control flooding of farmland, and improve irrigation, increasing Egypt's tillable soil by one-third. Cairo initially secured promises from the United States, France, Britain and the World Bank to underwrite construction of the dam, but when Nasser refused to negate Egypt's independence by submitting to US leadership, Washington—already irritated by Cairo's recognition of Communist China and support for a national liberation struggle in Algeria—withdrew its promises.

Undeterred, Nasser sought financing from the USSR. The Soviets were more accommodating, underwriting the dam project to the tune of $300 million.[10] To generate an internal source of revenue, Nasser nationalized the Suez Canal, with a view to using tolls paid by ships passing through the canal to help pay for the dam and to fund other infrastructure projects.

The canal had been built and owned by a British-French consortium. Two-thirds of Europe's oil was shipped via the canal and one-third of the canal's traffic was British. While Egypt had an incontestable legal right to nationalize the British-French infrastructure marvel,[11] London and Paris seethed with incandescent fury at what they saw as Nasser's insolence in expropriating Western capital.

The Third World reacted quite differently. Songs of praise were sung to a new hero. Leila Khaled wrote that Nasser's *lèse-majesté* against what Europe regarded as its property brought him "stardom in the firmament of the Third World." In recognition of this achievement, "the nationalists identified themselves with Nasserism and applauded his deeds for the next decade."[12]

Meanwhile, in the First World, Nasser was demonized. The British prime minister Anthony Eden denounced him as "the Mussolini of the Nile."[13] French premier Guy Mollet compared him to Hitler, as did *The London Daily Mirror*.[14] The British Labour leader Hugh Gaitskell agreed. *The Voice of Britain* condemned the Egyptian leader as a "barking dictator," while *The Daily Telegraph* complained that Nasser had a master plan to control the Middle East,[15] this, apparently, being considered the sole prerogative of the British government. For added measure, Nasser was called a crypto-communist and anti-Semite.[16]

"To the American, British, and European publics, and members of the US Congress," Nasser was "the Saddam Hussein of his day," recalled Said

Aburish.[17] Saddam, an Arabist in the vein of Nasser, would also later be compared to the Nazi leader. He was branded by Western governments as the "Hitler of Baghdad."[18]

Nasser's sins against the First World were multi-fold. He had overthrown Britain's puppet, King Farouk, ejected the British military from his country, and nationalized an important shipping route. But this was only the tip of the iceberg. He encouraged the colonial oppressed—not only in the Arab world, but farther afield—to throw off the chains of colonialism. He called for his Arab compatriots to overthrow the rulers the British and French had imposed on them. He funded their liberation movements. He inspired Arabs to dream of pan-Arab unity. Equally as disturbing for US, British and French statesmen, Nasser pioneered Arab socialism, which relied on publicly owned enterprises and economic planning, at the expense of First World free enterprise, to develop Egypt's economy. Were Nasserism allowed to thrive, the United States, France and Britain would be driven out of the Arab world, Western investors would be denied profit-making opportunities in the Middle East and North Africa, and Arabs would shake off European-imposed political divisions and coalesce into a strong, pan-Arab state. The whole Third World might take heart and rise as a single bloc in revolt.

Nasser denounced the rulers the West had imposed on the Arabs as "agents of imperialism," "agents of reaction and ignorance," and "the syndicate of monarchs."[19] He told Arabs that their leaders were traitors.[20] Nasser upbraided the Western-aligned president of Lebanon, Camille Chamoun as an "agent" of the West and a "slave," and hurled the same aspersions at the British-backed prime minister of Iraq, Nuri Said.[21]

Using the assets of the Egyptian state, Nasser built a strong propaganda machine that broadcast Arabist appeals throughout the Arab world, importuning Arabs to overthrow the quislings who governed them and to transcend the veiled colonialism the quislings represented.[22] Among the many targets of Radio Cairo's *Voice of the Arabs* was Nuri Said's government, which the Arabs of Iraq were called upon to topple.[23] These broadcasts, needless to say, consternated the Western-backed rulers of the Arab world, who became increasingly apoplectic as Arabs flocked to Nasser's anti-colonialism in growing numbers.[24]

Another target of Nasser's anti-colonial disdain was the Jordanian monarchy. Nasser referred to Jordan's King Hussein as "a descendant of traitors" and "a tool of the imperialists."[25] Hussein was a scion of the Hashemite dynasty, which claimed descent from Mohammad, and invoked this claim to justify rule over Islam's holy sites in the Hijaz region of Arabia. The Hashemites entered into a pact with the British in World War I. They would mobilize the Arabs to revolt against the Turks, Britain's enemy, in return for British-protected rule over the Arab world after the war. The British eventually installed the Hashemite prince Faisal as king of Iraq, a country the British created out of Mesopotamia, while his brother Abdullah was imposed as monarch of Jordan, a country artificially manufactured by carving territory out of Syria.

From the beginning, the Hashemite monarchy in Jordan was wholly unacceptable to the people over which it ruled, a condition that prevails today. This should come as no shock. The Hashemites are a foreign dynasty with no roots in Jordan. The monarchy was created by an outside power, Britain. The consent of the people over which the monarchy rules has never been solicited. The situation is tantamount to the Chinese arbitrarily creating a new country out of southwestern California, and imposing on it the rule of a Spanish king.

Devoid of legitimacy, the imposed Jordanian monarchy has, since its inception, relied on outside support to maintain its unacceptable rule. Its military was staffed at the highest levels by British officers who reported directly to London. The top military official, the British General Sir John Bagot Glubb, was effectively the uncrowned king of Jordan, or at least behaved as one. [26] Glubb ruled Jordan from behind the scenes, until Nasser demanded that Hussein dismiss him. Eager to counter Nasser's accusation that the Jordanian monarchy was nothing but a front for British imperialism, Hussein complied. Glubb returned to London, complaining that Britain was being chased out of the Middle East, anticipating US Senator John McCain, who in 2017 sounded the alarm that the Axis of Resistance, a coalition of Iran, Syria and Hezbollah, was trying to chase the United States out of West Asia. British prime minister Anthony Eden blamed Nasser for Glubb's removal and vowed to destroy the Arab leader.[27]

To shore up its rule, the Hashemite dynasty looked to Israel as a natural ally. Abdullah, as we have seen, machinated with the Zionists to divide Palestine in the First Settler-Native War.[28] Hussein, Abdullah's grandson, took the informal alliance further, beginning secret meetings with the Israelis in May 1963.[29] In those meetings, Hussein sought Israeli help to counter Nasser, while pledging to suppress anti-Israeli activity in the West Bank, at that time under Jordanian control.[30] At the same time, Jordanian intelligence entered into a cooperative arrangement with the Mossad, the Israeli intelligence agency.[31]

The monarchy also built an extensive security apparatus, whose operatives were—and continue to be—trained and equipped by Western powers, to suppress opposition to the Hashemites' tyranny.[32] Emblematic of the Pantagruelian dimensions of Jordan's secret police is the reality that the largest building in Amman, the country's capital, is the headquarters of the internal security service.[33]

To support a lifestyle befitting a king, and to cement Hussein's loyalty, the CIA made him a salaried employee.[34] While the fact that the CIA 'owned' the monarchy was kept a secret, Nasser called out the Jordanian quisling, openly accusing him of being a CIA agent.[35] CIA 'ownership' also extended to the Jordanian state as a whole; it operated under CIA supervision, and continues to do so today. Michael Hayden, the CIA director under George W. Bush, told *The Washington Post's* Bob Woodward that the CIA pumps "tens of millions of dollars into a number of foreign intelligence services, such as" Jordan's, "which he said the CIA... 'owned.'"[36] At the CIA's direction, Hussein unceasingly taunted Nasser, calling him a paper tiger, afraid to attack Israel, seeking to place him in a position in which inaction would lead to his humiliation and action would lead him to certain defeat (and humiliation) at the hands of the stronger Israelis.[37]

The "fabrication called Jordan," wrote Said Aburish, "would be unstable without an army to maintain it. For nearly thirty years this army was officered and equipped by the designers of Jordan, the British. Now, the US equips Jordan's native army for the same reason: to maintain" a pro-West monarchy "against the wishes of his people."[38] Nasser, intolerant of the 'owned' leaders who had been imposed on the Arab world by exploitative foreign powers, was indefatigable in denouncing them, and his broadsides against the local agents of imperialism aroused the indignation of the Arab people against their quisling rulers.

Nasser's opposition to the local agents of foreign powers, however, was more than rhetorical. On top of calling for Arabs to overthrow their imposed rulers, he provided arms and training to Arab guerrilla-based national liberation movements. "Nasser was the backbone of the Algerian rebels,"[39] fighting to free their country from French settlers. When the Algerians won their independence in 1962, after an eight-year struggle, Nasser regarded the rebels' victory as a personal triumph. At the same time, he made a signal contribution to the struggle of Palestinian Arabs to recover their homeland. Nasser played a decisive role in the creation of the PLO, the Palestinian Liberation Organization, instilling in it a mission to mobilize "the forces of the Palestinian Arab people to wage the battle of liberation, as a shield for the rights and aspirations of the people of Palestine and as a road to victory."[40]

Aid was also given to non-Arab Africans who, like their Arab brethren, were engaged in a struggle against the First World for freedom and democracy. Pointing out that Egypt was part of Africa, Nasser said that his country could not stand aside from the sanguinary and dreadful struggles raging in the heart of Africa.[41] The Third World leader invited hundreds of African students to attend Egyptian universities free of charge.[42]

Although he was the president of Egypt, Nasser's compass was the Arab world. He spoke less as an Egyptian and more as an Arab,[43] viewing his constituency as Arab speakers from the Atlantic Ocean in the West to the Persian Gulf in the East.[44] Unified into one large state, the Arab world would be, in territory and population, larger than the United States of America, and strong enough to put an end to the indignity and humiliation of (indirect) foreign rule. What's more, such a state would contain within it the petroleum riches of Mesopotamia and Arabia. "Arab oil for Arabs," was Nasser's slogan. Not only would a United Arab State be a geographic Brobdingnag, it would have the means to achieve economic independence and a high standard of living for all sectors of the Arab world. Nasser had no concrete plan for how to bring this about, but transforming the divided Arab land into a unified state was, all the same, a captivating dream, which he did much to instill in others.[45]

Throughout Nasser's years in power, numerous attempts were made by his followers to merge their countries with Egypt into a united Arab republic as a nucleus for an eventual pan-Arab state. The first such attempt came in 1958 when Syria joined Egypt. As we've seen, pan-Arab motivations may have played less of a role in the merger of the two Arab states than a desire to pre-empt the possibility of communists gaining ascendancy in Syria. In any event, the union was short-lived, lasting only until 1961. Once the communists were jailed, exiled and purged, the union collapsed.

The year 1958 also saw the Nasser-inspired overthrow of the British-installed monarchy in Iraq. While the Arab nationalist leader, and his Iraqi votaries, were keen on bringing Iraq into the United Arab Republic, the country's powerful communist party was opposed, and the proposed fusion failed to come to fruition. However, the potential for unification was tantalizingly or threateningly evident, depending on one's perspective. Nasser greeted the ouster of Iraq's Hashemite monarchy with these words: "My brothers, the flag of freedom which flies over Baghdad today will fly over Amman and Riyadh. Yes, the flag of freedom which flies over Cairo, Damascus and Baghdad today will fly over the rest of the Middle East."[46] These words, needless to say, sent frissons of fear down the spines of the Saudi and Jordanian kings, and their Western backers. Washington immediately sent Marines to protect the Chamoun government of Lebanon against a possible Arabist attempt at a *coup d'état*. The British dispatched troops to Jordan to protect the monarchy there. Zionist settlers in Palestine also reacted with alarm. The prospects for the survival of a First World outpost in the heart of a unified Arab world are dim indeed. But the more immediate concern for the Israelis was that the union of Egypt, Syria and Iraq would have created an Arab country able to match Israel militarily. The West, much committed to domino theories, also had cause for concern. Once the process of unification began, it might become self-perpetuating, with each Arab flag of freedom raised in an Arab capital making the next flag raising more likely.[47]

Despite the heady promise of 1958, the project of Arab unification failed to gain traction. In 1964, Egypt, Iraq and Yemen formed the United Political Command to pave the way for a political union to create a new United Arab Republic, but the project failed. In 1972, Muammar Gaddafi, a young Libyan army officer intensely devoted to Nasserism, attempted to create a political union of Libya, Egypt, Sudan and Syria, to be known as the Federation of Arab Republics, but this plan, too, advanced no further than a proposal, and remained a dream.

In her autobiography, Leila Khaled recalls a hortatory address she made as a member of the Nasserist Arab National Movement. I've included it here to illustrate Nasser's pan-Arab themes.

> I concluded with a plea to free Palestine. Such a state of affairs cannot continue and we must not allow it to continue. We can end it through Arab unity and the liberation of Palestine. Our goal can be reached if the [United Arab

Republic] was expanded and all the Arab states become one nation-state. We must fight for one Arab nation, for unity, for freedom, for socialism. We must defeat enemy number one, America, the [armorer of] Israel, and we must seize our own oil resources. We must learn to emulate our Algerian brethren in order to liberate Palestine.[48]

Khaled's reference to socialism points to an important aspect of Nasserism. Not all Arab nationalists are socialists, but Nasser, and the Ba'athists, (whose tripartite slogan, unity, freedom and socialism, indicate a socialist commitment), were. The socialism of Nasser and the Ba'athists has been called 'Arab socialism,' to distinguish it from the socialism of communist parties. The socialism of communist parties, contrary to what some Marxists believe, is only one possible socialism of many. Marx and Engels, in their *Communist Manifesto*, identified a number of socialisms, including feudal, petit-bourgeois, German, bourgeois and utopian. To be sure, they were critical of these socialisms, but recognized them as socialisms, even if, in their view, they were flawed.

It is often understood that Marxist socialism takes class as its basic unit of analysis, while Arab socialism brings nation forward as the primary consideration. Hence, while Marxists are concerned mainly with the liberation of the working class from its exploitation by capitalists, Arab socialists are concerned mainly with the liberation of the Arab nation from its exploitation by the West. These views, however, are oversimplifications.

Arab socialism has been as concerned with championing the cause of the subordinate classes within Arab countries, including workers and peasants, as Marxist socialism has. It would be an error to conclude that Arab socialists condone class oppression within their own countries and have done nothing to relieve it. Moreover, the understanding that Marxist socialism has focused exclusively on the struggle between the working and capitalist classes is too narrow. Marx and Engels saw the compass of class struggle as including more than the antagonism of capitalist and proletarian, feudal lord and serf, and master and slave. Instead, they saw class struggle as arising out of all economic relationships in which one group is able to command—and therefore exploit—the labor of another. This includes not only the aforesaid struggles, but also those between men and women over the division of labor within the household and the struggle between rich nations and poor ones over the division of labor on an international scale.[49]

The concept of slavery is central to the thinking of Marx and Engels. Workers are the wage *slaves* of capitalists. Women have often been and often remain the domestic *slaves* of men. Engels argued that, "the first class oppression coincides with that of the female sex by the male."[50] And Marx observed that a nation can grow rich at the expense of another and that those who are not equipped to understand this cannot understand how in the same country one class can enrich itself at the expense of another.[51] Lenin put it another way: Hundreds "of millions of working people in Asia, in the colonies in general, and in the small countries" had been *enslaved* by "a few select nations."[52] As Domenico Losurdo put it: "For Marx and Engels, the class struggle is fought around the division of labor at the international and national levels and within the family. The peoples who shake off the colonial yoke, the subaltern classes who fight against capitalist exploitation, and the women who refuse the 'domestic slavery' to which the patriarchal family subjects them, are the actors in emancipatory class struggles."[53]

Arab socialism was concerned with class struggle on all three levels, and did not restrict itself to overcoming the Arab world's enslavement by the West. On the contrary, it simultaneously tackled women's liberation, uplift of workers and peasants at home, and the Arab world's emancipation from the yoke of imperialism. In doing so, it was more faithful to the multidimensional thinking of Marx and Engels on class struggle than has been the practice of many people who call themselves Marxists.

Nasser secularized the religious courts, liberalized divorce laws, banned child labor, made education compulsory and free at the primary level, and began the process of ending institutional misogyny.[54] To overcome religious discrimination, he readmitted Shia, Alawites and Druze to the mainstream. They had been scorned and excluded as heretics and idolaters for centuries. To promote the integration of women into Egyptian society, he introduced mixed-sex, co-educational schools and began to promote female equality.[55]

The political Islamists were incensed. The Muslim Brotherhood, whose members and offshoots continue to comprise the main internal opposition to contemporary Arab socialism (see, for example, the war against the governments of Hafez al-Assad and Bashar al-Assad in Syria), bristled at the closure of Islamic courts and Nasser's moves to guarantee women's rights. The organization's chief ideologue Sayyed Qutub, wrote a book,

Signposts Along the Way, denouncing Nasser's Arab socialism as anti-Islamic.[56] Qutub's ideological descendants, the Syrian 'rebels,' were lionized by self-declared Western Marxists who sneered at Arab socialism.

Nasser also established a National Charter, to provide universal health care, public housing for the poor, vocational schools, and clean drinking water. Doctors were hired and hundreds of public schools were built. At the same time, rent controls were introduced, and basic foodstuffs were subsidized.[57] The Charter continued to expand women's rights, despite the often violent opposition of the Islamists. [58]

By design, half of the seats in the National Assembly were reserved for workers and peasants, and popular participation in the political life of Egypt was promoted by reserving assembly places for representatives of student groups, women's organizations, and trade associations.[59] Nasser strove to make the National Assembly as representative of all sectors of Egyptian society as possible, a departure from the practice of Western countries, in which legislative bodies typically over-represent the agents of an exploiting economic elite.

Nasser's economic policy closely hewed to socialist practice. He nationalized the commanding heights of the economy, including famously the Suez Canal, but also pharmaceutical, cement, phosphate, and tobacco industries, which had been owned by British and French investors. These were brought under state control. New state-owned enterprises were created, including a steel company, which became Egypt's largest enterprise.[60] Nasser paid special attention to indigenizing the Egyptian economy, making it as independent as possible, to safeguard Cairo's political independence. Strategic sectors—banking, transportation and overseas trade—were entirely publicly owned.[61] Private investment was permitted in some industries—mining, for example—but only by Egyptians. Foreign investment was allowed in some cases, but as joint ventures, with Cairo owning the majority of shares.[62] Enterprise employees were guaranteed an advisory role in their enterprise, and enterprises were mandated to provide programs of profit sharing.[63]

Arab socialism also championed the democratization of land, a vitally important reform in a region where most people were peasants.

Some analysts emphasize the differences between Arab socialism and communism, but the differences were more superficial than real. While Arab socialists, in contradistinction to the Soviets, tolerated some degree of free enterprise, not all communists have insisted that all enterprises be collectively owned. This is true, today, of Chinese communism. The main difference is that communists consciously accepted a Marxist paradigm, while Arab socialists rejected formal Marxist terms, categories and identification, in favor of wrapping the basic concerns of the political Left in an integument they saw as more acceptable to the conservativism of the Arab world.

Arabs were largely peasants, steeped in Islam. Arab socialists worried that Marxism-Leninism, associated strongly with atheism and Russia, would be rejected as anti-Islam and foreign, simply a new Russian imperialism to supersede the old imperialism of Western Europe. The project of advancing the goals of the political Left—emancipation from oppressions of class, nation, religion, and sex—could therefore be more easily achieved in the Arab world (it was believed) under the rubric of a home-grown political project. To this end, Nasser used the term 'Islamic socialism' to refer to what others have called 'Arab socialism,' appealing to a major cultural element of the Arab world, and the Arab nation's dominant religion, to legitimize his economic, political and social program. Whether consciously or not, he borrowed from the practice of Jesuit missionaries, who found that converting indigenous North Americans to Christianity was made easier by grafting Christian rituals and concepts upon indigenous ones.

Recognizing that the major internal opposition to Arab socialism was the Muslim Brotherhood, Arab socialists genuflected to Islam, even if they rejected it as the basis for organizing law and the state. In order to invest their project with legitimacy, they looked for ways to borrow the ready-made legitimacy of Islam. Nasser, the Assads, Gaddafi and Saddam, made clear that they were pious Muslims. It would be outstandingly strange for a communist leader to do the same. In a region in which Islam has great significance, communism as a doctrine associated with atheism, was at a disadvantage.

These surface distinctions aside, Arab socialists and communists shared "the idea that the government has direct responsibility for the welfare of the people," as Noam Chomsky once observed.[64] And the causes they pursued—anti-monarchism, anti-feudalism, agrarian reform, anti-imperialism, women's rights, overcoming discriminations based on religion and sect, use of the state to achieve poverty reduction, and economic development for all sectors—have been the same. The consequences of these policies—for the emirs, sultans and kings of the Arab world, and for Western investors—were also the same. For this reason, Nasser, Assad, and Saddam, while not identifying as communists, and maintaining a hostile stance toward local communist parties, were nonetheless known in US foreign policy circles as "Arab communists," which indeed they may as well have been from the point of view of Western investors.

Despite the vicissitudes of their relationship with the USSR, the Arab socialists were ultimately able to work with the Soviet Union and the Soviet Union with them, more so than the Arab socialists were able to work with the United States. A shared commitment to fundamental Leftist values accounts for why Arab socialist states became Soviet clients. While Nasser repressed the Egyptian Communist Party, his opposition to his Leftist rivals was more a matter of a tactical disagreement over how to advance the goals of the political Left in the Arab world and his fear that the ascendancy of the party would mean that Egypt would fall completely under the sway of Moscow as a Soviet satellite.[65] Nasser was willing to work with the Soviets, to accept Soviet aid, and accept the limits on Egypt's independence entailed in its reliance on the USSR for arms, military and technical advisers, food aid, and investment, but he was unwilling to forsake Egypt's independence completely by reducing Egypt to the status of a satellite. We might, then, think of Nasser as an Arab communist *au fond*, adamantly committed to his county's independence, who saw Egypt's communists as agents of Moscow and therefore as threats to Egypt's independence, and whose embrace of atheism and Marxism he viewed as guaranteed to marginalize the political Left in the Arab world. Of course, all of this was of no moment to London, Paris and Washington, and the Arab quislings who did their bidding. From their perspective, the efflorescence of either the communist or Arab socialist projects would have the same regrettable and entirely indistinguishable consequences for their ability to exploit the Arab world. Accordingly, both were regarded as dangers to be weakened, undermined and ultimately destroyed.

London and Washington looked to the Muslim Brotherhood as a naturally ally in the fight against both communism and Arab socialism.[66]

Founded in Egypt in 1928 by Hassan al-Banna, the Brotherhood, or *Ikhwan*, from the organization's Arabic name *Jam'iyat al-Ikhwan al-Mus-limin*, was intolerant of movements of the political Left, and regarded women's liberation, land reform, equality for minority religious sects, and socialism, as anti-Islamic.[67] In contrast to the Pan-Arabic dream of creating a network of unified Arab states, committed to secular modernization as the antidote to the colonialist poison of underdevelopment and the ongoing imperialist threat of recolonization, the Muslim Brotherhood advocated a network of Islamic republics whose political and legal foundation would be the Quran.[68]

The *Ikhwan* had no objection to the Egyptian monarchy and the country's feudal elite, so long as Egypt's aristocrats hewed closely to Islam. And while they were vehemently opposed to colonialism in the Muslim world—not because it was exploitative but because it diluted Islam—they were more strongly opposed to Nasser, whose secularism and cooperation with the Soviets, they found intolerable. In early 1953, the Brothers reached out to London to engage British assistance in undermining the champion of this repellent ideology. The Brotherhood's overtures were followed by missions to Riyadh to enlist the support of the Saudi monarchy. The Saudis were receptive, transferring cash to the organization's bank accounts, and signing on as one of its major bankers. Then, in late 1955, *Ikhwan* officials visited the deposed Egyptian king in exile in Italy. Would he work with the Brotherhood to overthrow Nasser? Jordan's King Hussein pitched in, allowing the Islamists to use his country as a home base and furnishing Brotherhood leaders with diplomatic passports to ease their movements through the Arab world as they plotted Nasser's demise.[69]

The Muslim Brotherhood's cooperation with monarchs and the major imperialist centers against Arab socialism inevitably led to fierce civil wars, not only in Egypt, but in Syria, where Hafez al-Assad and later his son and successor Bashar, were targeted by the *Ikhwan* for promoting Arab socialism.

As the Muslim Brotherhood actively sought alliances with the British, the Saudi kingdom, the Jordanian monarchy, and the deposed Egyptian king, Washington was reaching out to al-Banna. The Americans saw Islam as a potential bulwark against the spread of communism. US officials believed that Islam could be used as a counterweight to movements of the political Left and were therefore keen to strengthen Islam's grip on the

Arab world. The *Ikhwan,* in the estimation of the US State Department, could be a valuable cudgel to use against Arab communists. As early as the 1940s, US officials were holding regular meetings with al-Banna in Cairo.[70]

In the fall of 1953, Said Ramadan, al-Banna's son-in-law, had an audience with US president Dwight Eisenhower at the White House. At that point, or soon after or shortly before, Ramadan was recruited by the CIA. [71] The White House meeting would mark the beginning of a long and enduring relationship between the United States and the Muslim Brotherhood. Ramadan was a top *Ikhwan* official and one of the organization's key ideologues.[72] When his father-in-law died, he took over as the organization's chief spiritual guide.

With US assistance, the CIA asset set up an international affairs office in Geneva to propagate political Islam throughout the Arab and Muslim worlds. The office, little more than a CIA front, received tens of millions of dollars of funding from US intelligence.[73] One of Ramadan's jobs was to work with other CIA front groups, including Radio Free Europe and Radio Liberty, to turn Muslims in the Soviet Union against Moscow.[74]

In 1963, Ramadan contributed to the founding of the still extant Muslim World League, a Saudi-based pan-Islamist organization, whose goal is to establish a Muslim world union to be ruled by Islamic law, an obvious counterpoise to Nasser's vision of a secular Arab union. A year later, Ramadan issued a religious ruling condemning Arab socialism as apostasy.[75]

The CIA entrusted Ramadan with organizing Nasser's elimination.[76] An assassination attempt, the first of many against the Arab nationalist leader, was made on October 26, 1954 by Mohamed Abdel Latif, a Ramadan follower, as Nasser was giving an address celebrating the impending evacuation of British troops from Egypt. "Not a month passed without a new" Muslim Brotherhood attempt to assassinate Nasser, wrote Aburish. "They did it both on their own and also with British and occasionally American cooperation." The Brothers tried everything: nerve gas, poisoning Nasser's coffee, and hit squads.[77] Backed by the CIA and the Saudi monarchy, the Brotherhood made other attempts to undermine the Arab socialist leader. At least fourteen attempts were made to overthrow Nasser's government. In its efforts to do so, the *Ikhwan* blew up sixteen bridges and recruited members of the Egyptian military.[78] When Nasser

died, the Muslim Brotherhood ordered its followers to forebear from pray-
ing for an enemy they denounced as an infidel.[79]

If the Muslim Brotherhood was out to destroy Nasser, so too were the
Israelis. The Brotherhood objected to Nasser's domestic policies: land
reform, socialism, secularism, and freedom from discrimination based
on religion and gender. None of these policies, however, troubled the
Israelis. Their concerns were broader—even existential. Zionism was a
colonial movement whose success anachronistically coincided with the
Third World revolt against colonialism. Nasser was a rising champion of
the great wave of decolonization that was sweeping the world. "It was clear
to Israeli leaders from the early 1950s on that any radical movement aimed
at furthering the progress of decolonization in the Third World, and
within the Middle East specifically, was a threat, and Israel had to act
accordingly," observed Beit-Hallahmi.[80]

There were other reasons Zionist Jews sought Nasser's destruction. The
Egyptian leader inspired movements of pan-Arab unification. If these
movements succeeded, Israel would soon be outmatched militarily by a
unified Arab state. One of the reasons Israel had prevailed in the First
Settler-Native War was because the natives had been divided. Arab division was a *sine qua non* of Israeli survival, and the Israelis were prepared
to do all they could to keep the Arab world fractured. Hence, Israeli strategy from the very first moments of the settler state's existence was to build
alliances with groups within the Arab world that could be counted on to
oppose Arab unity. These groups included the Kurds and the Maronite
Christians, minorities that preferred an independent existence to absorp-
tion into a pan-Arab super-state. The Persian Gulf oil monarchs, who
preferred to keep Arab oil for themselves, and therefore opposed a movement whose slogans included 'Arab oil for the Arabs,' were also key allies.
So too were imposed leaders, such as the Hashemite king of Jordan, who
were unacceptable to their subjects, and would cooperate with the Israelis
in return for protection.

Another reason Israeli leaders conspired to destroy Nasser was to fulfill
the basic bargain that Zionists, from Herzl forward, had struck with
Western empires. Herzl, it will be recalled, promised that in return for
Great Power support that a Jewish state in Palestine would become a link
in Europe's "rampart against Asia," and "an outpost of civilization"
(Western colonialism) "against barbarism" (the Arabs.)[81] More than a

century later, the promise remained intact and undiminished. In the early 1990s, Israeli leader Benjamin Netanyahu described the Zionist state in his book *A Place Among the Nations* as "the West's outpost in the Middle East."[82] In Nasser's day, Gershom Schocken, editor of the liberal daily *Haaretz*, described Israel as a "watch-dog... capable of sufficiently punishing one or more of the neighboring countries, whose lack of courtesy towards the West [had] gone beyond the permissible limits."[83] There was no doubt that Nasser had committed multiple improprieties against the concept of a Western dictatorship over the people of the Arab world, and in challenging the dictatorship in the name of freedom and democracy he had gone well beyond the limits the imperialist West was willing to endure. Expunging Nasser and his Arab socialist movement would be a great feather in the cap of Israeli leaders, and would perhaps encourage Washington—which, until the late 1960s, preferred to rely on Arab quislings as the local enforcers of its imperial rule—to robustly support the Zionist state. To show Israel's commitment to protecting Western interests in the Middle East, the Jewish settler state would become the "rock... against which the waves of Nasser's Arab nationalism [would] be broken," as Moshe Dayan promised.[84]

Israel, as we'll see in a moment, would wage two wars against Nasser, the second of which broke the Arab leader and his movement, and, as a consequence, brought the Jewish Sparta to the attention of the United States as a potential extension of US military power in the Middle East. But prior to the Israelis initiating two outright wars of aggression against their Arab nemesis, they undertook a series of low-level aggressions against Egypt, designed to lure Nasser into a war with his more powerful neighbor. If Nasser took the bait, he would be destroyed in the subsequent fighting. If he didn't, his failure to respond would humiliate him before the hundreds of millions of Arabs who looked to him as their new Saladin.

In 1955, Ben-Gurion ordered an attack on an Egyptian army post inside the Gaza Strip. Code named Operation Black Arrow, the attack was led by Ariel Sharon, an Israeli general and later prime minister, who would become notorious as the architect of the 1982 massacre of Palestinian civilians by Maronite fascists at the Sabra and Shatila refugee camps in Lebanon. Sharon was infamous for excess, and his operation killed 56 Egyptian soldiers and wounded dozens. With an ill-equipped and poorly trained army, Nasser could do nothing.[85] Israel continued to mount a succession of minor aggressions against the impotent Egyptian military, knowing that with each attack the Arab leader ignored, the deeper would become his humiliation before his Arab compatriots, and the weaker would be his grip on the Arab street. If Nasser responded, better still. The Egyptian president would simply hand the Israelis the *casus belli* they sought to destroy him. Nasser sat tight. He had no choice but to allow the Israelis to taunt, torment and humiliate him.

CHAPTER SEVEN

Naksa

> *"For the Arabs, nothing has been the same since.*
> *In all likelihood, nothing will ever be the same."*
>
> Said K. Aburish[1]

Two years before Ben-Gurion ordered Sharon to pummel Nasser with a series of humiliating blows, and a year after the July 23 Revolution, Washington and London moved against another Third World leader, whose great crime was to nationalize his country's key economic asset. The prime minister of Iran had sought to bring a measure of economic sovereignty to Iranians. Nationalizing assets (that have been used by foreign owners to suck wealth out of a country), in order to use the wealth for internal development for this country, is a profoundly democratic policy, but, importantly, is inimical to the profit-making interests of foreign concerns. Attempts by Third World leaders to establish independent control of their economies, in preference to their economies being used as spheres of profit-accumulation for the sole direçt benefit of foreign investors, is almost invariably met by the opposition of investor-dominated foreign governments.

Like Nasser, Mohammad Mossadegh was a nationalist committed to asserting his country's political and economic sovereignty. As prime minister of Iran, Mossadegh, leading a National Front largely guided by the values of the political Left, nationalized the British-owned Anglo-Iranian Oil Company. Bringing the country's oil fields under public control was greeted in Iran by near universal approval, but provoked the ire of the British and US governments, which viewed Iran as little more than a vast oil field whose *raison d'être* was to furnish Western investors with sufficiently large quantities of black gold at sufficiently low prices to conjure Pantagruelian profits. These profits would be used to enrich the lives of investors in the West at the expense of Iranians, who were expected to forego any claim to the development potential inhered in the vast trove of oil beneath their feet.

The Dulles brothers, John Foster and Allen, Brahmins who, in civilian life, were partners in Wall Street's top law firm, persuaded US president Dwight Eisenhower that Mossadegh should be overthrown and replaced by a quisling who could restore Iran to its proper place as a sphere of Western profit making. The brothers, fanatical anti-Communists, charted US foreign policy as the United States' dual secretaries of state, John Foster as the *de jure* holder of the post and Allen, head of the CIA, as "the secretary of state for unfriendly countries," to use his own description of his post.[2] It should be noted that implicit in Allen Dulles's self-conferred title was a reference to what countries were unfriendly to, not the United States *per se*, but to a US investor class that sought to grow wealthy at their expense.

The brothers saw Mossadegh as a Persian communist and Soviet puppet. The reality, however, was not quite as black and white as that. Mossadegh was not a member of a communist party, though his political values were unquestionably of the political Left and largely overlapped those of communists. What mattered to the Dulles brothers was not Mossadegh's party affiliation, or his connections to the USSR, real or imagined, but that he embraced political values that contradicted those of the Dulles brothers and their class cohorts. More importantly, the Iranian prime minister acted on his values, and in doing so challenged the US Empire's self-declared prerogative to claim any part of the world as a capitalist playground for enriching the Dulles brothers' fellow Brahmins and the Dulles's law firm clients.[3]

At the Dulles brothers' behest, Kermit Roosevelt, the CIA's top man in the Middle East, organized a plan to destabilize Mossadegh's government. Working through the Iranian army, which had close ties with the Pentagon, the plan was brought to fruition. In August 1953, the army struck.[4] Mossadegh was arrested, and forced to yield to Mohammad Reza,

Shah of the Pahlavi dynasty. Until he was overthrown in 1979, the Shah would act as one of the chief guardians of US interests in West Asia.

The Dulles-organized *coup d'état* delivered an enormous pecuniary advantage to the duo's friends in the US oil industry. Prior to Mossadegh's democratization of Iran's oil industry, the British owned the Persian oil fields. With Washington's man, the Shah, in power, the ownership structure changed. Five US oil companies were now given 40 percent of Iran's oil.[5] Hence, in a short period, ownership of Iran's petroleum resources was transferred from British investors to Iranians *en bloc*, and then to British *and* US investors—or from private ownership to public ownership back to private ownership divided between the oil companies of a waning empire and the oil companies of a waxing one.

Mossadegh was the first victim of Western-engineered regime change operations of post-colonial governments headed by leaders of the political Left that sought to reverse the exploitation of their countries by the investing classes of one or more Western powers.[6] "My only crime," said Mossadegh, "is that I nationalized the Iranian oil industry and removed from this land the network of colonialism and political and economic influence of the greatest empire on earth."[7] Mossadegh, as would be true of regime-change victims to follow, was a post-colonial leader who sought to overcome neocolonial control of his country's economy. While post-colonial countries enjoyed a titular political independence, their economies remained tied to those of their former colonial masters, and existed, not for the people at home, but for a narrow band of private investors in remote First World countries. Efforts to redress this profoundly anti-democratic arrangement provoked Western governments to intervene in the affairs of their former colonies to pre-empt or reverse all attempts at democratization. Following the coup, the editors of *The New York Times* noted that, "underdeveloped countries with rich resources now have an object lesson in the heavy cost that must be paid by one of their number which goes berserk with fanatical nationalism."[8]

In 1955, British prime minister Anthony Eden established the Baghdad Pact, a grouping of anti-independence Middle Eastern governments that were to form a northern tier of West Asian countries to protect the region's oil fields from a possible Soviet invasion; in other words, a *cordon sanitaire*. The alliance originally included Iraq, Iran, Pakistan, Turkey, and the United Kingdom. However, when Nasser-inspired Arab nationalists overthrew the British-backed Hashemite king of Iraq in 1958, Iraq dropped out, and the name Baghdad Pact no longer fit. The organization's appellation was changed to CENTO (Central Treaty Organization), and the depleted body continued to exist, later under US leadership, until 1979, when Iran dropped out in the wake of the overthrow of the US-backed Shah.

While the ostensible purpose of the organization was to protect West Asia from the allegedly nefarious designs of the Soviet Union, the true purpose was to strengthen London's faltering hand in the region.[9] With Nasser and his Free Officers' Movement having ousted the British-controlled King Farouk, with the expulsion of British forces from Egypt, and with the United States displacing London's influence in Iran, Britain's once near total domination of the Middle East was rapidly collapsing. British influence receded further in 1958 when Iraqi nationalists deposed the British-installed Iraqi monarchy.

CENTO proved to be a colossal failure. While portrayed as an anti-Soviet alliance, Arabs saw it as a neocolonial organization aimed at undermining Nasser and anyone else, including the Soviets, who might want to help the Arab world break free from its subordination to the West.[10] Radio Cairo's *Voice of the Arabs* importuned Iraqis to rise against the Baghdad Pact and topple the quisling government that had joined it. According to Nasser's broadcaster, "the Baghdad Pact was nothing but colonialism in disguise. Why should Arabs join an anti-communist alliance, when the Israeli enemy was regularly attacking positions in Gaza and the West Bank?"[11]

Washington conditioned arms sales to Nasser on Egypt joining the Pact. Because Nasser refused to reduce Egypt to an anti-Soviet janissary of the US Empire, he was denied US arms and financing for the Aswan High Dam project—a denial that led to the nationalization of the Suez Canal and Egypt's accepting military and economic aid from the USSR. Hence, rather than eclipsing Soviet influence in Egypt, the Pact—and Washington's insistence that Nasser join it—enhanced Soviet influence in the north African country. Despite the attempt to prevent Moscow's influence spreading to the Arab world, the Soviet Union established close military and political ties with not only Egypt, but Iraq (an original Baghdad Pact member), Syria, the People's Democratic Republic of Yemen, Somalia, and Libya. By 1970, the USSR had over 20,000 troops in Egypt, and naval bases in Syria, Somalia, and Yemen.

In October 1956, Britain, France, and Israel invaded Egypt in a joint operation to destroy Nasserism. The war, known tendentiously in the West as the Suez Canal Crisis, but in the Arab world as the Tripartite Aggression, and presented here as the Second Settler-Native War, was ultimately aimed at arresting the disarticulation of the British and French empires under the Nasserist assertion of Arab independence.[12] Nasser, in the view of the co-conspirator aggressors, was a key facilitator of and direct participant in a great movement of equality aimed at toppling the ascendancy of Europe's elites over the Arab world. If the movement continued to gain traction, the British and French empires would be completely hollowed out, and Jewish settlers in Palestine would either be expelled by the Arab natives or forced to live as equals in a democratic state rather than as denizens of a *Herrenvolk* Jewish state with rights superior to those of the Arabs.

The British, to be sure, had a litany of grievances against Nasser, apart from his nationalization of the Suez Canal. Nasser's overthrow of Farouk had cancelled British political influence in Egypt, and his propaganda had shamed King Hussein into dismissing John Bagot Glubb, the British general who commanded Jordan's army. Then there were Radio Cairo's incessant calls for the people of the Arab world to overthrow the kings, emirs, and sultans the British had inflicted upon them. Would Nasser's assaults on British domination of the Middle East ever end? "At one point" according to Said Aburish, Eden "reacted to the mention of Nasser's name by saying, 'I want him destroyed, I want him removed!'"[13]

For the French, Nasser was equally a threat. French influence in the world was steadily declining. France had fought a long war in Indochina from 1946 to 1954 to reassert colonial supremacy over natives who were bent on liberating themselves from colonial tyranny, and had recently liberated themselves from the Japanese. Inspired by a vision of equality, and vehemently renitent to resuming lives as instruments of French economic and political interests, the Vietnamese put up a terrific struggle under the leadership of Ho Chi Minh. By 1954, the French were forced to admit defeat, and cede the fight to the new hegemonic force, the United States. In 1956, Morocco and Tunisia, French protectorates, won their independence. Meanwhile, native Algerians, whose country the French had stolen and begun to settle in 1830, and had annexed to metropolitan France, had launched a war for independence in 1954. Nasser established a pipeline to the rebels through which munificent aid flowed, and which the Israelis, at the request of France, tried to disrupt.[14] So invested was Nasser in Algeria's struggle for liberation, that when the natives finally succeeded in ridding themselves of French tyranny, Nasser considered their victory a personal triumph.

Until 1973, US strategy called for the integration of Arab quislings into a US-led regional alliance. As imposed rulers who were unacceptable to the populations they ruled, Arab quislings were disinclined to take any action that would unnecessarily agitate public opinion. Their rule was tenuous at best, and taking measures that would further weaken it was ill advised, to say the least. For this reason, Arab governments were officially anti-Israeli, even if some were willing to cooperate covertly with the Zionists. So indignant were Arabs at Jewish settler colonialism, that any Arab government that overtly cooperated with Israel would invite its own destabilization. For this reason, there was no room for Israel in a US security system that included Arab states.[15]

Recognizing that the United States had emerged from World War II as an empire of incomparable scale, the Israelis—true to the roots of the Zionist movement established by Herzl and cultivated by Weizmann—desperately sought the sponsorship of the imperial goliath. If nothing else, Zionism recognized that toadyish scraping before the world's greatest imperialist power, and sycophantically offering to do its dirty work in exchange for protection, was a necessity of achieving its goal of displacing the Arab natives of Palestine and preventing their return.

US president John F. Kennedy had explained to Israel's foreign minister Golda Meir that Washington couldn't rule the Middle East through Arab proxies and at the same time conspicuously back Israel.[16] Israel tried repeatedly to interest the United States in a military alliance, proposing to become Washington's main strategic asset in West Asia, but in vain. Washington remained committed to an alliance of Arab quisling states. This forced the Israelis into the camp of Britain and France, who were willing to enter into an alliance with the Zionist state.[17] The alliance was cemented by the opposition of the three states to Nasser. London sought to avenge the Arab socialist leader for driving British influence out of the Middle East, Paris wanted to put an end to Nasser's support of the Algerian rebels, and the Israelis wanted to destroy an Arab leader who threatened their colonization project by rallying the Arab world against it and providing aid to the Palestinian guerrillas. Finally, there was the Suez Canal. The British and French wanted to recover it, so that the profits of its operation could once again flow to its former British and French owners. And the Israelis wanted to fulfill the promise Weizmann had made to the British, namely, that a Jewish homeland in Palestine would safeguard Britain's control of the Suez Canal.[18]

Twenty-four hours after Nasser announced that he was nationalizing the canal, Eden obtained a favorable decision from the British cabinet to go to war.[19] There was no legal *casus belli* for the British decision. Cairo's right to nationalize the canal was beyond dispute.[20] Egypt had posed not the slightest territorial threat to Britain; Nasser had not mobilized the Egyptian army to attack Britain; and an authorization for war had not been obtained from the UN Security Council. On the contrary, the Security Council knew nothing of Eden's intention to attack Egypt. Preparation for the aggression was conducted in secret. Washington was deliberately kept in the dark. The British were preparing an unprovoked war, a war of aggression, no different in its violation of the principle of *jus ad bellum* (right to war), than the German invasions of multiple European countries a decade and a half earlier.

Representatives of the three co-conspirator states met at Sèvres, a Parisian suburb, to plan the crime. At the conference, Ben-Gurion articulated a Zionist vision for the Middle East. Jordan, he noted, was an artificial construct. At the time, it comprised territory west of the Jordan River (the West Bank), coveted by the Israelis, since it contained Judea and Samaria, home of the Jewish state of antiquity. Jordan also included territory to the east (the East Bank, today's Jordan.) In Ben-Gurion's vision, the East Bank would be annexed to British-controlled Iraq and become the new home of the Palestinian Arabs. Israel would absorb the West Bank. Britain, thus, would control an expanded Iraq. France would control Lebanon and Syria. And the Jewish state would control all of Palestine.[21]

The co-conspirators built their war preparations around a subterfuge. Israeli tanks would cross the Egyptian border into the Sinai Desert, and advance toward the canal, allegedly in pursuit of Palestinian 'terrorists.' The British and French governments would profess concern, condemn the Israeli aggression, and call for a ceasefire. London and Paris would order Egyptian and Israeli forces to withdraw to positions tens miles beyond the canal (the Egyptians to the west, the Israelis to the east.) The Israelis would comply. But the chances that Nasser would bow to the ultimatum were recognized as approximately zero. After all, Egypt was his country, and he had every right to position his forces wherever necessary to defend it against an invasion. Who were the British and French to issue an ultimatum to the Egyptians on a matter that unequivocally fell within the Egyptian purview? With Nasser's rejection of the Anglo-French demand, the British and French would be handed a pretext to intervene to 'protect the canal.' Egypt's weak military, putting up what resistance it could, would be completely destroyed by the far superior British and French forces, and the government of the new Saladin would quickly fall. Would-be imitators would discover what befalls Third World nationalists who challenge Western supremacy and encroach on the profit-making interests of Western investors.[22]

The plan went off without a hitch—almost. On October 29, 1956, Israeli tanks stormed into the Sinai and advanced toward the canal. A day later Britain and France, following the script their politicians and generals had worked out with the Israelis, ordered a cease-fire, and directed the belligerents to withdraw from the canal zone. As the triumvirate had predicted, Nasser rejected the ultimatum. On October 31, the British and French struck, launching a land, sea, and air attack against overwhelmed Egyptian forces, dishonestly presenting their intervention as a selfless campaign to restore peace and protect an international waterway from the disruptions of the 'Arab-Israeli conflict.' But before Anglo-French forces could occupy the canal zone, the Soviets intervened. Premier Nikolai Bulganin warned London and Paris that if they proceeded further, the USSR would come to Nasser's aid. Angered that his nominal allies had plotted an aggression in secret, and had blundered into a possible war with the Soviets, US president Dwight Eisenhower ordered the conspirators to withdraw their forces from Egypt. Chastened, the British and French withdrew, and the 'Suez Canal Crisis' was defused. By aborting their conspiracy, Washington let its former imperialist rivals know that the Middle East was now under US proprietorship. The Second Settler-Native War thus marked the end of Anglo-French colonialism in the Arab world and the beginning of US ascendancy in the region.[23]

The British-French-Israeli humiliation greatly elevated Nasser's standing in the Arab world and in the larger Third World. The Tripartite Aggression had tried to make an object lesson of the Arab socialist leader, but had failed. Instead of discouraging movements of national liberation, what was a debacle from the perspective of Paris, London, and Tel Aviv, had turned out to be an inspiration for peoples seeking to emancipate themselves from Western supremacy and economic subordination. Nasser had stood up to two imperialist powers and their settler colonial subaltern and survived. Of course, the reality was that without Soviet willingness to intervene on the side of Nasser—and the consequent US demand that the aggressors abandon their efforts at regime change through war—that Arab nationalism would have suffered a crushing defeat in 1956. The Arab nationalists were far too weak to achieve even a fraction of their goals without the support of the Soviet Union.

Nasser was a principal figure in efforts to build a non-aligned movement of Third World countries that would remain independent of the United States and the USSR. Reality, however, proved to be a pumice stone that ground away so many of Nasser's illusions. Increasingly he recognized that only with aid from the Soviet Union—the sole superpower that embraced political values that were simpatico with the Arab socialist project—could an Arab nationalist government even hope to survive.

If the failure of the Tripartite Aggression was the twilight of British and French domination of the Arab world, then the Eisenhower Doctrine marked the dawn of a new American era in the Middle East. It was also the beginning of another chapter in a story of unchecked US economic expansion throughout the world—one that began with the doctrine of

Manifest Destiny, which justified the annexation of the North American continent to the original 13 colonies that comprised the infant United States; was succeeded by the Monroe Doctrine, which laid claim to Latin America as a US sphere of investment; and was now joined by the Eisenhower Doctrine, a Monroe Doctrine for the Middle East, and a new chapter in US claims to economic *lebensraum*.

The Eisenhower Doctrine was promulgated by the US president in a January 5, 1957 "Special Message to the Congress on the Situation in the Middle East." In his address, Eisenhower requested "authority to employ the armed forces of the United States to assist to defend the territorial integrity and the political independence of any nation in the" Middle East "against Communist armed aggression." In seeking this authorization, Eisenhower announced *urbi et orbi* that the Middle East was a US sphere of interest that would be protected by force.

In his address, Eisenhower emphasized that domination of the Middle East was a long-standing Russian goal, "as true of the Czars and it is true of the Bolsheviks." Soviet aspirations in the Middle East, he told Congress, were unrelated to economic interests, for the Soviet Union was a net exporter of oil and sent barely any traffic through the Suez Canal. The USSR's interest in the region was related instead to its "announced purpose of Communizing the world."

The Middle East, Eisenhower continued, was important to the United States as "the crossroads of the continents of the Eastern Hemisphere." At the heart of it lies the Suez Canal, which "enables the nations of Asia and Europe to carry on the commerce that is essential if these countries are to maintain well-rounded and prosperous economies." The region is also "a gateway between Eurasia and Africa." Equally important, it "contains about two thirds of the presently known oil deposits of the world and it normally supplies the petroleum needs of many nations of Europe, Asia and Africa. The nations of Europe are peculiarly dependent upon this supply, and this dependency relates to transportation as well as to production!" Left unsaid was that the Middle East was also the source of immense profits for the US oil companies that sold Middle Eastern oil to European, Asian and African clients.

In view of the significance of the Middle East, Eisenhower sought Congressional authorization to deploy "the armed forces of the United States to secure and protect the territorial integrity and political independence of such nations, requesting such aid, against overt armed aggression from any nation controlled by International Communism."

The usual suspects—Arab leaders whose survival depended on currying favor with the hegemonic powers—immediately genuflected at the altar of the new Monroe Doctrine. The first to pay obeisance was President Camille Chamoun of Lebanon. King Saud of Saudi Arabia quickly followed, along with Prime Minister Nuri of Iraq, and King Hussein of Jordan. The Arab quislings correctly construed the doctrine, not as a warning to Moscow, but as a caution to Nasser to refrain from using his military to topple the proxy rulers the United States would depend on to enforce its hegemony over the Middle East. To be sure, the doctrine made US intervention contingent on an invitation from a country threatened by "Communist armed aggression," but Nasser was understood by Washington and its proxy Arab rulers to be an agent of 'International Communism.'[24]

Neither Arab socialists nor communists liked to be reduced to facsimiles of the other, for while they cooperated (some times, though not always) there were many differences between them that each regarded as significant. But there were many similarities as well that, in the view of Washington and its collaborators in the Arab world, were far more significant. The implications for US domination of the Middle East of an Arab socialist versus a communist program, were, for all practical purposes, indistinguishable. Both Arab socialists and Arab communists would replace quisling governments, enact land reforms, abolish religious discrimination, enforce women's rights, democratize ownership of the commanding heights of the economy, and put the interests of their country's citizens ahead of those of foreign investors. For imperialists and their local servants, Arab socialism and Arab communism were as different as Pepsi and Coke.

Eisenhower and the Dulles brothers were fairly certain that Soviet military intervention in the Middle East was not on Moscow's agenda. As Eisenhower acknowledged, the Soviets didn't need Arab oil; they had enough of their own. Nor were they driven by a profit-motive, as US foreign policy was, that would compel Moscow to lay claim to Arab oil fields as a rich bounty of profits for private Soviet investors (of which there were none.) What's more, the Soviets struggled militarily to keep up with the United States. Moscow wasn't interested in becoming embroiled in a war it could not win against its far stronger rival.

Instead of marching into West Asia and seizing control of the territory, Washington believed that Moscow's intervention in the Middle East would be limited to the provision of military and economic aid to Arab socialist states that sought to escape the Western neocolonial orbit. Of course, this was hardly welcome; it would frustrate US efforts to establish hegemony in the region. Egypt and Syria had already entered into agreements with the USSR. And there was a danger that other Arab states would follow.[25] But Washington wasn't going to go to war with the Soviets over military and economic aid. However, Eisenhower was letting the Kremlin know that the United States would not tolerate armed aggression by a Soviet client against any of its Arab proxies, especially the oil monarchs of the Persian Gulf.

During the Cold War, it was US standard operating procedure to define all revolutionary movements as a communist conspiracy organized by Moscow. This was an extension of a long-standing theory of the political Right that defined revolution as a conspiracy of the Jews. Except in the US reformulation of the thesis, the Jews were replaced by Moscow. Of course, in Hitler's view—and in the view of many revered Western statesmen of Hitler's era whose anti-Semitism has since been overlooked—Moscow was the international headquarters of a Jewish conspiracy. But the new US revolution-as-Soviet-conspiracy theory would not borrow from older political Right notions of Judeo-Bolshevism. Hitler had taken negative sentiment toward the Jews, and by equating Jews with communists, directed anti-Semitism at the Bolsheviks. Hatred of Jews, then, translated by association into hatred of communism. US Cold War ideologues took Moscow-phobia, which had been made a veritable mass psychopathology, and paired it with all revolutionary movements. Accordingly, anti-Moscow sentiment, as incandescent and irrational as anti-Semitism, was directed at revolutionary nationalism.

To be sure, Jews and revolutionary movements of the political Left weren't entirely disconnected, and nor were Moscow and revolutionary nationalist movements strangers. Jews were disproportionately attracted to movements of the political Left because such movements embraced equality and promised Jews surcease from the discriminations with which they were afflicted. Owing to the strong attraction of Jews to emancipatory movements, it was easy to demagogically attribute Leftist movements to a Jewish conspiracy.

Similarly, communists, as champions of universal equality, were disproportionately drawn to revolutionary national movements as organic manifestations of the search for freedom from national discrimination. Likewise, revolutionary nationalists were strongly attracted to communism, seeing in its commitment to universal equality a simpatico movement. Kim Il Sung and Ho Chi Minh, revolutionary nationalists, were inspired by Lenin's call for the oppressed peoples of the world to throw off the chains of colonialism, and for the workers of the First World to extend to them material assistance. They heard in the Bolshevik slogan, "Workers of the world *and oppressed peoples* unite!" a compelling rallying cry and program for national liberation.

The struggle for equality has always arisen in the intolerance that human beings have of being exploited, oppressed, plundered, cheated, debased, dehumanized and discriminated against—not in a conspiracy conceived by a cabal of Jews, as the political Right alleged, or in a plot hatched in Moscow by Soviet commissars, as US Cold War ideologues would have had us believe. Washington's contention that any gains by the Third World to liberate itself from colonial and neocolonial bondage represented 'Soviet expansionism' amounted to the negation of the independent initiative of human beings to take a recalcitrant stance against their exploitation. The vile and oppressive treatment to which South Africa's indigenous people were subject under the white supremacist regime of the Afrikaners was the goad for the anti-apartheid struggle, not a conspiracy cultivated in Moscow. Communists were intimately involved in that struggle, as they have been in all struggles against racism, and Moscow, befitting a center of a communist movement espoused to a vision of universal equality, extended a helping hand to the anti-apartheid movement, when the West—and Israel—supported it. But the African revolt against white supremacist oppression would have arisen all the same in a world in which Lenin's successors had not achieved primacy in Moscow, since the communist movement was only a collateral product of the conditions that gave rise to the fight against apartheid, not its cause. National hierarchy, imperialism, and exploitation were the common causes of both the communist and anti-apartheid movements.

Denying the independent initiative of revolutionary movements against exploitation and oppression was a way of denying the existence of exploitation and oppression.[26] If all uprisings could be attributed to Moscow-directed 'trouble-makers' stirring up discontent (as the French Revolution was attributed to by conservative intellectuals to Jewish trouble-makers enkindling disaffection), then all uprisings could be portrayed as illegitimate, and the exploitative and oppressive conditions that truly underpinned the uprisings could be covered up. *Mein Kampf* bursts with misattributions of this sort. The Nazi leader labored diligently to portray the attachment of German workers to Marxism as originating, not in their exploitation and dehumanization, but in their brainwashing by clever Jews whose highly developed skills of deception were used to mislead the stolid German worker. US Cold War ideologues borrowed liberally from Hitler, replacing clever Jews with clever Moscow agents. But as Yevgeny Primakov, a former Soviet foreign affairs official, explained in his 2009 book, *Russia and the Arabs*, while it "is widely speculated that Moscow lent a hand in bringing anti-colonial forces to power... this does not remotely stand up to scrutiny." True, acknowledged Primakov, the "Soviet Union did not stay on the sideline of events." But it only built links to anti-colonial forces "after their revolutions." Revolutionary nationalists "seized power not because of any plots orchestrated by Moscow," but because of the oppressive policies of the West.[27] With the Soviet Union's demise, Washington was forced to concede that Third World challenges to US domination continued. In its 1990 National Security Strategy, the George H. W. Bush administration acknowledged that threats to US domination of the Middle East could no longer "be laid at the Kremlin's door."[28] With the demise of the USSR, and the exit of all possibility of attributing recalcitrance against US tyranny to Kremlin conspirators, Washington had to find new bogeymen.

Israeli efforts to deny Nasser hero status failed. Despite raining humiliating blows upon him, knowing he was too weak to respond—and because of the failure of the Tripartite Aggression to crush him—Nasser's star as a Third World hero burned ever brighter. Nasser's biographer Said Aburish characterized his subject as "the most popular Arab leader since Mohamed and Saladin,"[29] and concluded that the Egyptian leader was as charismatic as Mohamed.[30] Nasser, Aburish observed, died on the same day of the year as the prophet did. The Lebanese writer Nejla Abu Izzidine opined that this was no accident.[31]

Leila Khaled wrote that "Mass adulation for Nasser became an Arab phenomenon; Nasserism became a world-wide doctrine.... Diplomats from the Third World made pilgrimages to Cairo to declare their solidarity with the Arabs...the Arab world applauded; the oppressed saw a spark of hope. Europe and America stood in awe while Nasser became the brown giant of the Third World."[32]

Like the French revolutionary, Maximilien Robespierre, and the Argentine communist Che Guevara, Nasser was 'an incorruptible,' who shunned the trappings of power. As president he continued to live in the same modest house he had occupied as an Army colonel.[33] While other members of the Free Officers' Movement sent their children to private schools, Nasser kept his children in public school.[34]

"Nasser owned the street, the people loved him," wrote Aburish.[35] He "gave voice to the historical frustration of the Arabs. The average Arab waited for Nasser's radio speeches like a groupie,"[36] as did not so average Arabs, like Muammar Gaddafi.

So too did—and do—Third World leaders find inspiration in Nasser. Nelson "Mandela referred to his first visit to Egypt in 1962 when he was still a freedom fighter. He... praised the late President Gamal Abdel Nasser, whom he met then, adding that Nasser was a great source of inspiration for him at the time," reported CNN in 1997.[37] According to *Al Arabiya*, Cuba's revolutionary leader Fidel "Castro confided that Egypt's resistance under Nasser against" the Tripartite Aggression "proved to be inspirational for the rise of his own movement."[38] And Hugo Chavez, leader of Venezuela's Bolivarian Revolution, was inspired by Nasser, long after the Third World hero's death. "Someone talked to me about his pessimism regarding the future of Arab nationalism," Chavez confided. "I told him that I was optimistic, because the ideas of Nasser are still alive. Nasser was one of the greatest people of Arab history. To say the least, I am a Nasserist."[39]

It was precisely because Nasser owned the Arab street and inspired revolutionaries in Syria, Iraq, Lebanon, Yemen, Algeria, Saudi Arabia (where Nasserist officers tried to overthrow the anachronistic Saudi monarchy),

Ghana, South Africa, Cuba and beyond, that he was feared and despised—by all the forces that sought to keep the Third World down, to plunder its resources, to expropriate its land, to displace its people, and to steal the product of its labor. Budding Arab revolutionaries memorized his speeches and repeated his slogans.[40] Syrian political leaders competing by claiming to be his most ardent followers.[41] The Arab monarchs, the Jewish colonists, and U.S. officials were acutely aware that Nasser was revered as a new Saladin. They were equally aware of Saladin's accomplishments, and feared that Nasser might lead a great movement to repeat them. Conservatives and reactionaries, then, labored mightily to undermine and destroy the Third World's new hero.

It was the Zionists, the European implantations in the Third World—Jewish settlers who had always pledged that they would look after the West's interests in the Middle East—who eventually destroyed Nasser. This they did in 1967, as the culmination of the Third Settler-Native War, an Israeli-initiated war of aggression they would win handily. The quick and decisive defeat of the new Saladin would humiliate Nasser beyond the limits of all humiliations inflicted on him theretofore. The Israelis left him a seriously diminished figure, an empty shell who would die not too many years later, as what Said Aburish would call "the most popular failure in history."[42]

By 1967, a half century had elapsed since the British cabinet, on no authority, moral, legal or otherwise, had promised Palestine, part of the Arab homeland, to nationalist Jews. Twenty years had elapsed since the United Nations, at the time dominated by First World states, many with long histories of colonial tyranny, promised 56 percent of Palestine to a Jewish state, even though Jews in Palestine, most of them recent immigrants, constituted a minority that owned no more than ten percent of the land. Their immigration to Palestine had been opposed by the Arab natives who recognized that the Jewish settlers had come not to live as equals but to displace the Arabs. Nineteen years had elapsed since the declaration of a Jewish state, ruling on nearly eighty percent of Palestinian territory, and the defeat of the Arab armies in the First Settler-Native War. The plunder of most of Palestine, by colonial settlers, abetted by colonial states, was attended by the forced exile of over 700,000 Arabs. For fifty years Arabs had been afflicted by one Zionist injury after another, and in the view of the Arab people, it was time for the injustices to end. Arabs pressured Nasser, the new Saladin, to carry out a war of liberation, to free the homeland from the European implantation in Palestine, and to recover Arab dignity.

In Arab aspirations for immediate redemption, however, lay the seeds of a disaster. The Arab armies were in no state to wage war against Israel. The Egyptian military, the largest of all, had an air force that lacked pilots; its army reserve was poorly trained; and Egyptian officers were largely incompetent.[43] The government's financial situation was so straitened that Nasser could afford a war that lasted no more than a few days.[44] A lightening war, a *blitzkrieg*, may have been possible if Egyptian military power was many orders greater, but it wasn't, and to make matters worse, Nasser's best troops were tied up in Yemen, fighting with republican forces against a monarchy supported by Israel, the Shah, and the Saudi royal family, coordinated by Washington.[45]

The Israelis welcomed a war with Nasser, were ready to start one, and knew they would win.[46] What's more, they were certain that if, by chance, matters should go awry, the United States would step in to prevent a Nasserist victory. More importantly, they had an ace up their sleeve—an atomic bomb. As *The New York Times* reported in 2017, in the weeks leading up to the war, the Israelis raced to assemble an atomic device. A secret plan, called a 'doomsday operation,' had been developed to force the Arab armies to back off if the tide should improbably turn against the Jewish state. In the event of an impending defeat, the atomic bomb would be detonated atop a mountain in the Sinai desert as a demonstration of the horror Israel could inflict on Cairo, Damascus and Amman.[47] Victory for the Arabs, then, was completely out of the question. The Israelis had a nuclear sword, and all Nasser had was a poorly-trained, ill-equipped, under-staffed and incompetently-led military, the best part of which was deployed over a thousand miles away. Everything augured against an Arab victory and everything portended a rapid Arab collapse. Leaving nothing to chance, the Israelis had even arranged for the Kurds, who they had been supplying with training and arms since 1958, to mount an offensive against Arab nationalist Iraq, to prevent the Iraqi army from rushing to Nasser's aid.[48] A trap had been set, and the Arab street was blindly pushing Nasser toward to it.

In March 1967, tensions grew between Syria and Israel over the demili-tarized zone separating the two states.[49] The Soviets warned Nasser that Israel was preparing an attack on his ally. In April, the Jordanians and Saudis, taking their instructions from the CIA, accused Nasser of cow-ardice. He talked big, they said, but his inaction belied his words. He was nothing but a paper tiger. Their intention was to goad the Arab leader into attacking Israel, or lose face before his adoring Arab supporters if he didn't.[50]

On May 12, Israel threatened to invade Syria to topple its Arab nation-alist government, and immediately moved troops to the Syrian border. Convinced that an Israeli strike on Syria was imminent, Nasser ordered UN forces to withdraw from the Sinai, to clear the way for a deployment of Egyptian troops to the Israeli border. The United Nations had deployed peacekeepers to the Sinai in 1956 in the wake of the Second Settler-Native War to separate the two countries' militaries. The withdrawal of UN forces would allow the Egyptian army to advance toward the Israeli border, positioning Egypt for an attack from the east if Israel pursued an attack on Syria from the south.[51] On May 18 and 19, Egyptian troops, dressed for battle, paraded in front of Western embassies in Cairo, before heading to the Sinai. In a further effort to deter Israeli aggression, the Egyptian presi-dent signed a defense pact with Syria and Jordan.

With Egyptian forces advancing on the Israeli border, Arab states importuned Nasser to close the Strait of Tiran, Israel's nexus to the Red Sea and to the Indian Ocean beyond, in order to pressure the Zionists to back off their threats to attack Syria. Nasser complied, blocking Israeli shipping from the Gulf of Aqaba into the Red Sea. The Israelis declared this to be an act of war.[52]

In an effort to lower tensions, the US and Soviet ambassadors to Egypt told Nasser on May 26 that the Israelis wouldn't launch an attack. Nasser assured the ambassadors that he too had no intention of firing the first shot.

As we have seen, Nasser was in no position to go to war with the Israelis and expect anything other than total defeat. The odds were stacked heav-ily against him. It's very unlikely that the Arab champion was ready to undertake a suicide mission. The Israelis knew this. Yitzhak Rabin, at the time Israeli chief of defense staff, noted that Nasser had sent only two divisions to the Sinai, hardly sufficient to launch an offensive war. "He knew it and we knew it," recalled Rabin. "I don't think Nasser wanted war."[53] Menachem Begin, a guerrilla leader and prime minister, and at the time an Israeli cabinet minister, said: "We must be honest with ourselves. We decided to attack him."[54]

On June 2, Moshe Dayan joined the Israeli cabinet as minister of defense. Dayan, the one-eyed Zionist Spartan who defined Israel's role as acting as the West's bulwark against Arab nationalism, was known for advocating war with Egypt to undermine Nasser.[55] Having lulled the Arab paladin into a false sense of safety by assuring him that Israel would not attack, Washington gave Dayan the green light to initiate an attack. Working with the Israelis, the CIA had developed the military plans that would guide the Israeli offensive.[56] CIA director Richard Helms assured the US president Lyndon Johnson that an Israeli victory was certain.[57]

On June 5, Israel struck, executing a plan that had "been in the making for ten years," according to Shimon Peres, an Israeli prime minister who years before had been involved in the planning of the Tripartite Aggression.[58] Israel destroyed 304 Egyptian warplanes of a total of 419, or 73 percent, in the first two hours of the war, most as they sat on ground.[59] Four days later, most towns and cities in the Sinai had fallen to the Israelis. On June 10, Israeli forces captured the Golan Heights in Syria, and prepared to march on Damascus. The Soviets warned the Israelis to go no further. Washington took the warning seriously and enjoined the Israelis to stand down.[60]

On June 11, a ceasefire went into effect. In just six days, the Israelis reduced the Egyptian army to ruins. According to Nasser's accounting of Egypt's war losses, eighty percent of its military equipment was destroyed.[61]

Israel significantly expanded its territory. "The June defeat," or *Naksa* (Arabic for set back), "led to the occupation of the whole of Palestine as well as of the Golan Heights and Sinai, the dispersion of hundreds of thousands of citizens and the humiliation of an entire nation," recalled the Popular Front for the Liberation of Palestine, a Marxist breakaway from the Nasserist Arab National Movement. Rather than moving forward to victory against the colonization of the Arab world, the Zionists had colonized even more of it.[62]

The consequences of the Third Settler-Native War for the Arab nationalist movement were staggering. Nasser, the movement's maximal leader, was humiliated. In a mere eighty minutes, the time it took the Israelis to wipe out his air force, the new Saladin and rising star of the Third World was reduced to a nullity. Prior to June 5, 1967, Nasser was, after the Prophet Mohamed, the most popular Arab in history. After June 5, he was the most popular failure in history. Today, he is hardly remembered.[63] Nasser's successor as Egypt's president, Anwar Sadat, wrote that while Nasser, the man, died in September 1970, Nasser, the conduit through which the hopes and aspirations of the Arab nation spoke, died "on 5 June 1967, exactly one hour after the war broke out."[64] "The Arab masses," wrote Leila Khaled, "had for over a dozen years pinned their hopes on Nasser to liberate them from Zionism and from their local oppressors. In 1967, after the June tornado, Nasserism lay in shambles."[65] Nasser, and Arab nationalism, wrote Said Aburish, "never recovered from the defeat."[66]

Some of Nasser's followers, like George Habash, drew a lesson from the *Naksa*, namely, that Nassersim had no viable plan for the liberation of the Arab world. Habash began referring to Nasser's government, and others inspired by Arab nationalism, such as those of Syria, Iraq and Libya, as "colonels' regimes"—governments that had been established by military *coups d'état*. While they were progressive, reformist, highly popular and committed to Arab emancipation, they were not based on organized mass movements—and that was a fatal weakness.[67] Indeed, while Nasser may have been wildly popular, he failed to build a mass organization to mobilize the energy of the Arab people and to direct it in methodical ways toward the goal of achieving Arab independence. His movement was largely a one-man show, backed by a small inner circle of 'Free Officers,' and reliance on the clearly inadequate Egyptian military. As Aburish remarked, Nasser failed to formulate "a revolutionary program that would harness the energy of the millions of people who believed in him."[68] There was no strategy, no master plan, and no mass organization. Instead, Nasserism was simply a vision articulated by a highly charismatic figure. It was not a movement. Mao Tse-Tung, Kim Il-Sung, Ho Chi Minh and Fidel Castro were also highly charismatic Third World figures, but in addition to their captivating personalities and ability to articulate the collective aspirations of their people, they possessed highly developed organizational skills which they used to build movements that did the work of making their inspiring visions a reality.

All the same, our appraisal of Nasserism should not be too harsh. Arabism wasn't a complete failure. On the contrary, it boasted many successes. Paradoxically, those successes played a role in its decline. Nasser and those he inspired had overturned the British influence in Egypt, Iraq and Yemen, while Morocco, Tunisia, and Algeria had achieved independence from France. With Arabs achieving some measure of freedom from overt foreign domination in some parts of the Arab world, pressure for a pan-Arab uprising against Western tyranny diminished.

At the same time, there were significant obstacles that stood in the way of an Arab nationalist advance. Minority populations within the Arab world had resisted the Arab nationalist tide from within. The Kurds, who the Israelis cultivated as allies, furnishing them with arms and training, saw Arabism as negating their aspirations for national self-determination. Joining the Kurds in opposing Arab nationalism were Shia Arabs. They were a minority compared to the much larger population of Sunni Arabs. The former were often discriminated against as heretics by the latter. Shias interpreted the strong attachment of Sunnis to Arabism as a sign that Arab nationalism was a stalking horse for advancing Sunni interests at the expense of the Shias. Of course, the United States and its allies did much to encourage these fissiparous beliefs. Arab nationalism also competed against the Muslim Brotherhood and the Islamist-inspired political movement of pan-Islamic unity, consciously promoted by the United States and its satellite Saudi Arabia as alternatives to Arab nationalism. Together, the *Naksa*, Arab nationalist successes, the opposition of ethno-religious minorities to Arabism, and competition from US- and Saudi-backed Islamist movements, reduced Arab nationalism to the moribund state in which it finds itself today, living on only in the Den of Arabism, Syria.

The Israeli annihilation of the Egyptian military disabused Nasser of his illusion that he could steer an independent non-aligned course between the two superpowers. Clearly, his only defense against further Israeli aggression was a military alliance with the USSR. The Americans were clearly against his program of freeing the Arab world from foreign oppression and exploitation, and were enemies, not potential allies. Nasser now came face to face with reality. Egypt's only hope for survival against a stalking Washington and its new henchman, Israel, was to ensconce itself firmly in the Soviet orbit.[69] Soviet troops, then, were invited onto Egyptian soil, and arrived in significant numbers.[70] Soviet naval facilities were established at Port Said, Alexandria and Marsa Matruh. Iraq, Algeria, and Syria followed suit, granting the Soviet navy basing rights on their territories.[71] The 'colonels' regimes' would now rely on the Soviet military for protection.

If the Israeli victory disheartened Arab nationalists and other Third World liberation movements, it had the opposite effect on the countries of the US Empire. Throughout the world, regimes of the political Right took heart, celebrating Israel as a First World outpost in the Third World, which was acting to impede the advance of communist and revolutionary nationalist movements. Israel's decisive 1967 victory was seen as a victory over a common Third World challenge to First World supremacy.[72] Among the right-wing regimes inspired by the Zionist state's victory was the white supremacist apartheid regime of South Africa, whose morale was greatly boosted.[73] The Afrikaners also saw themselves as a rampart of 'civilization' in the 'heart of darkness,' and believed they too had a providential right to expropriate the land they believed their deity had promised them. The Israeli victory, they concluded, augured well for their own cause.

Washington was equally pleased by the success of the Israeli aggression. US officials saw Nasserism as a virus (of independence.) Left unchecked, the contagion would spread from country to country, threatening US supremacy. The more countries to which the virus spread, the more difficult it would be to contain its outbreak.

The use of the term 'virus' as a metaphor for Nasserist Arab socialism echoed Hitler's liberal use of pathogenic metaphors to demonize Marxism, socialism and communism. Other Western statesmen also had a predilection for metaphorical allusions to communism as a contagion. Hadn't a 'cordon sanitaire' been established in Europe after World War I as a prophylaxis against the spread of the Bolshevik 'virus'? The Israelis also developed their own germ theory of national liberation. In the Zionist version, a democratic contagion infected anti-democratic Portugal. The contagion precipitated the collapse of the authoritarian regime in Lisbon and the fall of its African colonies. The virus soon spread to Rhodesia, where white supremacist rule was laid low, and yielded to democracy and racial equality. From there, it spread to South Africa, threatening white minority rule over the natives. If South Africa fell, so too, warned Zionist ideologues, would Jewish minority rule over the Arabs of Palestine collapse.[74] Of course, the fall of white supremacy in South Africa didn't lead to the fall of Jewish settler supremacy in Palestine, but all the same, the belief that Nasserism, the virus of independence, would sweep the Third World, agitated the minds of US planners. They were entrusted with the mission of preserving the Third World as a sphere for exploitation for US investors, and Nasserism threatened their mission. Israel's war of aggression proved to be a powerful physic against the contagion of independence, stopping the virus's spread before it reached the oil-rich Gulf states.

Not only did Israel's destruction of Nasserism overcome the threat to Western domination of West Asia's oil resources, it also struck a devastating blow against the nonaligned movement. Nasser had been one of the founders of the movement, along with India's Nehru and Yugoslavia's Tito, and he was perhaps the movement's most high-profile figure. The alliance of non-aligned countries stood for Third World independence. Nasserism's defeat, and Egypt's subsequent abandonment of non-alignment in favor of a partnership with the USSR, discredited the movement. Washington saw this as a major contribution to US power,[75] and a major contribution to the war against the movement for universal equality.

Israel's fulfillment of its promise to act as a rock against which the waves of Nasser's Arab nationalism would be broken,[76] confirmed the thesis in US foreign policy circles that the Zionist state could operate as a major strategic asset of the United States in the Middle East.[77] By destroying the Nasserite 'virus' and undermining the non-aligned movement, Israel recommended itself to US officials as a West Asian Sparta on which Washington could depend to pursue US strategic interests in the Middle East. Thus was the stage set for the 'special relationship' Washington would confer on Israel—a relationship that carries on to this day.[78]

The United States had long supported Israel ideologically. A strong strain of Christian Zionism had always run through US society, and this had been expressed in numerous Congressional declarations of support for Jewish settler colonialism in Palestine, dating to as early as 1922.[79] But until Israel performed its feat of crushing Nasserism and thereby safeguarding US oil profits from the Arab nationalist contagion, Washington had preferred to deal with its Arab quislings exclusively. Now, it was evident that Israel was of incomparable value to the imperialist project, and must be brought on board as a key asset. No longer would Washington deal with Israel in the background for fear of alienating the United States' Arab clients.

Washington now stepped up aid to Israel, from a trickle to a gusher. In the five-year period preceding the Third Settler-Native War, 1962-1966,

Washington sent Israel $129 million in military aid. In the five years following the Israeli aggression, 1968 to 1972, US military aid to Tel Aviv increased more than seven-fold, to $985 million.[80] At the same time, the Israel lobby, previously of little significance and hardly noticed, began to command attention in Washington. It was also at this point that commentators, journalists, and intellectuals in the United States, began to sing paeans to the Zionist state.[81]

It's worthwhile to recapitulate the events that led to Washington adopting Israel as a strategic asset in the Middle East, which, in the decades to follow, would receive countless billions of dollars of military, economic and other aid—more than any other country in US history. These events, and the fact that they recommended the Zionist state to Washington, speak volumes about US leaders, the role the United States plays in the world, and the orientation of the US state to movements for international democracy.

In 1967, a state established on land that Arabs had occupied for centuries, by an aggression that led to the exile of hundreds of thousands of Arab natives, carried out a premeditated attack on its neighbors, stole parts of their territory, and added to the Himalaya of refugees already driven into exile, barred from ever returning to their homes. At the end of the war, the settler state had expanded its borders to include the Sinai and the Gaza Strip (stolen from Egypt), the West Bank and East Jerusalem (taken from Jordan), and the Golan Heights (conquered from Syria.) This act of international piracy, by a colonial settler regime, which enforced Jewish supremacist rule over Palestine, the Sinai and the Golan Heights, led to the embrace of Israel by the United States as a strategic asset and key ally, so valuable that it warranted a special relationship. The attachment of US officials to Israel reflected a shared history of expansionary colonialism and ethno-religious supremacism; belief that both Americans and Jews are a chosen people with a providential mission; the prevalence of Christian Zionist thinking in US culture; and, most significantly, the systemic imperative of capitalism to keep the Third World open to US free enterprise and the role Israel could play in overcoming impediments created by local forces of independence to US profit-making in the Middle East.

In 1970, Israel once again acted as a guardian of US interests in the Middle East, this time by deterring a Syrian military intervention in Jordan. Syria was prepared to send tanks across the Jordanian border to protect Palestinians who were challenging King Hussein's rule. As we've seen, Hussein, the scion of the British-installed Hashemite dynasty, was unacceptable to Jordanians as a leader, but was protected by the British, and now the Americans, as a local proxy for Western rule.

Israel's crushing 1967 defeat of Egypt convinced Palestinians that they could no longer rely on the colonels' regimes, or any Arab government for that matter, to recover their country. Up to that point, they had waited for a new Saladin to win back their land. The events of June 1967 washed away their illusions that the Arab nationalist leaders could deliver on their promises to vanquish Zionist colonialism. The harsh reality seemed to be that Palestinians would have to liberate themselves.

Additionally, it had become evident that in view of Israel's clear military superiority—now all the more overwhelming given the hike in US military aid to Tel Aviv—that a conventional military confrontation with Israel was out of the question. Israel had handily won the First and Third Settler-Native Wars, and easily captured the Sinai in the Second. Arab armies were too weak to win a conventional war with the Western-backed Zionist state. What's more, Israel had the ultimate deterrent—a nuclear saber. It seemed, from this perspective, that the more promising route to recuperating Palestine and ending Zionist colonialism was to fight a guerrilla war—the option of the weak. Hence, the leadership of the Palestinian Liberation Organization passed from the now discredited Nasser, who had founded it, to Yasser Arafat, a self-identified Palestinian. In 1970, Arafat and his Palestinian guerrillas had taken up residence in Jordan, and were using it as a base from which to launch attacks on the Jewish settler state.

This state of affairs was, for obvious reasons, opposed by the Israelis, who didn't want the Palestinians using neighboring Jordan, or any other contiguous territory, as a base of operations. It was opposed too by the Jordanian king for a host of mutually reinforcing reasons, not least of which was that his rule was at risk of falling to the well-organized Palestinian guerrillas. In September, a bloody confrontation erupted between the Palestinian fighters and the Jordanian monarchy. The events that followed became known as Black September.

Hussein's forces, the stronger of the combatants, were on the verge of crushing the Palestinians, when the Syrians, under Arab socialist leadership, made infantry and tank incursions into Jordan on the side of the guerrillas. The Palestinians had waited in vain for 15,000 Iraqi troops, who had been in Jordan since the 1967 war, to spring to their defense, but Baghdad, led by Arab socialists who saw the Palestinian cause as their own, quailed. They feared that if they intervened on behalf of their Palestinian brothers—but more to the point, against the US protégé, Hussein—that Washington would order Israel to strike Iraq. In the interests of self-preservation, the Iraqis opted for inaction.

The same considerations stayed the hand of Damascus. When Israel mobilized its army in response to the Syrian incursions, fears were raised in Damascus that a line was about to be crossed that would trigger an Israeli assault on Syria. Just three years earlier, the Israelis had easily conquered the Syrian Golan Heights, and may have conquered Damascus had the Soviets not warned them off. Clearly, an Israeli assault was not to be invited. In order to live to fight another day, the Syrians decided not to proceed further.[82]

The greatest general, remarked the ancient Chinese military strategist, Sun Tzu, is the one who wins without fighting. Israel won an important victory in September 1970, without firing a shot. Because no shot was fired, the significance of its military accomplishment was overlooked. Had Israeli tanks crashed into Jordan and Syria, and Israeli warplanes bombed Baghdad and Damascus, September 1970 would have marked the beginning of the Fourth Settler-Native War. But does the reality that no shot was fired by Israel diminish the significance of its victory? It deterred two Arab armies and in the process saved the rule of an Arab quisling on whom Washington relied to enforce its domination of the Middle East. September 1970 was a clear victory for the forces of imperialism, and a clear defeat for the forces of democracy and independence. Washington recognized Israel's service to the US Empire by further infusions of aid. US military aid to Israel in 1970 was $30 million. A year later it climbed to $545 million, an increase of over 1,700 percent. In US foreign policy circles, the budding special relationship with Israel was hailed as a firm basis for US power in the Middle East.[83]

CHAPTER EIGHT

Progress

> *"The greatest and most significant achievement during the
> last decades has been the independence from colonial and
> alien domination of a large number of peoples and nations."*
>
> United Nations General Assembly Resolution 3201, 1974

If 1967 was a set back year for the Arab world, the 1970s were a *Naksa* decade for the US Empire. But what proved to be a setback for Washington, and its aims of exercising a Wall Street-friendly tyranny over as much of the world as possible, was, in contrast, a warm caress for humanity, as Victor Hugo once described the French Revolution.[1] During the US setback years, right-wing authoritarian rule was brought to an end in Portugal after forty-two years, after which quickly followed the independence of the Portuguese colonies of Angola and Mozambique. In 1974, a revolution in Ethiopia led by the Soviet-backed Marxist-Leninist Derg ended a feudal monarchy. In 1975, US forces withdrew from Indochina. Vietnam, Laos, and Kampuchea became independent states. At the end of the decade, the US-backed monarchy in Iran was toppled, and white supremacist rule in Rhodesia was brought to an end. Additionally, the Sandinistas ousted the US-backed dictator Anastasio Somoza in Nicaragua. The leaders of the United States and Israel regretted the loss of their ally, the Portuguese dictatorship; mourned the fall of Ethiopia's emperor, Haile Selassie, another ally; deplored the uprising in Tehran that chased the Shah, a friend, from power; and lost a long-time comrade in Somoza. The Israelis lamented the end of white supremacist rule in Rhodesia as an augury of what might befall Jewish rule of Palestine. And neither the Americans nor the Israelis saw any benefit in the fall of the US puppet regime in Saigon.[2]

Equally deplorable, from the point of view of Washington and Tel Aviv, was the growing predominance of Third World countries in the United Nations General Assembly. No longer was the world body a virtual monopoly of First World countries with colonial histories. General Assembly resolutions inimical to Third World interests, such as the infamous Resolution 181, which granted most of Palestine to European colonists, would no longer be ratified. Moreover, the socialist bloc and its Third World allies were combining to issue resolutions condemning imperialism and its concomitants—racism, white supremacy, and apartheid. In 1975, the General Assembly condemned Zionism as racism. Seventy-two states, all Third World or Communist, voted in favor of Resolution 3379, decrying Zionism as a form of racism and racial discrimination. Thirty-five countries, mostly states with ignominious histories of colonialism, including Britain, France, Germany, and Italy voted against it, as, of course, did the United States (along with the other British colonial off shoots, Canada, Australia and New Zealand) and Israel.[3]

In 1974, the General Assembly adopted two resolutions that were, concurrently, front-on assaults against imperialism, and a declaration of a global economic order expressing the values of the political Left. The first, General Assembly Resolution 3201, was titled Declaration of the Establishment of a New International Economic Order. The resolution was adopted on the heels of a special session called to consider ways to overcome the Great Divergence, that is, the widening gulf in wealth between the First World and the Third World. Europe's plunder of the Americas, beginning in the fifteenth century—its primitive accumulation as Marx called it—was the catalyst for a growing divergence between parts of the world that, to that point, had been roughly economically equal. In Marx's words, "The discovery of gold and silver in America, the extirpation, enslavement and entombment in mines of the aboriginal population, the beginning of the conquest and looting of the East Indies, the turning of Africa into a warren for the commercial hunting of black-skins"—this was the basis for "the rosy dawn of the era of capitalist production."[4] The rosy dawn of the era of capitalist production marked the beginning of the

take-off of Europe, and the complementarily stifled and distorted development of the colonies and semi-colonies that Europe, and later North
America, exploited as sources of raw materials, cheap labor, and *lebensraum*, living space, on which to settle surplus proletarian populations.
Like Marx, Sven Beckert, whose masterly 2014 book *Empire of Cotton*
traces economic development as a global history, reminds us that, "industrial capitalism and the Great Divergence ... emerged from the violent
caldron of slavery, colonialism, and the expropriation of land."[5]

> When we marshal big arguments about the West's superior economic perform-
> ance, and build these arguments upon an account of the West's allegedly superior
> institutions like private-property rights, lean government, and the rule of law,
> we need to remember that the world Westerners forged was equally character-
> ized by exactly the opposite: vast confiscation of land and labor, huge state inter-
> vention in the form of colonialism, and the rule of violence and coercion.[6]

All of this resonates with Palestinians for whom vast confiscation of
land, huge state intervention in the form of colonialism, and the rule of
violence and coercion, have been their lot since 1917, as it has been the
experience of the indigenous inhabitants of the Americas, Africa, and
Asia since the voyages of Columbus.

"The greatest and most significant achievement during the last decades
has been the independence from colonial and alien domination of a large
number of peoples and nations," declared the General Assembly resolution. All the same, there remained "vestiges of alien and colonial domination, foreign occupation, racial discrimination, apartheid and neo-
colonialism." These affronts to human equality, according to the Third
World and socialist bloc states that backed the resolution, were "obstacles
to the full emancipation and progress of the developing countries."
Overcoming these obstacles was "impossible to achieve...under the existing international economic order," for the existing global economic order
perpetuated inequality.

The resolution called for a new international economic order—one predicated, not on the unfettered access of free enterprise to the world's markets,
but founded on the notion that each nation or people had the right to determine its own economic future, including one in which access to markets
was restricted or conditional on meeting local needs. According to this view,
it was the prerogative of every state "to adopt the economic and social system that it deems the most appropriate for its own development and not to

be subjected to discrimination of any kind as a result." No state, therefore, could be blockaded or regime-changed because it nationalized its oil, incubated its infant industry, imposed performance requirements on foreign investment, ring-fenced certain sectors of its economy from foreign ownership, or outlawed free enterprise.

At the heart of the resolution was the idea that Third World states must have the latitude to put the needs of their own populations before the profit-making requirements of First World investors; otherwise the Great Divergence would continue *ad infinitum*.

The solution to the Great Divergence, the champions of the resolution proposed, was to accord to each state "full permanent sovereignty... over its natural resources and all economic activities," including the right to nationalize economic assets or transfer ownership to nationals of the state, without being "subjected to economic, political or any other type of coercion to prevent the free and full exercise of this inalienable right."

The resolution's demands, which also included the right of developing countries to regulate "the activities of transnational corporations" and accord "preferential and non-reciprocal treatment" to local enterprises, were an anathema to Washington, which had no intention of acceding to a plan to alter a global economic order that so munificently benefited US investors. As far as Washington was concerned, Third World development was all fine and well, so long as it proceeded along lines that benefited corporate America and posed no threat to Wall Street's supremacy in the global economic order. As an alternative, Washington proposed a development model that hegemonic economic powers always propose—one to preserve their hegemony. Rather than using tariff policy, state-owned enterprises, foreign-investment restrictions, and industrial planning to develop their economies, Third World countries were directed to create climates favorable to Western investment.

Later that same year, the General Assembly adopted another resolution that was no less distasteful to the idea that the proper role of US investors is to serve as masters of humanity. Titled a "Charter of Economic Rights and Duties of States," Resolution 3281 sought to clip, by legal means, the wings of the enforcement arm of Wall Street's primacy—the US military. This, the resolution sought to do, by establishing that the 'fundamentals of international economic relations' should include the following: "peaceful coexistence;" "non-aggression;" "non-intervention;" "the peaceful settlement of disputes;" and the "sovereignty, territorial integrity and political independence of States." In other words, Western governments should refrain from using their military superiority to do what they had regularly done—topple governments that had chosen to exercise "the sovereign and inalienable right to choose" their country's "economic system as well as it political, social and cultural systems in accordance with the will of its people."

The framers of the resolution knew well the history of imperialism. Hegemonic powers regularly used strong and overwhelming military advantage to violate the sovereignty, territorial integrity, and political independence of weaker states to obtain economic advantage for their captains of industry, titans of finance, and substantial landowners. These advantages were obtained at the expense of the citizens of the countries whose sovereignty was infringed. In other words, the will of the peoples of Latin America, Africa, and Asia to organize their political, social and cultural systems in their own way—that is, democracy—had regularly been thwarted by the will of Western industrialists and financiers to impose on the Third World favorable foreign investment climates. Profits trumped democracy.

It was a self-perpetuating cycle. As the imperialist powers sucked wealth out of the countries they exploited, they accumulated the means to build stronger armies, navies, and bomber squadrons. And as their military capabilities expanded, their ability to exploit their victims and extract more wealth grew accordingly. In proportion to the degree imperialists plundered their victims, they acquired the means to plunder them more.

Resolution 3281 called for this cycle to end. No more would Western powers use their militaries to obtain economic advantage for their economic elites. From now on, developing countries would be given the freedom to develop peacefully in accordance with the will of their people. What might the will of their people include? The right: "to regulate and exercise authority over foreign investment;" "to regulate and supervise the activities of transnational corporations;" and "to nationalize, expropriate or transfer ownership of foreign property." The practice of applying trade sanctions to coerce states to change their economic or political system—as the United States had done to pressure communist states such as China, Cuba, and North Korea to give up collective ownership and planning of their economies—was to be prohibited, as well.

Finally, the resolution called for the elimination "of colonialism, apartheid, racial discrimination, neo-colonialism and all forms of foreign aggression, occupation and domination." What's more, it demanded "restitution and full compensation" for the exploitation and damages inflicted on Third World peoples and territories by the practices of imperialism.

Together, resolutions 3201 and 3281 called for a sweeping change to the global economic system. They attacked a global economic order in which a few chosen countries, regarding themselves as model nations, based their own prosperity and primacy on despoliation and domination of the rest of humanity;[7] and they proposed in its place, a world economy that replaced hierarchy with equality, where democracy (the right of people to choose their own politico-economic system) superseded the international dictatorship of the West (the right of Washington to impose one by coercion.)

The political Left and the world movement for universal equality had advanced further than it ever had. Needless to say, there was alarm in Washington, world headquarters of the political Right. Washington stood for economic and political hierarchy and the ascendancy of those who command the labor of others and live on profits, interest, and rent. Zionist Jews in Tel Aviv were equally alarmed. Israel fell squarely within the sights of the resolutions' condemnations of colonialism, apartheid, and racial discrimination. Zionism was unquestionably a colonialist ideology; on this, Zionist leaders, including Herzl and Jabotinsky, agreed. Jewish settlers governed territories over which they had rights superior to those of the Arab natives. Jewish-only colonies—euphemized as 'settlements'— were being built in the West Bank, Gaza Strip, Golan Heights, and Sinai. That Israel was an apartheid state, as its ally South Africa was, was undeniable. The advance of the Third World, the global movement for universal equality, and the political Left, bode ill, equally for the continued domination and plunder of the world by corporate America and the maintenance of colonialism and racial discrimination in the Arab territories conquered by Zionist settlers.

During the 1970s, the political Left fought back against colonialism and neo-colonialism, not only in Africa and Southeast Asia, but also in the Arab world. Egypt and Syria combined to launch a war against Israel to recover territory the Zionist state had taken from them in 1967. The war, fought in October 1973, (thus becoming known as 'the October War'), would be the fourth war fought between settlers and natives over the settlers' displacement of native Arabs and the conquest of their territory.

When Nasser died in 1970, he was succeeded by his vice-president, Anwar Sadat, a fellow member of the Free Officers' Movement. In an effort to recover the territory Israel had taken from Egypt in the 1967 War, Sadat broke with the Soviet Union, and embraced the West, hoping his new political orientation would persuade Washington to pressure Israel to return the Sinai.[8] He offered Israel a peace treaty in exchange for Israeli withdrawal from Egyptian territory. Israel was certainly interested in a non-aggression pact—it would free Israel's hand to move aggressively against other Arab states—but it would also mean giving up territory that Israel preferred to hold on to.[9] That the Israelis had their eye on the Sinai as a territorial possession was clear in Ben-Gurion's vow that he would never return the territory after Israel captured it in the Second Settler-Native War.[10] Specifically, Israel was loath to relinquish the Jewish colony of Yamit, in the north-eastern Sinai. A political settlement entailing the surrender of Israel's territorial gains would militate against Israel's existing "according to the scale, spirit, and quality she now embodies," declared General Ezer Weizman, who would later become Israel's president.[11]

The Saudi monarch did his own part to help Sadat recover the Sinai, importuning the White House to intercede on Cairo's behalf. But Sadat's expulsion of Soviet troops to curry favor with Washington, his peace overtures to the Israelis, and King Faisal's entreaties to the Americans, proved futile. After Egypt's humiliating 1967 defeat at the hands of the Israelis, Egypt was seen in Washington as wholly without bargaining power. Sadat could be safely ignored.

Sadat and Faisal reluctantly concluded that war, backed by an oil embargo, was the only viable way to command Washington's attention. Washington and Israel were ignoring them, because they thought they could. Faisal would have preferred not to act, but inaction was not an option. Arab public opinion strongly favored measures to redress the egregious injustice Israel had inflicted on the Arabs in 1967, and Faisal's failure to accommodate the demands of the Arab street could very well lead to his overthrow.[12]

In 1967, Riyadh had imposed an oil embargo on the United States, Britain, Germany, and other countries that supported Israel, as a sop to the demands of enraged Arabs that the monarchy punish Israel's Western enablers. The embargo was maintained for a month, long enough for Arab passions to subside.[13] The monarchy's goal was to keep Arab anger from boiling over in order to secure the House of Saud's place atop Arabia's oil fields, not to alienate and harm its American protector.

On October 6, 1973, Egypt and Syria launched a surprise attack on Israeli forces in the Sinai and Golan Heights, with the aim of recovering their territories. The two armies initially met with considerable success. Iraq sent 30,000 troops, including an armored division, to reinforce Syrian troops in the battle to recover the Golan Heights. But Israel's technical superiority, backed by emergency airlifts of arms by the United States, negated Syria's early gains. By October 26, the fighting was over, with Israel still in possession of the territory it had captured in 1967.[14]

At this point the oil weapon was deployed. The Arab oil monarchies had announced that they would reduce output by five percent to pressure Israel's backers to press the Zionists to return Egyptian and Syrian territory. Soon, production was cut by 10 percent, with threats of additional cuts of five percentage points in each subsequent month, until Israel returned the territory it had stolen. The cutbacks led to soaring oil prices.

While the cutbacks caused some pain in the West, the embargo failed to achieve its objectives. The Saudis lifted the embargo in March 1974, seven months after it was initiated, without obtaining a single concession; Israel continued to hold onto Egyptian and Syria territory. Iraq, which had been excluded from secret pre-war discussions, increased its oil production during the critical seven-month period, limiting the measure's efficacy. The reputation of Washington's protégé in Arabia, King Faisal, was greatly enhanced in the Arab world by his perceived rebellion against his US masters. Faisal's concession to Arab public opinion saved him from possible overthrow and replacement by a government that would be responsive to local, rather than US investor, needs.[15]

In the end, the October War appeared to be a complete failure for Arab forces. The war's exoteric goal—recuperation of territory lost in 1967—had not been achieved. But that was only how matters appeared. Beneath the surface, Egypt had made it plain that it was not defeated, had not capitulated, and could not be ignored, and was prepared to inflict pain on Israel and the United States in pursuit of the project of recovering the Sinai. Washington now determined that the prudent course was to accede to Sadat's demand for peace in return for Egyptian territory. But Washington would make Sadat pay a heavy price. In exchange for the Sinai, he would have to abandon the Arab nationalist cause and join the alliance of Washington, Tel Aviv, and Saudi Arabia in the fight against the Arabist contagion.[16] Egypt, which not so long before, under the charismatic leadership of Nasser, had spearheaded the fight against foreign domination of the Arab world, would now switch sides. Under the leadership of Sadat, it would become a key US ally and stalwart of the anti-Arabist alliance.

The 1973 Arab oil embargo affected the United States by reducing the supply of oil on the world market. Restricting Saudi oil production affected the price of oil produced everywhere, since price is determined by the intersection of the supply and demand globally. Since the supply had shrunk, while at the same time demand continued to grow, the inevitable result was upward pressure on price.

US officials propagated the myth that the United States was dependent on Saudi Arabia for its oil. But the United States has always counted itself among the world's top producers of oil, and for decades was completely self-sufficient. By the early 1970s, the United States had started to become dependent on foreign sources of oil as demand grew sharply, outstripping domestic supply. Saudi oil was imported, but in small quantities compared to imports from other foreign sources, namely Canada, Mexico, and Venezuela. The goal of spreading the fiction of US dependence on Middle East oil was to garner the consent of US citizens for policies to keep Saudi oil under US control. The public relations message was that Saudi oil could not be allowed to fall into the hands of an unreliable steward, for fear of losing access to a vital natural resource on which the US economy depended. But the reality was that Saudi oil couldn't be allowed to fall into the hands of an unreliable steward for fear that the benefits of the resource would be directed toward Arabs rather than US oil company shareholders.

One of the biggest oil company shareholders was the Rockefeller family, which made its fortune in oil, through the Standard Oil Company, and in banking, through the Chase-Manhattan Bank. In 1973, the Rockefellers' man in Washington was Henry Kissinger, the US secretary of state. Kissinger had close ties to the Rockefeller family. He had been director of special studies for the Rockefeller Brothers Fund, a high-profile member of the Rockefeller-led Council on Foreign Relations, and foreign policy advisor to the presidential campaign of Nelson Rockefeller. Kissinger started to make noise about a US military intervention to seize the Saudi oil fields. James Schlesinger, the secretary of defense, seemed to back him up. Schlesinger told Lord Cromer, the British ambassador to the United States, that it was no longer obvious that the United States could not use force to end the oil embargo. Cromer reported his conversation with the US defense secretary to British Prime Minister Edward Heath, who asked British intelligence to look into the matter. Were the Americans really considering an intervention to seize the oil fields? MI-6 was undecided. A US military intervention was possible, it informed the prime minister, but if so, the costs would be high. The Arab world would be totally alienated, as would most of the rest of the Third World. A number of other factors also militated against the contemplated invasion. The White House's attention was focused on the Watergate scandal. The US military was still mired in Vietnam, and US citizens were surfeited of war. Moreover, Arabs resented foreign interference in their affairs, and an invasion of the Arab world could turn into a second Vietnam.[17] If the Americans were going to launch a military strike to seize the oil fields, they would create a world of trouble.

Despite the costs, Kissinger wouldn't let go of the plan. Using the pseudonym Miles Ignotus, the Rockefeller house-intellectual wrote an article for Harpers in 1975 to articulate what would later become known informally as the Kissinger Doctrine. The article was titled, "Seizing Arab Oil."[18]

Kissinger began the article with an attack on the Declaration of the New Economic Order, the vision for a global political and economic order of equality, non-aggression, and democracy, articulated by the UN General Assembly one year earlier—the vision of Resolutions 3201 and 3281. The new economic order would isolate the United States, Kissinger warned, reducing its independence. Of course, he was right to conclude that an economic order based on the right of all states to choose their own economic system would isolate the United States, if the term 'the United States' meant 'US investment.' The new economic order would isolate US investment, in the sense that it would limit it to those territories in which a state chose an economic system that freely welcomed US investment. But since many states could be expected to block or limit US investment, or subject it to performance requirements, big US banks and corporations would find their compass reduced and their profit-making opportunities attenuated. This was hardly a world in which the Rockefellers wished to live.

Next, Kissinger made the case that the "control of Saudi oil" was "a vital national and all-Western interest for the United States." He claimed that "dependence of the Western world on Arab oil is absolute," a reference to the reliance of Western Europe and Japan (but not the United States) on the Middle East as an important source of oil. From this, Kissinger made a leap of logic to conclude that, owing to the dependence of these two regions on West Asian oil, that the United States was "living at the mercy of the Arabs." Of course, it was not the United States that was living at the mercy of the Arabs, but the French, Germans, Italians, and Japanese, the consumers of Arab oil, but even they weren't living at the mercy of the Arabs, since there was no reason the Arabs wouldn't sell them oil and plenty of reasons they would.

Virtually the only source of income for Saudi Arabia and other Gulf oil monarchies is oil sales. The Arabs could no more make Europeans live at their mercy by refusing to sell them oil than Jeff Bezos could hold them at their mercy by refusing to sell them goods from the Amazon website. Bezos would put himself out of business if he shut down his website for very long, and likewise the Saudis would bankrupt themselves if they imposed an oil embargo with teeth. As we've already seen, Faisal's 1973 oil embargo was a public relations manoeuvre aimed at pacifying the Arab street's demand for blood, not the equivalent of a suicide bomb attack. The deeper the harm to the West, the deeper the harm to Saudi oil revenues, and with nothing but oil to sell, there's no way the Saudis are ever seriously going to use the oil weapon. Indeed, one of the advantages for the Saudi monarchy of the 1973 oil embargo was that it demonstrated to the Arab world that oil production cutbacks as a mean of coercion don't work; hence, the Saudi royal family would no longer be pressured by Arabs to use a weapon the House of Saud didn't want to use anyway. What's more, shoppers—of both online merchandise and oil—have alternatives. Amazon customers have plenty of other places from which to buy goods, and German, French, Italian, and Japanese oil customers have alternatives too: Russian oil and natural gas, for example.

Kissinger next turned to consider the proper function of the US military. Anticipating Madeleine Albright, who as US ambassador to the UN infamously asked the head of the US Joint Chiefs of Staff, Colin Powell, "What's the point of having this superb military if we can't use it?"[9] Kissinger questioned the returns on the United States' (then) $85 billion per annum expenditure on the Pentagon. The Rockefeller-backed foreign policy thinker demanded the muscular use of US military power. The function of the Pentagon should be power projection, he argued. Billions of dollars per year shouldn't be spent on the military for impotence. If Washington needed to seize Saudi oil fields, it should have the military wherewithal to do so. But the United States was impotent in the Persian Gulf. It had no military presence in the region. "Except for staging and refueling points in Israel itself, almost 1,000 miles away, there would be no friendly bases within easy reach," Kissinger complained. And so the Kissinger plan to seize Saudi oil wells and turn them over to US oil firms, was voided for want of US bases in the Persian Gulf. It would not be too long before the Persian Gulf teemed with Uncle Sam's military outposts.

CHAPTER NINE

Saddam

"Arab oil for the Arabs."

Saddam, 1972[1]

In late January 1980, US president Jimmy Carter promulgated a new Monroe Doctrine for the Middle East that built on the earlier Eisenhower Doctrine. The Carter Doctrine was a formal articulation of a US claim to what, from the perspective of US investors, was the most lucrative part of the Middle East—the oil-rich Persian Gulf. Carter declared that, "An attempt by any force to gain control of the Persian Gulf region will be regarded as an assault on the vital interests of the United States of America, and such an assault will be repelled by any means necessary, including military force." In promulgating this doctrine, Carter had declared the Persian Gulf an American *mare nostrum*, a US lake, as Mussolini had declared the Mediterranean an Italian lake. The Persian Gulf, in Carter's warning, was to be regarded as informal US territory. Washington was prepared to go to war with any force that repudiated this claim.

The ostensible trigger for Carter's reinforcement of the US claim to Arabia's oil fields was Moscow's decision weeks earlier to send troops to Afghanistan in support of a secular, socialist government that was under attack by Islamist guerrillas secretly armed, trained, and encouraged by the United States. Carter's National Security Advisor, Zbigniew Brzezinski, would many years later publicly acknowledge that he had encouraged the

Islamist war on Kabul, a Soviet ally, to draw the USSR into its own Vietnam. US intelligence services began to aid the Islamist fighters six months before the Soviet intervention, drawing the USSR into what Brzezinski called "the Afghan trap." The US national security advisor told *Le Nouvel Observateur* in 1998 that the "day that the Soviets officially crossed the border, I wrote to President Carter, essentially: 'We now have the opportunity of giving to the USSR its Vietnam War.'"[2]

However much the Soviet intervention in Afghanistan was cited as the motivation for the Carter Doctrine, it was, in point of fact, only a pretext. Carter's take on the Monroe Doctrine wasn't aimed at the Soviets at all, who, no one in Washington seriously believed, were about to use Afghanistan as a launch pad for an invasion of the Middle East to seize Saudi oil. US officials knew that Soviet forces had entered the Central Asia country, not with designs on the oil fields of Arabia, but to prevent the emergence of an unfriendly, US-aligned regime on its border. Had the CIA not deliberately strengthened the Islamist opposition to the Afghanistan government, intending to draw the USSR into a trap, Soviet forces would not have been present in the country in significant numbers. What's more, Washington had every reason to believe that Moscow would be too preoccupied with the imperative of extracting itself from the Afghan trap and the Soviet military would be too bogged down in its own Vietnam to as much as consider a military adventure in the Persian Gulf, let alone pursue one. Finally, Kabul was 2,000 miles from Riyadh. It wasn't as if Soviet forces were sitting on the Saudi's doorstep. If the United States could not act on Kissinger's plan to seize Saudi oil fields in 1973, because there were no staging and refuelling points except in Israel, almost 1,000 miles away, how could the Soviets use Afghanistan, twice that distance away, as a staging point for a Persian Gulf invasion?

In an 1981 article in *Foreign Affairs*, the unofficial journal of the US State Department, Christopher van Hollen, who had served as the deputy assistant secretary of state for near eastern and south Asian affairs, revealed that the Soviet Union was not "the primary threat to Western interests in the Persian Gulf area" and that a direct Soviet attack on the Gulf was "improbable;" instead, "the most likely challenges to Western interests," he wrote, were internal to the Persian Gulf or regional: "wars between regional states, trans-border incursions, civil disturbances, oil embargoes or production cuts, or the overthrow of existing regimes." He summarized the threat to US control of Arabia's oil resources as "local forces of independence and national assertiveness."[3]

Repeated allegations that the Soviets planned to seize Persian Gulf oil were nonsense—part of the standard practice of concealing Third World grievances by portraying movements to redress them as a conspiracy instigated in Moscow. No serious case was ever presented that the Soviets would risk a war with the United States to block US investor access to the oil riches of the Persian Gulf.[4] The reality was that indigenous forces of independence and national assertiveness threatened US plunder of the Arab and Muslim worlds. This became apparent with the dissolution of the USSR. Despite the USSR's demise, the United States continued to find that there were obstacles to its plunder of North Africa and West Asia, in Iraq (Saddam), Syria (Assad), Libya (Gaddafi), Iran (Khomeini and the Islamic Revolution) and Lebanon (Hezbollah).

Pointing to the Soviet intervention in Afghanistan as the impetus for the Carter Doctrine was, then, a misdirection designed to conceal the real audience Carter intended to reach with his warning. The intended audience comprised local forces of independence and national assertiveness, as van Hollen had called them. Read carefully, the doctrine addressed itself to *any* force, not just an external one, that might seek to bring Persian Gulf oil under its control. In reality, it was an internal force to which Carter's warning was addressed. Control of the Persian Gulf by anyone other than the United States and its approved lackeys, including by the people who lived there, was declared *verboten*. The Persian Gulf was to be recognized as territory under US management.

In 1980, the most significant local force of independence and national assertiveness in the Persian Gulf region was Iraq, led by Saddam Hussein. Saddam, as he'll be referred to here, the name by which he was known to Iraqis, has been so thoroughly vilified by the Western powers who opposed him and eventually sent him to the gallows, that his accomplishments (which were considerable) and his politics (which were admirable) have been concealed behind a demonic caricature and silence about his goals and achievements. Saddam redirected Iraq's oil away from Western investors to social reforms and economic development for Iraqis, part of an Arab socialist program to overcome the Great Divergence. Every member of Iraqi society was uplifted by the Arab socialist reforms Saddam implemented. That he should be maligned—and by the same Western powers whose investors he refused to accommodate in favor of advancing the interests of common Iraqis—is not only expected, it's virtually axiomatic.

There are no neutral appraisals, only evaluations that reflect the political forces with which the appraiser is aligned. Investor-driven governments and mass media sing paeans to world leaders who foster favorable investment climates, and quietly pass over their crimes. At the same time, they excoriate and diabolize leaders who put their people's interests ahead of Wall Street's, and pass over their accomplishments. As the US cultural historian Bruce Franklin once pointed out, from the perspective of the British "George Washington was an arrogant scoundrel and traitor to his country, king and God, a renegade who brought slaughter and chaos to a continent." To the Confederacy, "Abraham Lincoln was responsible for the deaths of millions and the destruction of a civilized, cultured, harmonious society based on the biblically sanctioned relationship with the black descendants of Ham." To US settlers, "Sitting Bull was a murderous savage who stood in the way of the progress of a superior civilization." To the US establishment, Jimmy Carter was a kindly peanut-farmer who championed human rights and "used force only when necessary to protect the treasured values of the Free World."[5] Figures of the political Left whose job is to overcome the political Right, will be demonized by the political Right in proportion to the degree they succeed. Saddam, as we'll see, was unquestionably a figure of the political Left, however much astigmatic portrayals of him would suggest otherwise. He did his job well. Consequently, he was thoroughly maligned by the Western mass media, the apparatus through which Western investors speak and propagate their point of view. Like Nasser before him, and for the same reasons, Saddam was caricatured as a butcher and Hitler redivivus.

To be sure, there was much about Saddam's personal conduct that was deplorable, brutal and shocking, but much about his politics and achievements during the 1970s that was admirable. He was not a model of Nasserite incorruptibility, and he used violent and brutal methods (as too did Nasser and today Bashar al-Assad, as yesterday did Abraham Lincoln.) But Saddam lived among wolves, and those who live among wolves, must act as wolves, or perish—and there is no question that Saddam was well versed in lupine ways. Eventually, Saddam perished at the hands of wolves that were stronger and more brutal than he, but it's doubtful he could have made the gains he did on behalf of common Arabs without resorting to lupine methods. He was, after all, engaged in a war—of an oppressed people against its oppressors—and war by nature is violent and brutal. Saddam was a dictator, who gassed the Kurds, and invaded Kuwait, and for this he has been transformed from a human being into an incarnation of pure evil, while Churchill, a man who possessed *de facto* dictatorial powers during the Second World War, vowed never to end the tyranny of the British Crown over hundreds of millions of colonial subjects, favored the gassing of rebellious natives,[6] and oversaw the terrorist bombing of German civilians, has been transmuted from a human being into a semi-deity. David Ben-Gurion used terrorism to ethnically cleanse Palestine, established a settler dictatorship over the natives, and invaded Egypt in 1956, and in the West is generally held in esteem. From this can be concluded that it is not the methods used that determine how a political leader is regarded in the West, but whether he or she acted for or against Western governments and the investor interests they represent. The ruling ideas about who deserves approbation and who deserves reprobation are, to cite a Marxist tenet, the ideas of the ruling class.

Saddam's personal conduct is often emphasized in appraisals of the Arab leader, and indeed there are aspects of it that are repellent. He once invited a cabinet minister to step outside a cabinet meeting for a word, personally executed him, and then calmly returned to the meeting. The minister was involved in a scheme to import defective vaccines into Iraq—a scheme that misappropriated public funds for the cabinet minister's personal enrichment and imperilled the lives of Iraqis. In contrast, Saddam's politics are almost never explored and his achievements are almost never acknowledged, for these are largely admirable, especially next to those of the oil monarchs Wall Street aligned itself with and protected and fawned over. Saddam embraced republicanism against the monarchism of the rulers the British imposed on the Arab people and the Americans protected. He propelled Iraq into the modern world, while the oil monarchies remained stuck in the Middle Ages and mired in superstition. Saddam was a fervent champion of women's rights while Saudi kings enforced a medieval misogyny that treated women as the property of men. Until 1962, the Saudis kept slaves and the practice wasn't formally abolished in Oman and Yemen until 1970; it was inconceivable that slavery could exist under a Saddam government. Saddam sought to overcome hierarchies based on social origin, religion and nation; the Saudis reinforced social and religious hierarchies, treated Shia as heretics, and accepted the subordination of Arabs within an informal US empire. The Arab oil monarchs chose collaboration with a foreign hegemon and engaged in a kickback scheme, in which they ceded Arab oil to US investors in exchange for a share of the take, while Saddam championed independence and used Arab oil to uplift all sectors of Iraqi society. Is it any surprise, then, that Washington reduced to a demonic caricature an Arab leader whose values were the very antitheses of those embraced by the Arab paragons of political reaction Washington chose to befriend and protect?

During the 1970s, Saddam used Iraq's oil wealth to pursue ambitious programs of social reform and economic uplift, earning him the plaudits of the cofounder of the Arab Ba'ath Socialist Party, Michel Aflaq.[7] "Everything Saddam did had a social and socialist basis to it," wrote Aburish, who wrote a biography of the Iraqi leader. Saddam was, in Aburish's estimation, a Marxist at heart who "gave Marxism a local meaning." While he pursued socialist policies, he insisted that his socialism was adapted to the Arab world and that "Mohamed came before Marx."[8] He "became loved for his thoughtfulness towards the poor and disenfranchised."[9]

In June 1972, Saddam nationalized the Iraq Petroleum Company, a move that was enthusiastically supported throughout Iraq, including by his most bitter local opponents.[10] Saddam declared, "Our wealth has returned to us."[11] Radio Baghdad, voice of the Iraqi government, broadcast the revolutionary message of 'Arab oil for the Arabs.'[12] Of Arab countries endowed with oil, it was only Iraq, under Saddam, and Libya, under Gaddafi, that implemented policies independent of the West to use their oil income to improve the lives of the common people. By contrast, the Persian Gulf oil monarchies directed their countries' oil wealth to the West while skimming off a percentage for themselves. The result was handsome returns for Western investors, pharaonic wealth for the oil monarchs, and poverty for ordinary Arabs.[13] In contrast, Saddam's nationalization of Iraq's oil industry spurred an enormous increase in Iraq's national income, furnishing him with the means to change Iraq beyond recognition,[14] and making the country a model of what the Arab world could achieve by bringing its oil wealth under local control to satisfy local needs.

Saddam's government brought electricity to thousands of villages and free refrigerators and television sets to go with it.[15] It developed agriculture and funded the Palestinian struggle for emancipation.[16] It also set out to eradicate illiteracy.[17] So impressed was UNESCO by Saddam's anti-illiteracy efforts that it awarded the Iraqi government its Kropeska Award. UNESCO used the Iraqi program as a model to be followed elsewhere.[18] "There is no denying the social and economic achievements of the Ba'ath's first decade in power, 1968-78, under the stewardship of Saddam Hussein'" wrote Aburish. "Iraq had become a welfare state which was envied by the other Arabs and admired by the USSR."[19] But in the West, nothing was written in newspapers or broadcast on radio and television about Saddam's eradication of illiteracy, about his health care programs, or about the improvements he brought to the lives of women.[20]

In Saudi Arabia—special ally of the self-declared beacon of liberty, the United States—women were sequestered, veiled, and forbidden to drive automobiles. But in Iraq, Saddam was overcoming centuries of oppression against women. In 1970, only one-third of Iraqi girls went to school. By the end of the decade, almost all of them did. Women were admitted to professions and occupations from which they had previously been excluded. They now made up almost 30 percent of the country's physicians, nearly half of its dentists and almost three-quarters of its pharmacists. The armed forces were opened to women, and some became fighter pilots. Saddam's pro-women reforms made him more popular with Iraqi women than with men.[21]

Saddam endeavored to promote equality among Iraqis in another way. Most Iraqis did not have family names, and instead were named after their place of birth. Saddam, for example, was Saddam al Tikriti. Tikriti referred to Tikrit, the town of his birth, not far from where Saladin was born. (Hussein wasn't Saddam's family name but his father's name.) Birthplace implied social status, so an individual was forever stigmatized by his or her last name, which acted as a caste-like marker of social status. People from Tel Keif in northern Iraq, poor Christians who were janitors and servants, were marked out as people fit only for the lowliest and most servile labor, and were thus spurned and ostracized. So Saddam issued a decree forbidding the use of last names to overcome this form of social prejudice and discrimination.[22]

Saddam also pursued pan-Arab goals, evinced in the way he presented the Iraqi state. Iraq, he said, was as a state of all Arabs, not just Iraqis.

Saddam's government welcomed workers from all Arab countries, who could enter Iraq without visas, and receive free public health care and social security coverage.[23] At the same time, Baghdad created the National Fund for External Development, to spread Iraq's oil wealth to Arab states that did not have their own munificent sources of oil. These actions made Saddam an Arab hero, and the Arab world resounded with praise for his generosity. Saddam was hailed as the 'hero-brother' and 'Arab knight.'[24]

The Arab knight believed that the Arab world should be totally independent, militarily, economically, ideologically, and politically, and during the 1970s, Saddam's government pursued this goal.[25] If Iraq were to be sovereign, it would have to produce its own arms. "No country which relies on importing weapons is completely independent," he observed.[26] No other Arab leader in the twentieth century had ever attempted to overcome this impediment to independence by becoming self-sufficient in arms, with the exception of Nasser, who had taken some small steps.[27] Since the overthrow of the British-installed monarchy in 1958, Iraq had relied on the Soviet bloc for its military gear, but the Soviets occasionally used their control over Iraq's arms supply to exert political pressure.[28] Saddam saw that the only way Iraq could ever achieve true independence would be by eliminating its dependency on other states for the arms it needed for self-defense.

Fearing Saddam's efforts to build Iraq's military forces might challenge its regional superiority, Israel launched an assassination program to eliminate the scientists and engineers Saddam hired to staff Iraq's defense industry. It did the same to Syrian and Iranian scientists and engineers who worked in their countries' defense industries. The Jewish settlers, keen to preserve their monopoly on nuclear weapons in the Middle East, particularly focused on atomic scientists. For example, Mossad assassinated Egyptian atomic scientist Yahya El Mashad in 1980, who was working on Iraq's nascent military nuclear program.[29] In 1990, they assassinated Gerald Bull in Belgium, a Canadian arms industry scientist working on Iraqi rocketry.[30]

To lay the foundations for a genuine independence, Baghdad had embarked on a program of developing nuclear arms, a move viewed with some favor in the Arab world. For underdeveloped countries that seek to chart a course independent of Washington, atomic weapons make sense. The West has always used its military superiority to tyrannize weaker countries; indeed, it was Europe's military superiority that allowed it to conquer and loot the East Indies, extirpate, enslave and entomb in mines the aboriginal population of the Americas, and turn Africa into a warren for the commercial hunting of black-skins. Military disparity, in other words, was a necessary catalyst of the Great Divergence. "We have got, the Maxim gun, and they have not," wrote the British writer, Hilaire Belloc. At the Battle of Omdurman in 1898, the British reconquered Sudan, despite being outnumbered two to one. But owing to the superiority of British arms, the invaders slaughtered 12,000 native warriors, while losing only 47 men. "It was not a battle," wrote one observer, "but an execution."[31] The Battle of Omdurman was emblematic of thousands of other battles, in which Western military superiority was used to slaughter poorly-armed natives. For centuries the West has been using its 'Maxim guns' against the spears of the natives. The result was always the natives' slaughter and despoliation.

The reality behind the alleged military prowess of H.R. McMaster, a decorated US general who, for a time, served as the National Security Advisor to US president Donald Trump, illustrates the West's overwhelming military superiority. During the 1991 Gulf War, McMaster, commanding a group of nine tanks, destroyed 28 Iraqi tanks in less than 30 minutes, without suffering a single casualty. This was hailed as a great feat of military prowess, and the young captain was awarded the Silver Star, the United States' third highest decoration for valor in combat. But as Dave Lindorff, writing in the *London Review of Books*, explained:

> McMaster's exploit (later embellished with a name, the 'Battle of 73 Easting') was little more than a case of his having dramatically better equipment. His tanks were several generations ahead of the antique Russian-built T-72s of his Iraqi opponents. They were protected by depleted uranium armor – a dense metal virtually impenetrable by conventional tank shells, anti-tank rockets and RPGs – and carried anti-tank munitions tipped with depleted uranium penetrators, which can punch through steel armor as if it were cardboard. They then ignite a tank's interior, exploding any ordnance inside and incinerating the crew. The Abrams main cannon also has a significantly longer range than the tanks McMaster was confronting, meaning he and his men were able to pick off the Iraqi tanks while the shells fired back at them all fell short.[32]

This wasn't a fair fight. But, then, when have the colonizers' fights against the natives ever been fair? "The United States must retain overmatch—the combination of capabilities in sufficient scale to prevent enemy success and to ensure that America's sons and daughters will never be in a fair fight," reads the United States National Security Strategy of 2017. "Overmatch," the strategy document continues, "permits us to shape the international environment to protect our interests."[33]

Overmatch is the key to the success of all movements that seek to loot the land, resources, and labor of other people. Why wasn't the population of Bavaria or Pennsylvania or Bretagne displaced to make room for a Jewish state? Because overmatch wasn't a possibility against the people of these regions. "Settler colonialism," observed Beit-Hallahmi, "is only possible when the natives suffer a clear technological inferiority. Could Zionism," he asked, "have been possible in a Palestine inhabited by French farmers?"[34] The Arabs of Palestine were over-matched by Jewish settlers. Their weakness made them the perfect victims.[35]

Because they are light-years behind the West in wealth and technological development, Third World countries cannot possibly hope to compete with the US military Leviathan, and therefore are forever at the West's mercy. Their only hope is to lay their hands on an equalizer—and atomic weapons fit the bill. We're told that Third World leaders who seek to build nuclear weapons are crazed madmen who want to terrorize the West to realize (unspecified) nefarious aims; the truth of the matter is that they need nuclear arms for the same reasons Western powers claim they need them—self-defense. Only they need them more urgently; they don't have overmatch. Would the United States have "dared deal with Qaddafi or Saddam Hussein if they had a nuclear capability?" asked Major General Amir Eshel, chief of the Israeli army's planning division. "No way," he replied.[36] If we shudder at the thought of Third World governments building nuclear arsenals, we should put an end to the conditions that lead them to reach for a nuclear sword. The roots of contemporary nuclear proliferation lie in the West's use of its military superiority to impose its will on the Third World. So as long as the US Empire encroaches on the rights of other states to use their resources, markets and labor for their own benefit—and to choose their economic, political and cultural systems in accordance with the will of their people—local forces of independence and national assertiveness will lean toward building nuclear arsenals to defend their imprescriptible rights to independence. Only in the abolition of exploitation and the flowering of democracy on an international scale will the proliferation of nuclear arms be arrested.

Iraq purchased a small nuclear reactor from the Soviets in 1975, but Moscow stymied Iraqi nuclear ambitions by building safeguards into the reactor to make it proliferation-safe.[37] The French, however, proved to be more amenable, and agreed in 1976 to sell Iraq a uranium reactor.[38] In April 1979, Mossad agents blew up a ship carrying atomic reactor cores to Iraq.[39] Eventually, however, reactor cores arrived at Osirak. Not to be deterred, the Israelis tried again to disrupt Saddam's attempts at acquiring an equalizer. On June 7, 1981, using aerial photographs of the Osirak site provided by the CIA, Israeli pilots, flying US-provided F16 and F15 warplanes, destroyed the atomic reactor. To reach Iraq, they flew through the airspace of Saudi Arabia, (a US, and covert Israeli, ally).[40] The bombing derailed Iraq's nuclear weapons program. By this point, Iraq was mired in an exhausting war with Iran, and US war and sanctions in the subsequent decade left Iraq so weakened that it was unable to resurrect its program. Once again, Israel had done a great service for Washington. By preventing Saddam from acquiring an atomic equalizer, the United States was able to do what Amir Eshe said it would never do if Saddam had successfully developed an nuclear deterrent—invade Iraq.[41]

A number of developments marked Saddam as a danger to US investors: he restricted their opportunities to profit from Iraqi oil by ensuring that the preponderant benefit was directed to the local population; he built Iraq into a paragon of Arab socialist development, thus inspiring other Arabs to follow the same path, threatening the viability of US quisling regimes; he struck an alliance with the Soviet Union, formalized in a fifteen-year friendship treaty; and he began efforts to build a domestic arms industry, including nuclear weapons, in order to make Iraq truly independent. There was a risk to Washington that the latter development might furnish Saddam with the military means to achieve pan-Arab goals. Our "aims and ambitions do not lie in Iraq," announced Saddam in 1979, shortly before Carter declared the Persian Gulf an American *mare nostrum*, "but extend throughout the whole Arab homeland." Saddam saw Iraq as the state of the Arabs and himself as more than an Iraqi leader. He was an Arab leader whose program, like that of Nasser, was Arab oil for the Arabs.[42] With a nuclear saber he may have been in a position to raise the Arab flag of freedom in Kuwait and Saudi Arabia, and to bring Arabian oil under Arabist rule. Thus, it was Saddam and the common Arabs inspired by him, not the Soviets, who Carter sought to deter with his doctrine. The Eisenhower Doctrine was a US reply to, what might be called, the 'Nasser Doctrine.' Nasser declared that the Arab world and its oil belonged to the Arabs. Eisenhower rejoined that anyone who tried to make this so would be met by force. The Carter Doctrine was a restatement of the Eisenhower Doctrine, updated for the times. It was also a reply to what might be called the 'Saddam Doctrine.' Nasser was gone, but there was a new Arab socialist leader on the scene whose doctrine—that the Arab world and Arab oil belonged to the Arabs—was objectionable to the profit-making imperatives of US investors and therefore needed to be challenged. The subtext of the Carter Doctrine was that Arab oil belonged to the government of the United States and the investors it represented and anyone who said differently would have to contend with the combined services of the US Air Force, US Navy, US Army and US Marine Corps. They would also have to deal, as the Arab knight found out, with the Mossad and the Israeli air force.

CHAPTER TEN

Syria

"Jesus Christ was a Syrian Jew."

Hafez al-Assad[1]

Before the British and French divided Turkey's West Asian possessions in 1920, Syria comprised territory covering today's Palestine, Israel, Jordan, Lebanon, the Syrian Arab Republic, and parts of Turkey. These territories were inseparable parts of Syria, and their denizens were Syrians. Faisal, the Hashemite prince who would be installed by the British as the king of Iraq, told his British patrons that Palestine was an integral part of Syria.[2] Until the 1930s, Palestinians called themselves southern Syrians,[3] and Hafez al-Assad, the Arab socialist leader of the Syrian Arab Republic from 1971 to 2000, consistently claimed Palestine as Syrian territory. The 1911 edition of the Encyclopedia Britannica agreed with Assad. Palestine, it said, was "the southern third of the province of Syria." The territory was called Southern Syria.[4]

The international frontiers that partitioned Syria into four separate countries date to 1918-1923, when the British and French carved up the historically united region into entities they could control indirectly through imposed leaders. Jewish settlers were given Palestine. The French created Lebanon as a country to be ruled by their Maronite Christian allies. And the British created Jordan as a kingdom for a Hashemite prince.[5] In the 1980s, Hafez al-Assad complained bitterly to the French president François Mitterrand that, "When France entered our countries they were united [as one: Syria]. When it left they were disunited [partitioned into four separate countries.]"[6]

Determined not to submit to the imperial division of Syria, the Syrian Arab Republic asserted its claim to Palestine, Lebanon, and Jordan.[7] Damascus refused to recognize the armistice line that divided Arab and Zionists forces at the end of the First Settler-Native War as an international border.[8] During the Third Settler-Native War of June 1967, the Syrian representative to the UN Security Council defined Israel as a country illegitimately created by severing Palestine from Syria.[9]

In the mid-1980s, Damascus's claim to all of Greater Syria was evidenced in its maps. Daniel Pipes, the unapologetically pro-imperialist US specialist on Middle East affairs, wrote in 1986:

> The observant traveler entering Syria for the first time is startled as he goes through passport control and sees a military map of the country on the wall, for this map contains several obvious anomalies. It shows the province of Hatay, a part of Turkey since 1939, included in Syria. It shows the Golan Heights under Syrian control, though it has been occupied by Israel since 1967. Syria's boundaries with Lebanon and Jordan appear not as international borders but as something called 'regional' borders. Israel does not even exist on this map. Instead, there is a state called Palestine. And Palestine is separated from Syria by a line designated as a 'temporary' border.[10]

Damascus's claim to Palestine was vehemently contested by Yasser Arafat, the guerrilla leader who led the Nasser-created PLO, after Nasser relinquished control of it in the wake of June 1967 war. Assad and Arafat hated each other, their mutual enmity rooted in the question of who represented the Palestinians.[11] For Assad, the answer was clear: "There is no Palestinian people," he said, "no Palestinian entity. There is only Syria. [Palestinians] are an integral part of the Syrian people and Palestine is an integral part of Syria. Therefore it is we, the Syrian authorities, who are the real representatives of the Palestinian people."[12]

There is no question that the Syrian Arab Republic is the most militantly anti-Zionist of the Arab states.[13] The reason why lies in its irredentist claim to Palestine. Other Arabs see Palestine the way Germans see Austria—as territory inhabited by members of the same ethnic community. Syrians see Palestine the way North Korea sees South Korea—as territory to which they have a legitimate claim, on which, through the intervention of a foreign power, has been installed a usurper regime. By this argument, Israel, Jordan and Lebanon are the products of colonialism, and inasmuch as colonialism is illegitimate, so too are Israel, Jordan, and Lebanon. The Syrian Arab Republic, then, plays the lead role in Arab opposition to Israel.[14]

The Syrians were no less committed to recovering the territory the French had designated the state of Lebanon.[15] "Syria and Lebanon are a single country," observed Hafez al-Assad. "We are more than brothers."[16]

Lebanon was a semi-autonomous part of Syria under the Ottoman Empire. It became an independent state when France redrew its borders to create a Maronite Christian state, allied with France against the Muslims. Syrians understandably rejected this. The creation of Lebanon implied the partition of their country. Lebanon was a cudgel to be used against the Arabs. The state gave Christians' rights that Muslims were denied. In these respects, Lebanon has something of the character of Israel.

The Maronites are adherents of a Christian Roman Catholic sect of Syrian origin, whose historical region is the territory around Mount Lebanon. Maronites are named after the Christian Saint Maron, whose followers migrated to the region from the area around Antioch.

The French created Lebanon by annexing Syrian territory inhabited by Muslims to Mount Lebanon, while elevating the Maronite community to political primacy. Political power was distributed according to a formula imposed by French colonial authorities called the National Pact. The formula vested the Lebanese presidency in the Maronite community, the office of the prime minister in the Sunni Muslim community, the defense ministry in the Druze community, and the office of the parliamentary speaker in the Shia Muslim community.[17] The result was a *de facto* Maronite state, since only a Maronite could hold executive power. In the 1980s, Maronites made up only 15 percent of the population.[18] The French, thus, had created a *Herrenvolk* democracy in which their Maronite puppets exercised influence far in excess of their numbers. Lebanon was a democracy for Saint Maron's followers, and a Maronite state for its Muslims and Druze inhabitants. Shia Muslims, the largest of Lebanon's ethno-religious communities, comprising 40 percent of the population, were assigned the least consequential political office. Sunni Muslims, making up only 25 percent of the population, received a more significant post—that of the prime minister.

Zionist settlers looked to the Maronites as allies. The main political movement of the community, the Phalanges (phalanx), rejected an Arab identity. Modeled after the Spanish Falange and Italian Fascists, the Phalanges saw the Maronites as a nation separate from the Arab community in which it was embedded. In this, it shared characteristics with the Zionist movement. Both identified as non-Arab peoples implanted in the Arab homeland, sponsored by, and dependent on, the West. Both saw themselves as outposts of civilization in a land of Arab barbarism. And both were fervently anti-Arabist, anti-Palestinian, and anti-communist.

The Phalange was founded by Pierre Gemayel, a Lebanese apothecary who, while studying in Europe in the 1930s, encountered the Spanish and Italian fascist movements, and was smitten. Returning to Lebanon, he established a knock-off fascist party in 1936, adopting the classic reactionary slogan, "God, Fatherland and Family," a sharp contrast to the Arabist "Unity, Liberty, Socialism." The party was backed by wealthy Maronite families whose fortunes were often made in the illegal trade of drugs.[19]

Vladimir Jabotinsky recognized the potential for a Zionist alliance with the Maronites in the 1930s. In 1948, Ben-Gurion envisaged a Christian state in Lebanon whose southern border would be the Litani River,[20] 25 miles north of the current Israeli-Lebanon frontier. That same year, Israel made its first contact with the Phalanges. Three years later, Tel Aviv made a small contribution to the Phalanges' election campaign. In 1955, Moshe Dayan, the chief of the Israeli Defense Forces, proposed that Israel invade Lebanon, annex southern Lebanon—which was inhabited mainly by Shia Muslims—and create a puppet state in Beirut presided over by Israel's Phalangist allies.[21] Israel didn't act on Dayan's proposal, but it came close. In the mid 1970s the Zionist state spent $150 million arming the Phalangist militia. Beginning in 1976, Phalangist fighters were trained in Israel alongside Israeli paratroopers.[22] It's likely that all of this was paid for by the United States. The Beirut-based reporter Robert Fisk wrote that, "old American tanks employed by the Lebanese Christian Phalange... were gifts from the Israelis who received them from the US.... 'American-made, Israeli-supplied' used to be the mantra."[23]

The injustice of the French guarantee of political power to its Maronite confederates inevitably provoked a reaction. In 1975, the community most bitterly disenfranchised by the National Pact, the Shia, organized a movement of the political Left dedicated to overcoming Lebanon's French colonial-sanctioned inequalities. Named Amal (Hope), the movement espoused social justice, advocated non-sectarianism, and promoted political equality. Amal had tens of thousands of members, was the largest organization in the Shia community, and was possibly the largest Lebanese political organization.[24] The movement paralleled the communist and Arab Ba'ath Socialist movements in two respects: It appealed to communities that had been victimized by ethno-religious discrimination and it advocated political equality, regardless of religious and ethnic identity.

While the United States and Israel originally ignored Sadat's proposal to establish an *entente* in return for the Sinai, the events of October 1973 persuaded US secretary of state Henry Kissinger to negotiate a peace between the two countries. The negotiations culminated in the Camp David Accords of 1978-1979. The Nasserist project of recovering Palestine on behalf of the Arab nation would be shelved in exchange for the return of Egyptian territory and the establishment of self-governing Palestinian territories in the West Bank and Gaza Strip.[25]

Sadat had arrived at the conclusion that recovery of Egyptian territory conquered by Israel in 1967 could best be accomplished by turning away from the Soviet Union and ingratiating Egypt with the United States. As we have seen, the strategy failed to gain traction until Egypt and Syria attacked Israel in 1973, and the Saudis deployed the oil weapon. At that point, Kissinger recognized that there was much to be gained by granting Sadat his wish. At the cost of returning the Sinai to Egypt, the Arab world's most populous country, and its largest army, would be neutralized. No more would Israel face the possibility of a two-front war (with Egypt on a western front and Syria on a northern one.) What's more, by eliminating Egypt as a threat, Israel could pursue the Palestinian guerrillas, who, having been driven out of Jordan during Black September, were now using Lebanon as a base of operations. Egypt, then, would be eliminated as an Arab socialist threat to US imperialist ambitions in the region. The Arabist movement would be weakened by Egypt's defection. And Israel would be afforded space to attack the Palestinian guerrillas in their lair.

There was another advantage for Washington in the deal it worked out with Sadat. US-Egyptian cooperation sent a signal: Washington could extract Israeli concessions to the benefit of an Arab government or movement that was willing to cooperate with the United States. If Sadat could recover Egyptian territory in return for cooperation with the Americans, maybe the Palestinians could recover part of their country if they worked with Washington. "Sadat's success in retrieving Egyptian territory by aligning with the United States in the region bred what can be described as a political illusion within the Palestinian camp," observed Abu-Manneh Bashir. "The belief was the following: national rights could only be retrieved by becoming politically moderate and gaining American acceptance. If Sadat could do it, why couldn't Arafat?"[26]

Israel, thus, was making an important contribution to US foreign policy. As a settler state that threatened the Arab natives, Israel encouraged the Arabs to turn to Washington for protection. The level of protection the USSR could afford was always limited; Egypt's and Syria's alliances with the Soviet Union didn't prevent the Israelis inflicting the great setback of 1967. After 1991, even the modest protection afforded by the Soviets was gone. Only Washington could realistically shield the Arab states from Israeli aggression. By incessantly threatening its Arab neighbors, the Zionist state fostered the cooperation of Arab West Asia with the only force that could keep the Israeli Doberman on its leash, and rein it in—the White House. Of course, not every state cooperated with Washington fully, but the presence nearby of a state with a penchant for territorial expansion, created pressure to cooperate. Israel thus played the role of threat-maker in a protection racket.

On June 6, 1982, Israel invaded Lebanon, initiating the Fifth Settler-Native War. Its objectives were to destroy the 15,000 Palestinian guerrillas who were operating out of southern Lebanon; to eject the PLO leadership from Beirut; and to force the Syrians—who regarded Lebanon as Syrian territory—to end their military occupation of the country. The latter objective, if achieved, would frustrate Syrian irredentist aims.

The invasion and occupation of southern Lebanon proceeded swiftly. Within a few days, 78,000 Israel troops occupied most of southern Lebanon up to Beirut. By September, the PLO had been driven out of the country. Even so, Israel announced it would not end its occupation until the Syrian Arab Army withdrew to its borders. Since the Syrians had no intention of complying with the Israeli demand, the Zionist state was effectively announcing that it intended to remain in southern Lebanon indefinitely. The Israeli Defense Forces left 20,000 troops behind to enforce the occupation and to prop up the Maronite government.[27]

The occupation of Lebanese territory was attributed by Tel Aviv to the need to deny Palestinian guerrillas territory from which to launch attacks on Israel, and more broadly, to eliminate an organized movement of secular Arab nationalism, the PLO. But territorial expansion into Lebanon meshed with longstanding Zionist aspirations to absorb southern Lebanon into a Jewish state. Israel occupied Lebanon for 18 years, until 2000. Over nearly two full decades of occupation, the resistance of the Arab natives to the Israeli presence mounted, until, for Israel, the costs of the occupation outweighed its benefits. The resistance was led by an organization that originated in the Amal movement. Its name was Hezbollah.

Hezbollah, literally the "party of God," emerged in embryo in late June 1982, as a split from Amal. It was led by Amal's second-in-command, Hussain Mussawi, a secular Shia leader. Initially, the Shia community supported the Israeli goal of ejecting the PLO. While the Shia were sympathetic to the Palestinian cause, the PLO's presence in southern Lebanon was a source of tension, and Amal took a generally favorable stance toward the settler invasion, hoping it would rid southern Lebanon of its Palestinian interlopers. Mussawi, and a small group of followers, were aghast at Amal's passive acceptance of the invasion. Looking to Iran for inspiration and support, they formed an organization called Islamic Amal. In Iran, followers of the Shia cleric Ayatollah Ruhollah Khomeini had overthrown the US-backed Shah in 1979 and instituted an anti-imperialist state that was a combination Shia theocracy and democratic republic. Iran immediately accommodated Mussawi's request for aid, sending approximately 1,000 Revolutionary Guards to Lebanon. These were militiamen dedicated to the Islamic revolution. In the meantime, the Amal offshoot set to work organizing armed resistance to the Israeli invasion.[28]

Israel's press into Lebanon left as many as 5,000 Shia dead and 80,000 homeless. While the Shia community welcomed the ejection of the Palestinian guerrillas, the deaths, homelessness, and the fact that the Israelis were settling in for a long occupation, turned the community against the Israeli invaders. Shia grievances escalated when US, French, and other Western troops arrived in the country as 'peace keepers.' Lebanon had become captive to a joint occupation by Israel and its Western sponsors, in support of a Maronite minority that had tyrannized the country since its founding by colonial France. As the tide of public opinion turned against the Israelis, Hezbollah's membership grew.[29]

The organization's aims were formalized in a February 1985 'Open Letter.' Hezbollah's "great and necessary objectives were to put an end to foreign occupation and to adopt a regime freely wanted by the people of Lebanon" and "to expel the Americans, the French and their allies definitely from Lebanon, putting an end to any colonialist entity on our land."[30]

Hezbollah thus began as an anti-colonialist organization. The Open Letter identified Israel as "a great danger to our future generations and to the destiny of our nation, especially since it embraces a settlement-oriented and expansionist idea."[31] The evidence for Israeli expansionism was found in Israel's behavior. The Zionist state had settled Jewish colonists in the Gaza Strip, the West Bank, and the Golan Heights—territory that had been obtained by military conquest. After the 1967 War, Israel had settled Jews in the Sinai, as well. The regional Leviathan continued to occupy southern Lebanon, despite having achieved its main war aim of ejecting the PLO. And, consistent with its previous behavior of settling Jews on conquered territory, the self-appointed Jewish state was now settling Jews in the Shia heartland of Lebanon. Small wonder, then, that the Party of God attributed to Israel the aim of creating an expanded Jewish settler state, a Greater Israel, from the Euphrates to the Nile.[32]

One of Hezbollah's most spectacular resistance operations was the suicide bombing of the barracks housing US and French occupation forces, an operation that killed 241 US and 58 French soldiers, and which triggered the withdrawal of Western armies from the country. It was this event that led the US government to label Hezbollah a terrorist organization. A more fitting description would have been 'resistance' or 'anti-colonial' organization.

For Hezbollah, attacks on Israeli and Western forces, both combatants and non-combatants, were justified on a number of grounds.

First, backed by the United States, Israel had committed heinous atrocities against the people of southern Lebanon. Hezbollah's 1985 Open Letter said that: "America, its Atlantic Pact allies, and the Zionist entity [i.e., Israel]... invaded our country, destroyed our villages, slit the throats of our children, violated our [religious] sanctuaries, and... committed the worst massacres against our nation... perpetrated with the tacit accord of America's European allies."[33]

Second, Israel was viewed, not as an independent entity, but as an instrument of the United States. Sayyid Muhammad Husayn Fadlallah, who has been called the spiritual mentor of Hezbollah, said: "We believe there is no difference between the United States and Israel; the latter is a mere extension of the former.... The two countries are working in complete harmony."[34]

Third, the Lebanese did not have the means to confront the United States and Israel with conventional weapons. The US-Israeli alliance had decisive military power, and could easily crush a conventional military response to their aggression. The Americans, French, and Israelis had the Gatling gun, and the Lebanese Arabs did not. The oppressed people of southern Lebanon had a choice: either acquiesce to the US-backed Israeli occupation and plunder of their land, or use whatever means were available to defend themselves.[35]

Moreover, the distinction between combatant and non-combatant was regarded as artificial. Israeli and US citizens supported Israel's settler colonialism. They elected governments that formulated, implemented, and defended Israeli aggression, expansion, and colonization. They paid taxes to these governments, and they expressed popular support for them. Without the backing of Israeli citizens, the self-declared Jewish state could not invade Lebanon, occupy its territory, prop up its fascist Maronite allies, and colonize its territory. Without the backing of US citizens, Washington could not enable, protect, and encourage Israel to attack the Arabs, dispossess them, and undermine their movements of national liberation.

Hezbollah's argument meshed with one put forth by the moral philosopher Tomis Kapitan. In an essay titled "Can Terrorism be Justified?"[36] Kapitan argued that under certain circumstances, terrorism is a morally justifiable tool of resistance for oppressed people facing an oppressor state whose aggression is supported by its civilian population. Defining terrorism as the deliberate politically-motivated use or threat of harm aimed at civilians, Kapitan pointed out that terrorism had been pervasively used by the United States throughout its history. Indeed, the establishment of the country was predicated on the systematic use of terrorism against indigenous people, whose land was despoiled through massacres and forced expulsions. Kapitan further cited US strategic bombing of civilians in Germany and Japan during the Second World War, including campaigns of incendiary and atomic bombing, with hundreds of thousands of civilian fatalities in aggregate, as clearly defined instances of terrorism on a grand scale.

US state-directed terrorism was also evidenced in the bombing of civilians in US wars of aggression on Korea, Vietnam, Cambodia, Iraq, and Afghanistan. Non-combatant deaths and injury were the known predictable consequences of US bombing campaigns, yet they were ordered by US state officials and were popularly supported by US citizens. These campaigns produced civilian casualties on a scale many orders of magnitude greater than those caused by all the terrorism campaigns in history that had been pursued by oppressed people in the pursuit of their freedom.[37]

The yawning disparity between the number of non-combatant casualties produced by state-directed versus resistance movement-directed terrorism revealed a significant reality: States have an immense technological advantage that allows them to kill civilians on a colossal scale. The gross disparity in power between oppressor and oppressed means that the oppressed have few means of resistance. Terrorism is one of the few ways they can realistically fight back in a manner that has any chance of making a difference.

Terrorism, it is often said, is the weapon of the weak. This is not true. Deliberate, politically-motivated harm of civilians is the weapon of the strong as much as it is the weapon of the weak. It is more accurate to say that civilian-aimed political violence is uniquely labeled as terrorism only when it is practiced by the weak. Since terrorism carries with it the stigma of moral opprobrium, the use of perhaps the only effective method of harm-infliction available to the oppressed in pursuit of the legitimate goal of emancipation is uniquely defined as morally repugnant. Thus, the effective resistance of the oppressed is, in practice, morally proscribed. By contrast, the terrorism of oppressors evades both the terrorist label and the stigma of moral turpitude.[38] The US Air Force can send millions of civilians to early graves by disarticulating, crushing, and incinerating them, and be celebrated as 'a force for good in the world,' but the death of a dozen civilians who support the oppression of another people, or of soldiers engaged in the occupation of a country, is condemned as an act of iniquity. But it has ever been thus. Outrages against the oppressed arouse no indignation, but assaults on oppressor populations instantly cause an outraged uproar.[39]

The terrorism of the strong—the deliberate use or threat of harm against civilians to achieve political objectives—is not limited to the use of strategic bombing (once known appositely as 'terror bombing'). The regular practice followed by US politicians of threatening to annihilate through nuclear attack the civilian populations of states that, asserting their independence, refuse to comply with US demands that are against their national interest, conforms to the definition of terrorism. On multiple occasions, Washington has threatened North Korea with nuclear annihilation; that is, it has deliberately threatened to harm North Korean civilians to achieve political aims.[40]

Imperialist states have also used their economic strength to inflict severe harm on the civilian populations of states that have chosen political and economic systems at odds with the interests of Western investors. Sanctions, blockades, and embargoes have led to the deaths through disease and malnutrition of millions of civilians, typically the weakest: children, the elderly, and the infirm. For example, *The New York Times* reported in 1996 that as "many as 576,000 Iraqi children" were believed to have died between 1991 and 1996 "because of economic sanctions imposed by the Security Council."[41] Because Washington continued to punish Saddam's Iraq economically until the US invasion of the country in 2003, sanctions deaths accumulated for another seven years. It's likely that well over one million Iraqi children died as a consequence of a program implemented by the US government to achieve its political goals. Writing in *Foreign Affairs*, John Mueller and Karl Mueller showed that the US-led sanctions produced more deaths than all the weapons of mass destruction in history, including all the chemical weapons used in the First World War and the atomic bombings of Hiroshima and Nagasaki. Indeed, the Muellers found coercive economic measures to be so devastating to qualify as instruments of mass destruction, even more injurious to civilian populations than weapons of mass destruction.[42] Considering that the number of deaths attributable to the atomic bombings of Hiroshima and Nagasaki (200,000) are less than half as large as the number of sanctions-related children's deaths in Iraq to 1996 (more than

500,000), the implication is that the economic element of the war on Saddam's Iraq was tantamount to an attack of two atom bombs.[43] While this form of political coercion does not involve the direct use of violence against civilians, it does involve the deliberate infliction of harm upon them, and therefore accords with Kapitan's definition of terrorism. Moreover, its effects are qualitatively the same as massive state violence and are often quantitatively greater.

Kapitan argued that if the members of a community have a compelling reason to believe that they are the target of an existential threat posed by an aggressor state, and that the aggression is supported by the state's adult citizens, that the use or threat of violence against those citizens is morally justified.[44] He used the case of the Palestinians to illustrate the principle. The Arab community in Palestine faced an existential threat from Zionist settlers, beginning in the twentieth century, and persisting to today. In 1948, Arab residents of Palestine were exiled from their homes, denied repatriation, and dispossessed of their property. Since then, Israel has established Jewish colonies in the territory it failed to acquire by force in the First Settler-Native War. In response, Palestinians used pacific means of self-defense, from diplomacy to negotiations to non-violent resistance. None of these measures made the slightest difference in ending the harm inflicted upon them. Instead, the expansionary Zionist state continued to settle Jewish colonists on what little territory had not already been pirated from the Palestinians. Arab terrorism, however, raised awareness of the Palestinian cause, mobilized world-wide support, and forced the self-declared Jewish state to withdraw from Gaza and southern Lebanon. Considering the intentions of the Zionist leadership, as evidenced by their record of colonial expansion, failure to use terrorist methods would have led to the extinction of the Palestinian community.[45]

Hezbollah is a resistance organization, born out of the Amal movement. Amal sought to transform a Maronite *Herrenvolk* democracy into a state in which all citizens are equal, regardless of their ethno-religious identity. Its descendant, Hezbollah, successfully drove Israel and Western invaders from its soil. The organization "was born as a resistance force in the reaction to the occupation," as its current leader, Hassan Nasrallah explained.

"It sought assistance from any party."[46] Two countries stepped up: Iran and Syria. Thus was born the Axis of Resistance: The alliance of Iran, Syria and Hezbollah, against Western domination of the Middle East.

CHAPTER ELEVEN

Settlers

*"Israelis are colonial fighters
and settlers, just like the Afrikaners."*

Benjamin Beit-Hallahmi, 1987[1]

S ettler colonialism is a system in which natives are displaced by immigrants. Under this system, the natives are defined as foreigners, or
non-persons, without rights to the land on which they live. The immigrants, in contrast, are defined as the true natives, the legitimate posses-
sors of the land.[2] This system prevails under Zionist rule in Palestine, and
prevailed under the rule of followers of the Dutch Reform Church, the
Afrikaners, in South Africa, and under the rule of Protestant settlers in
North America.

"The biblical Christian of European race and origin, who had settled
overseas among non-European peoples, identified inevitably with Israel
in obeying the will of Jehovah by taking possession of the Promised Land,"
wrote the historian Arnold Toynbee. "On the other hand, he identified
the non-Europeans, whom he encountered during his progress, with the
Canaanites who were given into the hand of the Lord's chosen people, to
be destroyed or subjugated. With this belief the English Protestant settlers
in the New World [decimated] the North American Indians in the same
way as the bison, from one coast of the continent to the other."[3]

The original first chapter of Laura Ingalls Wilder's 1935 novel *Little
House on the Prairie*, the story of the Wilder family's settlement on the

US plains, begins with a description of the land on which the family settled: "There were no people. Only Indians." Echoing US president Theodore
Roosevelt's genocidal pronouncement on American Indians—Roosevelt
had said, "I don't go so far as to think that the only good Indians are dead
Indians, but I believe nine out of every ten are, and I shouldn't like to
inquire too closely into the case of the tenth"[4]—characters in Wilder's
works opine that the only good Indian is a dead one.[5] America's aboriginal
people were equated implicitly if not explicitly with the Canaanites.

The Canaanites were members of the indigenous population of Canaan,
the area now called the Levant, or which was once called Syria, before
colonial France and Britain partitioned it. In the Old Testament Book of
Joshua, Canaanites were included in a list of seven nations slated for extermination by the Jews, on the order of their god, Jehovah. In the Bible, the
Land of Canaan was renamed the Land of Israel, after the Israelites, the
settlers, conquered it.

In the Old Testament Book of Deuteronomy, the Jews are told that they
have "been chosen out of all the people on the face of the earth to be his
people, his treasured possession," and that when he (the Lord) brings them
into the Land of the Canaanites they must destroy the native inhabitants
totally, showing no mercy. The Old Testament also recounts how Joshua,
who the Jews' deity commanded to take possession of the Canaanites'
land, "took all these royal cities and their kings and put them to the sword.
He totally destroyed them, as Moses the servant of the Lord had commanded. ... The Israelites carried off for themselves all the plunder and
livestock of these cities, but all the people they put to the sword until they
completely destroyed them, not sparing anyone that breathed."

The myth has resonances with the German conquest of *lebensraum* in
Eastern Europe. While Hitler did not offer a divine mandate to justify the
conquest of Germany's 'East Indies,' or the merciless extermination of its
inhabitants, he did invoke a social Darwinian imperative to legitimate
Germany's march into Eastern Europe. Germany, according to Hitler, had
the right to subdue the weak, as given to it by 'nature,' a kind of deperson-
alized god. Germans may not have been a chosen people by virtue of a
deity conferring on them a mission, but they were an elect people by virtue of what the Nazi leader deemed their advanced civilization and culture. The very same justification of racial or civilizational supremacy was
invoked by other imperialist powers, as well; the British, for example, in

the figure of Winston Churchill, used it to defend British settler colonial-ism. "I do not admit for instance," harrumphed Churchill, "that a great wrong has been done to the Red Indians of America or the black people of Australia. I do not admit that a wrong has been done to these people by the fact that a stronger race, a higher-grade race, a more worldly wise race to put it that way, has come in and taken their place."[6] What distin-guished Hitler's settler colonialism and its attendant exterminations from those of the British, French and others, was that he turned on Europe the very same system of a chosen people taking the place of non-elect natives, that, until then, had been wielded as a European weapon against non-European populations. In the West, Hitler's great crime, observed Aimé Césaire, was not that he used settler colonialism, but that he used it against the white man. He "applied to Europe colonialist procedures which until then had been reserved exclusively for the Arabs of Algeria, the 'coolies' of India, and the 'niggers' of Africa."[7] For this, the West could never for-give him. On the other hand, the West has found it in its heart to forgive colonial powers doing in 'the heart of darkness' what Hitler did in the 'heart of Europe.'[8]

The United States is a settler colonial nation as much as Israel is and apartheid South Africa was. Hitler looked to Britain for inspiration, see-ing its vast empire as a model for Germany. But he also looked to the United States. Hitler "sought his Far West in the East," observed Domenico Losurdo, "and identified the 'natives' of Eastern Europe and the Soviet Union as 'Indians' to be stripped of their land, decimated and, in the name of the march of civilization, pushed ever farther back beyond the Urals. The survivors were permitted to work like black slaves in the service of the white, Aryan race."[9] The Nazis even went so far as propose a *Judenreservat*, a 'reservation for Jews', modeled after the reservations to which the aboriginal peoples of North America were displaced.[10]

"The United States of America has long viewed itself as an exceptional nation, even as God's New Israel, sent to redeem the world," observed the economist Jeffrey D. Sachs.[11] US president George W. Bush declared the United States to be "chosen by God" and endowed with "the historical mission to be a model for the whole world,"[12] a theme traceable to the ear-liest Puritan colonial settlers. In 1630, John Winthrop, preparing to leave England to sail to the Americas, delivered a sermon. Winthrop used words from the New Testament Book of Matthew to outline his vision of the new

American colonial settlements. They would be a 'city on the hill'—a model to be admired by all humanity. The idea of the United States as a moral paragon recurs in the public discourse of US leaders. In a 1961 speech, president-elect John F. Kennedy quoted Winthrop directly. "We must always consider that we shall be seen as a city upon a hill." In a 1980 speech, US president Ronald Reagan said that "Americans in 1980 are every bit as committed to that vision of a shining 'city on a hill,' as were those long ago settlers." In 2006, US president Barack Obama referred to the early settlers who "dreamed of building a City upon a Hill."

The invocation of a Biblical justification for displacing natives and possessing their land is present too in the development of the Afrikaner colonial settlements on the southern tip of Africa. The Afrikaner settlements became the basis for the state of South Africa, with its system of settler supremacist rule and settler-native separation, or apartheid. Drawing on the ideology of the Dutch Reformed Churches of South Africa, the Afrikaners, Dutch settlers, saw themselves as the chosen people, laying claim to land they believed was promised to them by their deity. The Church had anti-Enlightenment views, resonant with those of the Nazis and other reactionary movements against universal equality. In the Church's view, nations were to be kept apart, in their own separate spaces, and protected from the dangers presented by the ideas of revolutionary movements that championed the equality of peoples. The Dutch settlers set out from their Cape Colony on a great trek into the interior to escape Britain's colonial administration. 'The Great Trek' was conceived as a parallel to the Jews' Exodus from Egypt to the Promised Land.

Thus, the United States, South Africa and Israel, began as European implantations in land beyond Europe, justified by reference to the mythology inhered in the Bible. The respective states assigned to the settlers, rights that were superior to those of the natives. They were *Herrenvolk* states, in which the settlers, though constituting a minority, exercised political supremacy over the natives. The United States was a state for white Europeans, Israel a state for the Jews, and apartheid South Africa a state for the Afrikaners. The natives were second-class citizens or non-persons.

Israelis, their supporters, and those who struggle to understand the 'Israeli-Palestinian problem,' will protest that Jews are not a minority in Israel, but constitute a majority. "What this claim fails to take into account," observes Beit-Hallahmi, "is that until 1948, Arabs were a majority in Palestine, and turning then into a minority was indeed one of the aims of Zionism."[3] It was only by the exile of 700,000 Arabs, and the prevention of their repatriation, that it was possible to create a Jewish majority in Israel. But the domain over which the self-declared Jewish state rules encompasses more than simply Israel. What of the Jews-only colonies established in the Palestinian territory of the West Bank and Jerusalem? The Gaza Strip, the West Bank, Jerusalem, and the Golan Heights, are all under Israeli control. If we consider these territories together, Arabs constitute a slight majority. Were the exiles to be repatriated, Arabs would constitute a decisive majority.

Even within Israel proper, Jews have more rights than the natives. The Jewish National Fund holds land within the 1948 armistice line on behalf of the Jewish people—land that Israel purloined from the Arabs at the end of the First Settler-Native War. A Jew who immigrates to Israel from anywhere in the world has the right, as a Jew, to own this land. An Arab resident of Israel does not. During the South African apartheid era, a Jew of European origin who immigrated to South Africa would likewise have had more land ownership rights in South Africa than would a native. The parallel was a source of solidarity between Israelis and white supremacist South Africans.

Both apartheid South Africa and the Zionist state were based on a hierarchy of peoples in which the state was identified with one people alone. While in reality the states ruled multinational populations, they ruled in the interests of only one of its nations. Likewise, their official ideologies identified the dominant people as doubly victimized—first by British colonialism and second by the hostility of the natives.[14] The mythology of double victimization is also seen in the experience of the American colonial settlers.

The American War of Independence was an uprising against British restrictions on the colonial settlers' expansion to the West and displacement of the natives. The British Crown had become surfeited of drawing on its treasury to fund wars against the natives for the benefit of colonial settlers who begrudged taxation. Western expansion, then, would be prohibited. "The chief factor in producing the Revolution ... was ... the ... Quebec Act of 1774 ... designed with the purpose of keeping the English-speaking settlements permanently east of the Alleghenies, and preserving the might and beautiful valley of the Ohio as a hunting ground for savages," wrote US president Theodore Roosevelt.[15] Losurdo notes that the colonial settlers' "priority was to rid themselves of the restrictions imposed by the British Crown on their westward expansion at the expense of the Native Americans. This was an absolutely intolerable limitation for those ruled by an 'expansionist vision of the future—a vision of manifest larceny that was especially dear to property speculators like George Washington.'"[16]

While the British sponsored the Zionist colonial settler project in Palestine, they also tried to restrict it when the resistance of the natives made British rule of Palestine a costly affair. This triggered a Zionist rebellion against Britain, and the war of 1948 has ever since been presented as a war of independence against British tyranny rather than a war of dispossession waged against the natives. In this the Zionists have aped the US experience of claiming dual victimization.

Losurdo saw the parallels extending further. The rebellion of the American colonists against King George and the Zionists against Britain can be compared "to the secessions, or attempts at secession, made shortly after the mid-twentieth century by French colonists in Algeria and British colonists in Rhodesia." In the case of the American colonists and the Zionists, "it was a question of sweeping away the obstacles to the process of colonization erected by a [metropolitan] government; in the other two, of blocking at any price the de-colonization that a [metropolitan] government felt compelled to initiate." All these "instances involved movements whose protagonists were the most fanatical supporters of colonial expansionism and rule."[17]

In 1971, *The New York Times* noted the similarities between the settler colonial state in Palestine and the settler colonial state on the southern tip of Africa: "There is a remarkably close if little known partnership between Israel and South Africa. This relationship between the nation controlling Africa's southern tip and the nation still holding the gate to its northern tip affects political, economic and military matters.... [South Africa's] Prime Minister [John] Vorster, even goes so far as to say Israel is now faced with an apartheid problem—how to handle its Arab inhabitants. Neither nation wants to place its future entirely in the hands of a surrounding majority and would prefer to fight."[18]

One US journalist pointed out the parallels between the two states of 'chosen people': "To Afrikaners, the parallels are as obvious as they are embarrassing to the Israelis. They and the Israelis are essentially white, Europeanized peoples who have carved their own nations out of a land inhabited by hostile non-European majorities that would destroy the two nations if the Afrikaners, and the Israelis, listened to the United Nations or world opinions. Their religions are similar, each being a 'chosen people.' Israel, to [South Africa's apartheid] government is the other Western outpost in the Third World."[19]

The two allies "understood and sympathized with each other's existential struggles," observes Sasha Polakow-Suransky, who explored the alliance between the two states in his 2010 book *The Unspoken Alliance: Israel's Secret Relationship with Apartheid South Africa.* For example, in 1987, Rafael Eitan, Israeli military chief of staff, and later an Israeli cabinet minister, explained that South Africa's indigenous population wanted "to gain control over the white minority, just like the Arabs here want to gain control over us. And we too, like the white minority in South Africa, must act to prevent them from taking over."[20]

Beit-Hallahmi cited a letter written to the editor of Haaretz in November 1985, to illustrate the ideological affinity between Zionism and apartheid. The letter was written at the height of the global anti-apartheid campaign.

> Events in South Africa are constantly in the news. [South Africa's] President Botha does not want to hand over control to representatives of the majority. Fifty years ago, in 1935, the British High Commissioner wanted to set up a legislative assembly in Palestine. As far as I remember, Jews were allocated two seats ... and the Arabs eleven [proportional to the size of their respective populations] ... Our representatives turned the idea down out of hand the day it was submitted. Is it so hard to understand President Botha?[21]

How was the Jerusalem-Pretoria Axis seen from the South African side? "Israel and South Africa have much in common," stated a 1968 editorial in the Cape Province newspaper of the governing South African National Party. "Both are engaged in a struggle for existence, and both are in constant clash with the decisive majorities in the United Nations. Both are reliable foci of strength within the region, which would, without them, fall into anti-Western anarchy. It is in South Africa's interest that Israel is successful in containing her enemies, who are among our most vicious enemies."[22]

South Africa and Israel also shared contempt for international law and a determination to defy UN resolutions demanding that they bring their malign practices into conformity with international legal standards. For example, South Africa conquered Namibia during the First World War, and occupied it until 1990. Namibia was, before its conquest by South Africa, a German colony, and the site of the genocide of the Herero people, an extermination of a native population that David Olusoga and Casper W. Erichsen called the 'Kaiser's holocaust' in their 2011 book by the same name. The book explored the continuity between the colonial practices of Wilhelmine Germany in Africa and Nazi Germany in Europe. South Africa's occupation of Namibia transgressed international law and Pretoria defied multiple UN resolutions to withdraw from the country. Similarly, Israel is notorious for defiance of international law. It continues to prevent the repatriation of Palestinians to their homes, in disregard of numerous UN resolutions. Additionally, it refuses to withdraw from the West Bank and Golan Heights, regularly violates the sovereign territory of its neighbors, and has launched multiple wars of aggression, all in violation of international law.

In 1975, the Organization of African Unity drew a parallel between Israel and the white supremacist colonial settler states of South Africa and Rhodesia. It denounced Israel as a "racist regime in occupied Palestine." The three states were declared to "have a common imperialist origin, forming a whole and having the same racist structure and being organically linked in their policy aimed at repression of the dignity and integrity of the human being."[23]

In December of 1973, two months after the close of the October War, Chaim Herzog, the chief of Israeli military intelligence, and later Israel's president, recommended that Israel enter into an alliance with white supremacist South Africa and authoritarian Portugal. At the time, Portugal was the only country that retained colonies in Africa.[24] Tel Aviv and Pretoria entered into a secret military alliance in 1975, signing an agreement of which neither side would disclose the existence.[25] The alliance may have come about at the suggestion of the United States. In 1975, US secretary of state Henry Kissinger asked Israel to help South Africa invade Angola. Tel Aviv complied, sending military advisers to the front. The magazine *The Economist* speculated that Kissinger's request was part of a general policy of using Israel "as a clandestine conduit to South Africa."[26]

Israel would become South Africa's second most important ally, after the United States, as a top political commentator in Israel's leading liberal newspaper, *Haaretz*, put it. So closely connected were the two governments, that the alliance was dubbed the "Jerusalem-Pretoria Axis,"[27] an alliance of two European settler states surrounded by a sea of dispossessed, oppressed, reviled, degraded and therefore hostile natives. It might have been called the 'Zionism-Apartheid Alliance.'

In 1984, South Africa was the top destination for Israeli arms by a large margin. Most Israeli arms shipments were US manufactured, sold to Israel, and then passed along to South Africa.[28]

On top of furnishing the South African military with US-supplied weapons, the Israeli Defense Forces trained their South African counterparts in the methods Israel used to suppress Palestinian guerrillas. South African military personnel were sent to Israel to be trained in Israeli military academies, while Israeli military advisers were sent to South Africa to serve as on-the-spot instructors. In 1986, the Israeli Labor Party daily newspaper wrote that, "It is a clear and open secret, known to everybody, that in army camps one can find Israeli officers in not insignificant numbers who are busy teaching white soldiers to fight" African guerrillas "with methods imported from Israel."[29] In other words, Israeli advisers were training South Africans in methods to suppress guerrillas who were fighting to throw off the hated yoke of apartheid, drawing on their experience in suppressing Palestinian guerrillas who were fighting to throw off the hated yoke of Zionism. One of Israel's main functions was to show South Africa how a small country could overcome the hostility of the natives by using advanced weapons and sophisticated tactics.[30] *The Nation* magazine observed that "Functionally and visibly, Israel is South Africa's only important ally in the world, providing Pretoria with the material, training, technical advice, and logistical support other Western nations have felt obliged to withhold."[31]

The Israeli effort to build a nuclear arsenal began only one year after the country's founding, in 1949, and depended on the assistance of France, its main imperialist sponsor until Israel demonstrated its value as a US strategic asset in 1967. David Ben-Gurion decided that Israel needed nuclear arms as the only way to avoid the fate of the Crusaders. A secret agreement on nuclear cooperation was reached between Israel and France in October 1957, leading to the construction of the Dimona nuclear reactor in the Negev desert by 1960. Israel's bomb may have been tested by the French in the Sahara sometime in the early 1960s. The US government didn't learn of Israel's nuclear arms cache until 1968,[32] a year after Israel had secretly planned to detonate an atomic device in the Sinai desert if its invasion of Egypt, Jordan, and Syria went awry. Israel has never acknowledged the existence of its nuclear arms, but any doubt was laid to rest when researcher Sasha Polakow-Suransky obtained South African government documents showing that Israel offered to sell the apartheid regime nuclear arms in 1975.

Soon after entering into its clandestine military alliance with Israel, South Africa asked Israel for atom bombs. In a 1975 meeting with Israeli defense minister, Shimon Peres, South Africa's defense minister, P.W. Botha, inquired into the willingness of Tel Aviv to sell Pretoria Jericho missiles with warheads. Peres indicated that Israel was agreeable to selling the missiles and that there were three types of warheads available: conventional, chemical, and nuclear. The South Africans, who would later develop their own nuclear arms, possibly with Israeli assistance, were interested in the nuclear warheads. The sale, however, fell through, partly because the cost was considered too steep.[33] But the South Africans did buy Israel's Jericho missiles, which they could outfit with nuclear warheads they developed independently.[34] Throughout the 1980s, Israel and South Africa jointly developed missiles, which they tested off the South African coast.[35] The two states had similar reasons for developing nuclear weapons, rooted in their displacement of the natives and the consequent hostility this engendered. Both were threatened by the indigenous populations, and the only way to guarantee their survival was to acquire the ultimate deterrent.[36]

Israel retains the vestiges of a socialist reputation owing to its kibbutzim, the world-renowned Jewish socialist communes, based, it is said, on equality and directed toward the project of ending the exploitation of humans by humans. If the communes were a means to end human exploitation of humans it was only the exploitation of Jews by Jews that fell within its compass. The exploitation of Arabs by Israeli Jews and Africans by Israeli Jews was an altogether different matter.

Zionism clashes with the values of equality, progress, and the perfectibility of humans, values at the core of the political Left's project. Israel's vestigial association with genuine socialism is illusory. This can be observed in multiple ways, including in the relationship of the Zionist communes to white supremacist South Africa, with which they did a booming business. A number of communes allied with the historically Marxist kibbutz federation found South Africa's business climate, based on the naked exploitation of the native population, to be particularly congenial.[37] TAKAM, a kibbutz federation of 150 kibbutzim, refused to join a cultural and economic boycott of white supremacist South Africa, both for the injury this might cause their South African partners, and out of solidarity with a fellow settler community threatened by global condemnation. Kibbutz Lohamei Hagetaot, founded by anti-Nazi fighters of Europe's Jewish ghettoes, operated a chemical plant in the Kwa Zulu Bantustan, a South African ghetto for blacks.[38]

Far from being progressive, the settler communes were an important tool in the dispossession of the Arabs and the creation of a Jewish-supremacist state. The "kibbutz was the most efficient way of taking over the land, through semi-military settlements. The main goal of the kibbutz was colonialist settlement and it was the vanguard of settler colonialism," remarks Beit-Hallahmi. "Settling the land with groups of young, vigorous and committed individuals having attachments only to the collective was more promising than the traditional way of family homesteading. It was also more efficient from a military point of view. The kibbutz was the first line of confrontation with the Palestinians." On whose land were these paragons of Marxist commitment established? Mainly "on land taken from the dispossessed Palestinians."[39]

The leading country in the number of emigrants to racist South Africa relative to its population was Israel.[40] Jews, with white complexions, were doubly blessed in being able to settle in either Israel or South Africa, enjoying privileges and rights denied to the natives.

Israel also maintained friendly relations with apartheid Rhodesia, acting as an arms supplier and conduit through which US arms could be covertly shipped to the Rhodesian army, which was attempting to suppress a guerrilla war waged by the black majority, backed by the Soviet Union and China, to win (gasp!) universal suffrage. The reasons for Israel's solidarity with this struggle on the side of the Smith regime against universal suffrage should be plain. Zionism presupposes either the absence of universal suffrage, or demographic engineering to create an artificial majority, as two possible routes to *Herrenvolk* rule. The Afrikaners in South Africa and the British settlers in Rhodesia chose restricted suffrage over demographic engineering to impose their political and economic ascendancies over the natives, while the Zionists chose demographic engineering to do the same. Zionists have also used interminable occupation of the West Bank and military control of the Gaza Strip as tools to create the illusion that Israel has universal suffrage. There is no suffrage for Arabs in these territories, even though the territories are, effectively, part of Israel, since Israel controls them, and appears to have no intention of ceding control of them, ever, without more demographic engineering. It is now routinely remarked that Palestinian refugees cannot be allowed to return to their homes for this would mean either the end of the Jewish state or the end of universal suffrage within it. These are presented as legitimate reasons to prohibit the repatriation of the natives and defy countless UN resolutions that demand repatriation. Implicit in this reasoning is the notion that a Jewish state is a greater good than the fate of Palestinian exiles, and that it is also a greater good than universal suffrage. People who believe that a Jewish state at the center of an Arab majority is a greater good than universal suffrage are also likely to believe that a white state at the center of a black African majority is a greater good than universal suffrage. This accounts for why Israel had little difficulty backing the Rhodesians and Afrikaners.

Zionists control all of Palestine but they only allow suffrage in those parts of Palestine in which they have engineered a Jewish majority, through expulsions, prevention of repatriation, and Jewish immigration. They deny suffrage for the natives in those parts of Palestine in which the natives are in the majority. Thus, they create the illusion that Israel is a democratic state with universal suffrage. The illusion depends on a gerry-mandering exercise involving the drawing of borders around a demo-graphically-engineered Jewish majority and calling it Israel, while declaring the remainder of conquered Palestine a territory under occupa-tion. The reality is that like apartheid Rhodesia and apartheid South Africa, Israel is a colonial settler state in which an ethno-religious minor-ity has assigned to itself rights senior to those of the native majority. The Zionists have simply engaged in legerdemain to create the illusion that their apartheid project is a model of democracy in the Middle East, when, in reality, it is a model of ethno-religious supremacism.

Israel kept the Rhodesians well stocked with Israeli-manufactured Uzi submachine guns, and granted the white supremacists the right to manu-facture the Uzi under licence. The 'Ruzi' (Rhodesian *Uzi*) became standard issue for the Smith regime's military and police forces. The United States evaded official embargoes on exporting arms to the Rhodesian racists by shipping them through Israel. By this means, 205 US-manufactured heli-copters were exported to the Smith regime for use in counter-insurgency operations. The helicopters were sold to the Israeli air force. Israel shipped the helicopters to its South African ally, which passed the aircraft along to its Rhodesian neighbors.[41] And so military gear manufactured by the United States was passed to one colonial settler state (Israel) for distribu-tion to another (South Africa) and eventual delivery to a third (Rhodesia).

CHAPTER TWELVE

Iran

> *"I am telling you with all honesty that the hand of the*
> *Americans is spurring [Israel] on. This hand is behind the*
> *Israeli aggression. It is imperialistic aggression. The real*
> *threat to the world is the imperialistic threat posed by the*
> *U.S., and Israel is one of its imperialistic instruments."*
>
> Hugo Chavez, 2006[1]

Iran's Islamic Revolution of 1979 toppled a major supporter of US domination of the Middle East, Mohammad Reza, Shah of the Pahlavi
dynasty. The Shah, as discussed earlier, was installed by Washington following the 1953 CIA-engineered *coup d'état* that overthrew Iran's nationalist
prime minister Mohammad Mossaddegh. Mossaddegh's 1951 nationalization of the Anglo-Persian Oil Company galvanized London and Washington
to work together to replace the Iranian prime minister with a biddable leader
who would return Iran's oil industry to the hands of private Western investors. The US-backed monarch became a stalwart supporter of US investor
interests, not only in Iran, but in the wider Middle East. The Shah's ouster
was a serious set-back for Washington. It removed Iran as a sphere of
exploitation for US investors, and created a new pole of resistance to the US
imperialist project, which attracted Syria, Libya and elements of the disenfranchised Shia population of Lebanon.

The revolution was carried out by communists, secular nationalists, and
Islamists led by Ayatollah Ruhollah Khomeini, with the latter playing a

decisive lead role. While political Islam—specifically of a Shia stamp—was used to mobilize Iranians to overthrow the monarchy, the revolution was driven by the same grievances that compelled secular Arab nationalists to overthrow Egypt's King Farouk in 1952 and Iraq's King Faisal in 1958. All three revolutions were ebullitions of native anger against foreign forces that ruled through imposed monarchs.

The kings organized their economies to suit their foreign backers at the expense of their own people; they ruled, not on behalf of local populations, but against them. While there were differences in the outward forms of the revolutions—two of them secular Arab nationalist, the other Islamist and Persian—the underlying causes were the same: colonial rule lurking behind the veil of a nominally independent local ruler, his independence a constitutional fiction. The revolutions were aimed as much against piratical foreign powers as they were against the local monarchs. Thus, not only were the monarchs overthrown and the institution of monarchy dissolved, but the countries' economic assets were repatriated, or patriated for the first time, from foreign investors, who had grown rich at the expense of the natives.

In Iran, the country's oil wealth would now be returned to Iranians, and the government would organize the economy for the benefit of the country's citizens, not US investors. Revolution would involve measures of economic *dirigisme*, including state ownership of the commanding heights of the economy. Washington would label and denounce these measures as 'socialist.' Iran would, in many respects, follow Iraq's Arab socialist model, but without the socially progressive elements of Saddam's administration, such as the promotion of women's rights and abolition of sectarian discrimination. All the same, the condition of women in Iran would be far more advanced than in Saudi Arabia, whose official Islamism carried with it harsh misogynistic oppression, as well as sectarian intolerance. Accordingly, Washington found itself allied with the most reactionary and oppressive forces in the region, and at odds with the most progressive ones.

Iran's revolutionary constitution prescribed socialization of the economy at its commanding heights, supported a cooperative sector, and carved out limited space for a private sector. The private sector was to buttress the public and cooperative sectors, which were to be the primary modes of economic organization. The state sector included all large-scale industries, foreign trade, natural resources, banking, insurance, power generation, dams, and large-scale irrigation networks, radio and television, post, telegraph and telephone services, aviation, shipping, roads, railroads and the like—all the meaty, lucrative, sectors US investors were eager to dominate and make king's ransoms from. The cooperative sector included enterprises concerned with small-scale production and distribution. The private sector comprised agriculture and small-scale industry, trade, and services. Their role was to fill in the interstices of the economy that the state and cooperative sectors didn't fill.

Despite stories of Iran undergoing a neo-liberal revolution in the twenty-first century, the public and cooperative sectors remained strong enough to lead *The New York Times* in 2017 to describe the country's economy as "quasi-socialist" and its official ideology as based on "anti-Western socialism."[2] Tehran's commitment to strong state and cooperative sectors was rooted in the goal of achieving true political independence—which is to say, to make Iran invulnerable to economic pressure from outside. This meant decoupling the economy from the West as far as possible, and refashioning it to specifically serve Iranian goals. The country's supreme leader defined the program as one of achieving political independence through economic self-sufficiency.[3]

The self-sufficiency program led to the development of home-grown industries that are rare in the Third World. Unusually for the Middle East, Iran developed its own automobile industry, producing 1.6 million vehicles per year. The market was almost wholly divided between two domestic firms,[4] and Western automobiles were a rarity. Tehran erected a high tariff wall to incubate national industry and protect it from foreign competitors.[5]

The revolution's goals, however, were not focused solely on fostering Iranian independence. Iran was only a small part of a larger Muslim world. Khomeini envisaged a Muslim sphere that was independent of the secular West. Like the Ba'athists who sought the parallel goal of Arab independence, and defined unity as the path to it, so too did Khomeini emphasize the significance of unity in achieving his goal. His vision was to lead the Muslim world in uniting against US domination. In the view of Khomeini's successor, Ayatollah Sayyid Ali Hosseini Khamenei, "a billion and a half Muslims" united, controlling "Islamic countries with all" their vast "resources" would be strong enough to prevent Washington imposing its will on the Middle East. With US hegemony checked, the

Muslim world could achieve "its own path and goals,"[6] free from US insistence on world leadership. Replace "a billion and half Muslims" with "400 million Arabs" and "Islamic countries" with "Arab countries" and you have the central idea of Nasserism.

Central to the project of Muslim unification was the liberation of Palestine. "Even if Muslim and freedom-seeking nations have different viewpoints and opinions," observed Khamenei, "they can gather together with one goal which is Palestine and the necessity to liberate it."[7] In other words, since all Muslims could agree on the desirability of liberating Palestine's Muslims, it was on this question that Islamic unity would turn. Part of Tehran's effort to rally all Muslim sects around the emancipation of Palestine was its sponsorship of an annual Al Quds (Jerusalem) day, to commemorate the Palestinian struggle.

As regards Iran's anti-imperialist project, it was pithily expressed by Mahmoud Ahmadinejad, Iran's president from 2005 to 2013. "We tell [the United States] that instead of interfering in the region's affairs, to pack their things and leave."[8] Iran's "ideology of independence from world powers"—evocative of Nasser's attempt to avoid entanglements with either the United States or Soviet Union—was widely embraced by Iranians.[9] The Persian state's resolve to pursue a course independent of US meddling was alluded to by US Senator John McCain, a major figure in the US foreign policy establishment, shortly before his death. "The Middle East is vitally important to ... the American people," intoned McCain. "And right now, a network of anti-American groups—at times working together, at times on their own—is trying to drive American influence out of the Middle East. They are doing so," he warned, in a way "that makes it harder and more dangerous for the United States to maintain its presence... [W]e could wake up in the near future and find that American influence has been pushed out of one of the most important parts of the world."[10]

Ejecting the United States and its quislings from the Muslim world was precisely what Tehran aspired to do, as much as the French Resistance sought to drive Nazi German influence out of France during World War II. In other words, the Iranian Islamic Revolution sought to mobilize local forces of independence and national assertiveness to free the region from its unacceptable domination by a foreign power. It did so under the banner of the Crescent, where Nasser and Saddam pursued the same goal under the banner of the Arab nation. The 2017 US National Security

Strategy declared that the "United States seeks a Middle East that is …
not dominated by any power hostile to the United States." The power that
Washington bristled against was not Tehran *per se*, but the forces of local
independence and national assertiveness that Tehran mobilized. Clearly,
forces of local independence and national assertiveness were hostile to US
assertion of world leadership. And for good reason. US leadership is syn-
onymous with denial of sovereignty.

Although Saddam and Khomeini pursued the same anti-imperialist goal
of liberating the region from foreign domination, they had different ideas
about how to achieve their common goal, and different visions of the kind
of independent society they wanted to create. Saddam wasn't anti-Islam.
He was a Muslim who tried to make Marxism acceptable to a Muslim
population. He emphasized his piety and insisted that Islam came before
Marx. In short, he rejected politicized atheism. At the same time, he
rejected politicized Islam. If the official denial of theism could not become
an organizing principle of politics, nor could Islam be the foundation on
which to establish a modern society. Saddam's rejection of politicized
Islam reflected multiple concerns. First, liberation presupposed unity. The
foreign rulers of Mesopotamia—the Persians, the Turks, and the British—
had used the sectarian divisions within Islam to keep Iraqis disunited.
The British in particular had labored diligently to aggravate sectarian
cleavages to keep Iraq weak and divided. Arab nationalists, like Saddam,
sought to bridge the sectarian differences between Arabs that were rooted
in Islam by appealing to common ethnicity. Rather than speaking of Iraqis
as Shia Muslims and Sunni Muslims, Saddam drew attention to their
identity as Arabs. A population that was fractured over the question of
who was the legitimate successor to the prophet Mohamed—the question
on which the split between Sunnis and Shias turns—would never achieve
the unity necessary to free itself. Second, Saddam—a man of very humble
origins—identified with the underclass and the exploited. He was born
into abased conditions, despised as the lowliest of the low of an Arab community that itself was among the world's most despised and abased. He
identified with the underdog and had a vision of society that reflected his
lowly origins. Traditional social and sexual hierarchies would be toppled

by reformist programs. Women would be liberated from their oppression by men. The underclass would be lifted up. Yet as appealing as Saddam's views and program were to women, the poor, the persecuted, and the marginalized, they were denounced by conservative Muslims as hostile to Islam.

Persia and Turkey fought over Iraq in the seventeenth and eighteenth centuries. Persia was Shia Muslim and the Turks Sunni Muslim. Both powers looked to their Iraqi co-religionists as allies and worked to use their influence to confer advantages and privileges on their sectarian cohorts. The Turks prevailed over the Persians, and ruled Iraq over a longer period. The result was that Iraq's elite was drawn from the Sunni community (most of which, however, remained poor), and the allies of the Turk's Persian rival, the Shia, were oppressed (along with poor Sunnis). The wealthiest and most highly educated Iraqis, then, were Sunnis, members of a minority community.[11]

The association of wealth, education, and political power with the Sunni community was strengthened further by the British, who imported the Hashemite prince, Faisal, as monarch. Faisal, who had never visited Iraq until the British installed him as ruler, was a Sunni.[12] Faisal's sectarian affiliation may have been of little consequence had the Persians and Turks not made sect a significant matter in Iraqi politics. But they did, and the reality that the Sunni Muslim Faisal was now backed by the untitled Sunni nobility, left the Shia majority feeling marginalized.[13]

The British, keen to cement their control over the Iraqi population, did all they could to further widen the sectarian divide. London maintained separate lines of communication with Iraq's three major communities: the Kurds, the Sunnis, and the Shia. Each community was played off against the other. To add to the divisiveness, the British reserved for the Jewish community the post of minister of finance (apparently reflecting the anti-Semitic trope that Jews are good with money.) There were, then, five significant communities in Iraq under British rule: the untitled Sunni nobility and the Sunni king, on which the British depended, along with the Jewish community, which was given a role in the country's finances. These were accompanied by three marginalized communities: the Kurds— Sunnis, but non-Arabs—who aspired to a nation-state of their own; the Shia community, which looked to their co-religionists in Iran for support; and poor Sunnis, who hated the British.

Arab Ba'ath Socialism was a response to the politicization of sectarian and other divisions within the Arab world that foreign powers used to keep Arabs internally divided and at war with each other. The monarchical system designed for Iraq at the 1921 Cairo Peace Conference—and London's pitting one community against the other—not only ensured that the country would be badly governed, but intended that it be badly governed.[14] The British had spent four decades working to inflame sectarian animosities, building on sectarian divisions that had already been inflamed by the Persian-Turkish rivalry over Iraq. This was the Iraq Saddam inherited. Sectarian tensions couldn't be abolished by fiat; they would have to be overcome gradually through painstaking reforms to undo the damage the British, Turks and Persians had inflicted. And efforts to remedy the illness would be slowed by a counter-narrative propagated by the West, that Saddam, a Sunni, was carrying on a tradition of Sunni political privilege in Iraq, with the aim of keeping the Shia community on the margins. With Shias making up the largest community in Iraq, the best strategy for Washington to undermine Saddam's Arab socialism was to inflame Shia animosity.

Ruhollah Khomeini spent fourteen years in exile, mainly in Iraq, where he witnessed Saddam's transformation of Iraq into a secular Arab socialist state allied with the Soviet Union. Khomeini was no fan of Saddam's government. The Shia spiritual leader wanted to break the chains of foreign domination by unifying the Muslim world and mobilizing it under the banner of Islam, not Arabism. He wasn't enamored of Saddam's 'anti-Islamic' social reforms either. Khomeini's presence in Iraq, and his influence in Iraq's Shia community, was making life difficult for Saddam and his goal of confining Islam to personal matters. Finding intolerable Khomeini's efforts to agitate the Shia community, Saddam expelled the Islamist leader in 1978.[15] This bode ill for Iraq-Iran relations when Khomeini came to power shortly thereafter.

Khomeini returned to Iran on February 12, 1979 at the head of a successful revolution. Saddam sent his congratulations, expressing his wish for regional peace. The new Iranian leader rebuffed the Arab knight. "Peace is with those who follow the righteous path," retorted Khomeini to the secular Saddam. Religion, not peace, was on Khomeini's mind.[16]

Syria, Libya and the PLO were in favor of the Iranian revolution. Having exited the US orbit, Iran was now firmly in the anti-Israeli camp, and they saw Iran as a potential ally in the struggle against the Zionist state. Baghdad saw matters differently. Khomeini was anti-Ba'athist, promoted sect over Arab identity, urged Shias to topple the Iraqi government, and wasn't interested in peace. Shortly after assuming power in Tehran, Khomeini announced that Iraq's Shia holy city of Najaf should fall under Iranian control.[17] Saddam, for his part, insisted that Arabism was senior to religion.[18] By contrast, Khomeini believed that Islam was "a force entitled to push aside everything" in its path, especially Iraq's 'heretical' Arabist government.[19] Iran's spiritual leader thought he was going to liberate Iraq from an oppressive secularism.[20]

Whereas Nasser's Radio Cairo had called on Arabs to arise and overthrow the imposed rulers of the Arab world, including Faisal in Iraq, now Khomeini exhorted Iraqis to overthrow the "non-Muslim" Arabists in Baghdad. He was joined by Iraqi Shia leader Sadr, who warned that "other tyrants [beside the Shah] have yet to see their day of reckoning," a clear reference to Saddam. Khomeini's calls for religious rebellion invariably sparked riots, not only in Iraq, but in other countries—Saudi Arabia, Bahrain and Kuwait—with large Shia populations.[21]

In April 1980, Khomeini's followers, who had murdered several Iraqi government officials in 1979, tried but failed to assassinate Tariq Aziz, Iraq's Christian deputy prime minister. The botched assassination attempt produced scores of dead and wounded. Four days later, the same group attacked the funeral of the victims, killing more people. Baghdad immediately cracked down on Khomeini's followers, executing hundreds of them. Along the Iraq-Iran border, skirmishes broke out between the two countries' militaries.[22]

Exasperated by Khomeini's attempts to overthrow his government, Saddam ordered the Iraqi army to invade Iran in late September of 1980. Washington was ecstatic. The *Wall Street Journal* expressed its support for Iraq, which it said believed in "Western values and technology."[23] The rest of the US media also sided with Saddam.[24]

Khomeini saw his agitation against the Baghdad government as the spark that would lead to Iraq's 'liberation' from 'secular tyranny' and believed that the war would precipitate a Shia revolt against the secular Arabist government. But the Shia uprising never materialized. Washington, which abhorred Khomeini for deposing their puppet, the Shah, and the Saudis, who abhorred him just as intensely for stirring up Arabia's Shia population, showered Iraq with arms and military intelligence.[25] The Pentagon trained Iraqi pilots secretly in the United States.[26] US warships in the Persian Gulf jammed Iranian radar.[27] US aircraft flew over Iran and sent targeting information back to Iraqi forces. The US Navy harassed Iranian warships.[28]

The United States calibrated its support for Iraq based on how well the war was going for Saddam's forces.[29] Support was to be given to Baghdad in sufficient quantities to keep the war going as long as possible, but not enough to allow Baghdad to achieve victory.[30] If Iraqi forces were making advances, support would be scaled back; if they suffered setbacks, support would be stepped up. The idea was to draw out the war so that each side bled the other white. Kissinger lamented that both sides could not lose.[31]

While Washington was helping the Iraqis, it was also helping the Iranians. It was secretly selling arms to Iran and using the money to illegally finance the operations of its Contra guerrillas in Nicaragua.[32] Meanwhile, Israel, with the full knowledge of the United States, was selling Iran US-manufactured F-4 warplanes and spare parts.[33] "The evidence is clear," observed Aburish. "The United States was indirectly supplying both sides with arms," operating through their accustomed Middle Eastern henchmen, the Saudis and Israelis.[34] Many countries did what they could to keep the war going. The one exception was the Soviet Union, which refused to supply either side.[35]

On July 18, 1988, after eight long years of war, Khomeini accepted a UN organized peace. The war had set the Iraqi clock back. The country was mired in debt. Baghdad owed $35 billion to the West, $11 billion to the USSR, and over $40 billion to Saudi Arabia and Kuwait.[36] The prospects for recovery were dim. Revenue from oil sales was insufficient to meet Iraq's current needs, let alone to service its debt.[37] No one was willing to extend Baghdad credit, except on exorbitant terms. The United States and Saudi Arabia spurned Baghdad's entreaties for help. The USSR, dealing with its own economic difficulties, was in no position to offer a bail out. Meanwhile, Iraq's million-strong army was being demobilized to a civilian economy that had been reduced to ruins.[38]

From Saddam's point of view, the other Arab states were indebted to Iraq for the protection they received from the dangers of Khomeinism. But rather than forgiving Iraq's debt, the other Arab states exacerbated Iraq's economic travails. Kuwait and the United Arab Emirates increased their oil production, driving down the price of oil, at a time Baghdad desperately needed oil prices to remain high. The Kuwaitis and Emiratis were crippling Saddam's ability to recover from the war.[39] It was at this point that the Arab knight realized that he had stepped into a trap of Washington's devising.[40] He had become a target for regime change.

On July 17, 1989 Saddam threw down the gauntlet. Kuwait, he said, was engaged in a conspiracy against Iraq, to make its people "live in famine."[41] In February 1990, Saddam denounced the US presence in the Persian Gulf, and proposed that the Gulf and its oil resources be brought under Arab control and under the leadership of Iraq. Later that month, he launched another broadside against US interference in the Arab world, accompanied by a demand that the Arab states cancel Iraq's war debt.[42]

At an Arab League meeting at the end of May 1990 Saddam accused Kuwait, which was producing 2.1 million barrels of oil a day, rather than its OPEC-allotted 1.5 million, of waging economic warfare against Iraq. He appealed to Kuwait to refrain. The Kuwaiti emir demurred, and insisted that Iraq pay its war debt immediately.[43] British prime minister Margaret Thatcher cabled her support to the Emir.[44]

On July 25, 1990 Saddam had a meeting with the US ambassador to Iraq, April Glaspie. He told her that Kuwait was overproducing oil and that the Emirate's policy, which the US supported, amounted to a campaign of economic warfare against Iraq. He then threatened to retaliate against Kuwait. Glaspie repeated the US State Department line: There were no treaty obligations for Washington to protect Arab countries. The United States has "no opinion on Arab conflicts."[45] Saddam took Glaspie's failure to voice an objection to his threatened retaliation against Kuwait as a signal that he could move against his tormentor with impunity. On August 2, Iraqi forces invaded Kuwait, taking control of the country in four hours.[46] Saddam justified the invasion as an Arabist measure to distribute Kuwait's oil revenue among all Arabs.[47] Washington denounced the invasion, and the UN Security Council ordered Iraqi forces to withdraw. On August 12, 1990, Saddam said he would comply with the UN directive if Israel complied with long-standing UN resolutions ordering the Zionist state to withdraw from the territories it had occupied since 1967.[48] Needless to say, Washington exerted no pressure on Israel, its strategic asset, to comply with UN resolutions. Compliance with UN directives was a discipline reserved for Third World leaders who challenged US supremacy.

Washington organized a war, the First US-Iraq War, to drive Arab nationalist forces out of Kuwait. The war marked the beginning of the Pentagon's heavy footprint in the Persian Gulf. Prior to Saddam overtly threatening to bring Persian Gulf oil under Arab nationalist control, the closest Washington could get to a military presence in Arabia was to store gear, weaponry and ammunition in Oman. Worried that a US military presence in their countries would be viewed by the Arab street as an occupation, the imposed rulers of the Persian Gulf resisted the deployment of US forces to their countries. But alarmed by Iraq's ouster of the Kuwaiti emir, the region's monarchies now saw a heavy US military presence as a pressing necessity for their political survival.[49]

While the movement of US troops, warships, and aircraft into the Persian Gulf solved Washington's problem of how to prevent local forces of independence from taking control of Arabia's and Mesopotamia's oil wells, it created a new problem: al Qaeda. Al Qaeda, the brainchild of a scion of a wealthy Saudi family, Osama bin Laden, was used as an instrument of US foreign policy in Afghanistan, receiving support from the CIA. But despite its association with US intelligence in Afghanistan, the Islamist organization evolved into a form of resistance to US occupation of the Persian Gulf. The impetus for the jihadist war against the Soviet presence in Afghanistan was to drive the infidel out of a part of the Muslim world, and the jihadists were prepared to accept the generous aid offered by the US government to achieve their goal. The organization's commitment to freeing Muslim countries from foreign occupation, however, also led it to wage a jihad against its former ally. Like the USSR, the United States was a foreign power obtruding itself on the Muslim world; its meddling in the Islamic sphere's affairs would be met by a determined al Qaeda resistance.

In a 1996 declaration, bin Laden said that pushing "the enemy ... out of [Saudi Arabia] is a prime duty .... It is a duty on every tribe in the Arab Peninsula to fight ... to cleanse the land from these occupiers."[50] In June of that year, the al Qaeda leader told Robert Fisk that Washington had turned Saudi Arabia into an American colony, had Westernized its society, drained its oil wealth, and was waging a war on Muslims. For these reasons, he explained, the United States was "the main enemy" and Muslims would resist Western occupation of their countries, as Europeans had resisted occupation of their countries by foreign fascist forces during the Second World War. Bin Laden added that, "the Americans must leave Saudi Arabia, must leave the Gulf." Washington's "attempt to take over the region" and "its support for Israel" were the causes of attacks on Western military forces in the region. The United States had turned Saudi Arabia into "an American colony."[51]

In 1998 Bin Laden called for attacks on the United States. He explained: "The call to wage war against America was made because America [is] sending tens of thousands of its troops to [the Arabian peninsula], over and above its meddling in [Saudi] affairs and [Saudi] politics, and its support of the oppressive, corrupt and tyrannical regime that is in control. These are the reasons behind the singling out of America as a target."[52]

Bin Laden's "principal organizational innovation" was "to reorient various local resistance movements away from local grievances in the short term so as to bring an accumulation of violence against the common enemy, the United States," concluded the political scientist Robert A. Pape.[53]

After the Gulf War, US General Wesley Clark, who would lead NATO's air war on Yugoslavia in 1999, met with Paul Wolfowitz, at the time the under-secretary of defense for policy. The war had coincided with the dissolution of the USSR. Without the Soviets to check its ambitions of world domination, Washington was now free to eliminate local forces of independence and national assertiveness in the Middle East. Wolfowitz informed Clark that:

> With the end of the Cold War, we can now use our military with impunity. The Soviets won't come in to block us. And we've got five, maybe 10, years to clean up these old Soviet surrogate regimes like Iraq and Syria before the next superpower emerges to challenge us. [...] We could have a little more time, but no one really knows.[54]

Ultimately, it was the Iraq-Iran War that destroyed Saddam's Arab socialism. It so weakened and indebted the country that Saddam's only hope for recovery was to invade Kuwait to oust the Kuwaiti monarch whose oil production policy represented a campaign to condemn Iraq to perpetual poverty. But the invasion was a second *faux pas,* fatal this time; it handed Washington a pretext to go to war with the Arab socialist state to drive it out of Kuwait. As Iraqi forces withdrew from Kuwait on the single highway to Baghdad, the US military launched strikes against the retreating Iraqi forces, ensuring that Iraq would be weakened even further militarily.

The Soviets' exit from the world stage allowed Washington to go even further. The Pentagon unilaterally established no-fly zones over Iraqi airspace, from which airstrikes against Iraqi targets were undertaken with impunity. Saddam was ordered to dismantle all weapons of mass destruction, and a crippling regime of international sanctions was imposed to ensure that he complied. The sanctions lasted for more than a decade and killed millions. By 2003, Iraq was so drained by war with Iran and sanctions of mass destruction, that the United States was able to easily conquer the country and topple Saddam. As Wolfowitz had predicted, the 'old Soviet-surrogate regime' was 'cleaned up.' Washington oversaw the writing of a new constitution to strengthen the ethno-sectarian divisions Saddam had labored so assiduously to efface. Iraq's economy was returned to private hands and foreign investors, and Arabists were purged from the state and banned from ever again participating in Iraqi politics.

Having toppled the Arab Prussian *manqué,* Washington now turned its attention to the second pole of resistance to its hegemonic grip on the region, Iran. It started with Iran's ally, Syria, another 'old Soviet-surrogate regime,' which Washington planned to invade as a follow up to its invasion of Iraq. But the Americans discovered that Iraqis didn't see US invaders as liberators. Having planned for an easy occupation with little resistance, Washington was stunned to discover that Iraqis were fighting back. Plans needed to be changed. Resources that would have been channeled to an invasion of Syria, were now redirected to the pacification of Iraq. The task of toppling Arab socialism in Damascus would be hired out to Islamists, who would be recruited to destabilize the Den of Arabism.

In the meantime, Israel launched a failed 2006 war to destroy Hezbollah, the Sixth Settler-Native War. Washington disliked Hezbollah because the

Tehran-backed organization was a force of local independence. It opposed US domination of the Middle East and worked against the National Pact that allowed the Maronites, allies of the West, to dominate Lebanon. Washington also resented Hezbollah for having driven US and French occupation forces out of Beirut in the 1980s. Israel's enmity to Hezbollah was rooted in the organization's willingness to block the expansion of Jewish settler colonialism into Lebanon.

With generous funding from Iran, Hezbollah's ability to resist Israeli expansionism and to challenge the ethno-sectarian disparities of power in Lebanon, were ever growing. By 2018, the resistance organization had almost 50,000 full-time fighters in Lebanon, along with 8,000 deployed to Syria and Yemen. It had an arsenal of 150,000 rockets, up from less than 5,000 only 12 years earlier.[55]

At the same time, Israel worked to deter Tehran from developing nuclear weapons by assassinating Iranian scientists, cooperating with the United States in cyber-warfare attacks on Iran, and threatening to launch air-strikes against Iranian nuclear sites.

Lacking the technological prowess of the West, the only reliable self-defense within the grasp of Third World countries keen on remaining free from Washington's control are nuclear weapons. If local forces of independence are to resist re-absorption into the system of Western domination, they must have credible means of self-defense. Iran's civilian nuclear energy program contained within it the seeds of a credible self-defense; it could be readily converted to a militarized nuclear program if necessary. From Washington's perspective, it was vital to deny Tehran not only nuclear weapons, but even the capability of developing them.

In 2007, Washington orchestrated the imposition of UN sanctions on Iran in order to "rein in what U.S. officials saw as 'Tehran's ambitions to become the dominant military power in the Persian Gulf and across the broad Middle East,'" wrote Mohsen M. Milani in *Foreign Affairs*.[56] In 2018, Iran's military budget was an inconsequential $11 billion per annum,[57] a little over half of Israel's $20 billion.[58] There was little chance that Iran would surpass Israel as the dominant military power in the region. But that wasn't what really vexed US officials. Washington's fear was that nuclear weapons—if Iran developed them—would make the leader of the Axis of Resistance virtually immune to re-colonization.

In order to mobilize Western public opinion against measures to undermine Iran, the US target would have to be presented as a unique danger. Western politicians and shapers of public opinion relied heavily on comparisons with Hitler to demonize leaders of Middle Eastern independence movements. Nasser and Saddam had both been analogized to the Nazi leader. The Iranians would get the same treatment. Iran would be accused of seeking nuclear weapons to finish the job Hitler had left undone—exterminating the Jews. Israel, as the self-appointed representative of the world's Jews, thus played another role in the US project of tyrannizing the Middle East. Leaders who opposed US neo-colonialism almost invariably opposed Zionist settler colonialism. Owing to this correlation, anti-imperialists of the Middle East could be presented as anti-Semites through the false conflation of anti-Zionism with anti-Semitism. Zionists had long played the anti-Semite card to discredit anyone who challenged Jewish settler colonialism. This was a way of derailing discussion before it landed on the essential moral indefensibility of the Zionist project: its displacement of the Arab natives and its subordination of indigenous people to the category of aliens in their own land. Better, from the perspective of Zionists, to present all challenges to Israel's settler colonialism as modern Hitlers.

This is what Nazila Fathi did when she filed a story with *The New York Times* in October, 2005, claiming that Iran's then president Mahmoud Ahmadinejad had called for Israel to be wiped off the map.[59] Ahmadinejad had said nothing of the sort. Instead, he had quoted Khamenei, who had defined Iran's goal, not as destroying Israel in war, but dissolving Israel as a Zionist state through a popular referendum[60]—a proposal that was tantamount to 'destroying' South Africa's apartheid regime through the implementation of universal suffrage. While implacably opposed to the colonial nature of Zionism, Khamenei was not proposing Israel's physical destruction. He was instead proposing the replacement of a *Herrenvolk* democracy with self-determination for Palestinians. In October 2011, Khamenei said:

The Islamic Republic's proposal to help resolve the Palestinian issue and heal this old wound is a clear and logical initiative based on political concepts accepted by world public opinion, which has already been presented in detail.

We do not suggest launching a classic war by the armies of Muslim countries, or throwing immigrant Jews into the sea, or mediation by the UN and other international organizations. We propose holding a referendum with [the participation of] the Palestinian nation. The Palestinian nation, like any other nation, has the right to determine [its] own destiny and elect the governing system of the country.[61]

To be sure, a referendum would inevitably spell the end of Israel as a Jewish *Herrenvolk* state, in the same way a referendum would have spelled the end of South Africa as a white supremacist state. Israel's prime minister Benjamin Netanyahu balked at this proposal, accusing the Iranians of seeking to destroy Israel. Indeed, they were seeking to destroy Israel *qua* Zionist state, though Netanyahu, a peerless demagogue, was knowingly making the point in a way that suggested quite inaccurately that Tehran was plotting Israel's physical destruction and planning the extermination of the Jews.

Predictably, Netanyahu ignored what Ahmadinejad said and Khamenei meant, and played up the erroneous *New York Times* story. Netanyahu's zeal for embellishing Iranian threats to Israel knew no bounds—or shame. "Iran," he portended, is "arming itself with nuclear weapons to realize that goal [the obliteration of Israel], and until now the world has not stopped it. The threat to our existence, is not theoretical. It cannot be swept under the carpet; it cannot be reduced. It faces us and all humanity, and it must be thwarted."[62] The Israeli leader would frequently equate Iran with Nazi Germany and raise the specter of a second anti-Jewish holocaust.[63] Iran's objectives, Netanyahu declared repeatedly, "are clear: It wants to destroy Israel and is developing nuclear weapons to realize that goal."[64] Finding the Nazi genocide infinitely useful in mobilizing support for Israel, Netanyahu also said: "It's 1938 and Iran is Germany, and it's racing to arm itself with atomic bombs."[65] And this: "Seventy years after the Holocaust, many in the world are silent in the face of Iran's pledges to wipe Israel off the face of the earth. This is a day in which the leaders of the world must commit not to allow another genocide."[66]

Behind the scenes, Tamir Pardo, the chief of the Israeli intelligence agency, Mossad, was dismissing Netanyahu's fear-mongering as arrant nonsense. Pardo told a gathering of a hundred Israeli ambassadors that Israel was using various means to disrupt Iran's nuclear program, but even if Iran did develop nuclear weapons, Israel's existence would not be threatened. "What is the significance of the term existential threat?" Pardo asked. "Does Iran pose a threat to Israel? Absolutely. But if one said a nuclear bomb in Iranian hands was an existential threat, that would mean that we would have to close up shop and go home. That's not the situation. The term existential threat is used too freely."[67]

In a closed 2007 discussion, Israeli Foreign Minister Tzipi Livni had also dismissed an Iranian atom bomb as an existential threat. Israeli leaders, she admitted, were arousing the country's citizens by appealing to their most basic fears in order to mobilize their support for military action against Iran.[68]

But Israeli leaders were also arousing the fears of the West's *menu peuple*—and for the very same purpose: to mobilize support for Western action against Iran. And in doing so, they were once again doing, as they had done so many times before, a great service for Washington; they were using an emotionally powerful appeal to the symbols of Hitler and the anti-Jewish holocaust, to equip their imperial sponsor with a *casus belli* to be used against Iran to bring the lead country in the Axis of Resistance under US control.

Few ideas are as effective in galvanizing support for international intervention as the necessity of preventing another Nazi-style holocaust. And no country could invoke an impending holocaust as a goad for action as credibly as could Israel, the self-appointed representative of the victims of the Nazi-instigated genocide. The anti-Jewish genocide had been raised to the pinnacle of all genocides, from 'a holocaust' to 'The Holocaust.' Israeli leaders had successfully convinced the world that they were the spokespeople of all Jews. An Israeli leader who could invoke the necessity of preventing a second holocaust against the Jews as a pretext for coercive measures against any state that resisted US hegemony, was indeed a valuable strategic asset.

But this wasn't the only role Israel played in the campaign to reclaim Iran as part of the US Empire. Another role was to dangle a sword of Damocles over Tehran by incessantly threatening military intervention. Repeated warnings of impending attack might cow Iran into backing off its nuclear program, which, even if it were authentically civilian, would still furnish the Iranians with the means to develop an atom bomb—a latent capability it could nurture as a deterrent if pushed too far. Accordingly, Israel defined its red line as "Iran's development of a nuclear weapons 'capability,' rather than the actual assembly of an atomic weapon," according to *The Wall Street Journal*.[69]

This is a key point. A country which intends to live peaceably with its neighbors will have no objection to its neighbors developing the capability to defend themselves. On the other hand, a country that intends to dominate its neighbors will object strenuously to their developing effective measures of self-defense. In order to prevent the development of their neighbors' deterrent military capabilities, they will launch preventive military interventions under the pretext of subduing a threat.

The Chinese military strategist Sun Tze had remarked: the greatest general is the one who wins without actually fighting. The Israelis had already done the US Empire a great service in 1981 by destroying Iraq's nuclear reactor at Osirak. In 2007, they added to their service by destroying Syria's nuclear reactor in the Deir ez-zor desert. Now, Tel Aviv would attempt to do another great service—intimidate the Iranians into aborting their nuclear program through the threat of attack. In June 2008, Israeli prime minister Ehud Olmert declared: "Israel will not tolerate the possibility of a nuclear Iran."[70] Led by Shaul Mofaz, an Iranian-born member of Olmert's security cabinet, and former Israeli military chief and defence minister, Israel collaborated on a strategy with Washington. Mofaz said: "If Iran continues with its programme for developing nuclear weapons, we will attack it."[71] Israel's ambassador to the United States at the time, Sallai Meridor, added his own warning. Iran, he said, "should understand that under no circumstances will the world allow it to obtain a nuclear capability."[72]

In 2008, the Israeli historian Benny Morris warned Iranians that Israel would reduce their country to nuclear ash if Tehran continued along the road to nuclear development. "Iran's leaders would do well to ... suspend their nuclear program," he wrote in *The New York Times*, otherwise Iran will be "turned into a nuclear wasteland."[73] Hillary Clinton, at the time a candidate in the Democratic primaries, let Tehran know that Israel was an extension of the United States. If Israel attacked Iran, she said, and Iran retaliated, the United States would treat the retaliation as equivalent to an attack on the United States. The United States would "totally obliterate" Iran.[74] In 2012, then Israeli defense minister Ehud Barak sought to allay fears that an Israeli attack on Iranian nuclear facilities would provoke a devastating Iranian counter-strike. The retaliation, he said, "would be bearable. There will not be 100,000 dead or 10,000 dead or 1,000 dead. The state of Israel will not be destroyed."[75]

Israel's neighbors have never posed much of a threat to the self-proclaimed Jewish state, and have never inflicted much damage upon it, through all the settler-native wars, to Saddam's threats in 1991 to "burn half of Israel." Saddam's minatory words were vacuous. Iraq fired forty Scud missiles at Israel. They did little damage. In 2006, Hezbollah fired 4,000 rockets into Israel. The damage was barely noticeable.[76] Israel grossly exaggerated the threats it faced to justify the police actions it took on behalf of its US patron. And some of its neighbors grossly exaggerated the threat they presented to Israel in order to earn the respect and admiration of the Arab and Muslim worlds.

In 2009, the Pentagon began to transfer to Israel 'bunker-buster' bombs, known as Massive Ordnance Penetrators.[77] The 30,000-pound bombs were specifically designed to take out "the hardened fortifications built by Iran and North Korea to cloak their nuclear programs."[78] Since North Korea is not within range of Israel warplanes, it was clear that the Pentagon was equipping its Israeli annex with the means to wipe Iran's nuclear facilities off the map. The Pentagon redesigned the bunker buster bomb, reported *The Wall Street Journal*, with "advanced features intended to enable it to destroy Iran's most heavily fortified and defended nuclear site."[79]

Sheldon Adelson, the billionaire hotel and casino magnate, is a US Jew who zealously supports Israel. Adelson prefers to live outside Israel, despite the Zionist claim that anti-Semitism is ubiquitous and unceasing and Jews can therefore be safe only in a Jewish state. A friend and supporter of US president Donald Trump, he was influential in persuading the Trump administration to move the US embassy to Jerusalem and recognize Al Quds (Jerusalem) as the capital of the self-declared Jewish state. Adelson is not shy about publicly voicing his ideas on how to handle the 'Iran problem.' "What I would say is: 'Listen. You see that desert out there? I want to show you something,'" Mr. Adelson said at Yeshiva University in Manhattan in October 2013. He then argued for detonating an American nuclear weapon where it would not "hurt a soul," except "rattlesnakes and scorpions or whatever," before adding, "Then you say, 'See, the next one is in the middle of Tehran.'"[80]

In 2018, John Bolton, the zealot of the political Right who successfully led a campaign to reverse the UN's Zionism-is-racism resolution, and a key figure in the George W. Bush administration's destruction of Arab socialist Iraq, became the US National Security Adviser. The moustachioed Bolton, who had threatened International Criminal Court prosecutors and judges with sanctions and prosecution under the US legal system if they ever dared pursue investigations of Israel or the United States,[81] had been a decades-long advocate of overthrowing "the mullahs' regime" in Tehran.[82] Former US ambassador to Russia Michael McFaul argued that by hiring Bolton, the Trump administration sent a clear signal of the direction in which it was heading. "He's very clear that there should be regime change in Iran and North Korea, and military force should be used to achieve those goals," McFaul said.[83] Bolton advocated airstrikes on Iranian nuclear facilities, invoking the Israeli airstrikes on Iraq's Osirak reactor and Syria's Deir Ezzor reactor, as models.[84] Equipped with US-supplied bunker-busters and F-35s, it was well within the Israeli military's capabilities to destroy Iran's facilities.

If Bolton's long-standing opposition to Iran was an indication of the direction in which US Middle East policy was heading, so too was the hiring of Jim Mattis, a former Marine Corps general, as secretary of defense. Mattis had been relieved of his post as leader of US military forces in the Middle East by Barack Obama, who worried Mattis' aggressive streak and animosity to Iran would escalate US aggression against the country beyond the limits the White House considered strategically tenable.[85] Mattis believed that Iran "remained the greatest threat to the United States' interests in the Middle East."[86] In 2012, he named the United States' three top threats as "Iran, Iran, Iran."[87] However much Mattis' actions and beliefs are deplorable, the Marine can be commended for his clarity of thought and presentation. He conceded that the United States seeks to dominate the Middle East. Since Iran rejects US supremacy, and is the one country in the Middle East most able to resist it, it follows, he argued, that "those idiot raghead mullahs,"[88] as he refers to Iran's leadership, must be dealt with.[89]

To deny Iran the means of a nuclear self-defense, Israel conducted a "covert campaign of assassinations, bombings, cyber attacks and defections," according to *The New York Times*.[90] Over the five-year period 2007 through 2012, Mossad assassinated five Iranian nuclear scientists. Under the direction of Kidon, a Mossad unit meaning "Tip of the Spear" in Hebrew, Mossad operatives placed magnetized bombs on the vehicles of four of the scientists and filled the house of the fifth with carbon monoxide, killing all five.[91] Between 2005 and 2009, Mossad was also responsible for "the disappearance of an Iranian nuclear scientist, the crash of two planes carrying cargo relating to the project, and two labs that burst into flames," according to *The Wall Street Journal*.[92]

The US cyber-intelligence agency, the NSA, and its Israeli counterpart, Unit 8200, worked together "to sabotage centrifuges for Iran's nuclear program," according to *The Wall Street Journal*, infecting Iranian computers with the Stuxnet worm. The worm disabled about 1,000 centrifuges.[93] Israel tested the worm on its own centrifuges at its Dimona nuclear facilities in the Negev desert, before the malicious code was deployed against Iran.[94]

Prior to inflicting Stuxnet on Iran, the United States and Israel targeted Iran with a sophisticated computer virus named Flame, which they had jointly developed. The "malware secretly mapped and monitored Iran's computer networks, sending back a steady stream of intelligence to prepare for" the Stuxnet cyber warfare campaign aimed at sabotaging Iran's centrifuges, according to *The Washington Post*.[95] Thus, Israel has played a major role in weakening the ability of Iran—the top challenger to the United States' hegemonic role in the Middle East after the demise of Saddam—to defend itself.

In 2011, Muammar Gaddafi, a former Soviet client, Arab socialist, admirer of Nasser, and 'resource nationalist,' to use the disapproving language of the US State Department, was overthrown by jihadists (with massive NATO support), the main internal opposition to his rule. Gaddafi had welcomed the 1979 Islamic Revolution in Iran, and was part of the Tehran-centered Axis of Resistance to the US dictatorship over the Muslim world. Washington had long targeted Gaddafi for removal. After the Soviet Union's dissolution, the Libyan colonel worked out a *modus vivendi* with the West. Part of the bargain was that Libya would dismantle its weapons of mass destruction. Gaddafi disarmed, and was hailed in the West, and held up as model for the North Koreans to emulate. But Gaddafi's nationalist inclinations irritated Western investors, who wished the colonel's influence in Libya brought to an end. With an Islamist insurgency in full swing, Gaddafi was accused of planning to massacre his opponents, providing Washington with a pretext to organize a NATO intervention ostensibly to prevent the alleged impending carnage. Having earlier surrendered his means of self-defense, Gaddafi was left at the mercy of NATO. Acting as the jihadists' air force, NATO quickly dispatched the resource nationalist from the scene.

Next up was Bashar al-Assad, son of, and successor to, Hafez al-Assad, the Syrian air force colonel who led the Den of Arabism under the banner of liberty, unity and socialism until his death in 2000. Hafez al-Assad was anti-West at the best of times, observed Aburish.[96] Western opposition to him was "the result of his studied refusal to accept Western hegemony."[97] During Hafez al-Assad's years in power there was "a four-way alliance of the West, Israel, the traditional regimes and the Islamic movements" to oust him,[98] paralleling the same four-way alliance assembled in the 1950s and 1960s to eliminate the Arab socialism of Nasser in Egypt.

Bashar largely followed his father's policies. He was not an inflexible ideologue, but, like Hafez, a realist, who recognized Syria's limitations, and did not try to push beyond them. While the senior Assad distrusted the West and rejected its hegemony, he accepted the need to occasionally work with it.[99] The same was true of Bashar. Bashar recognized that compromise was a *sine qua non* of survival. At the same time, his flexibility didn't go quite far enough for Washington and Tel Aviv. They sought a biddable ruler for Syria, preferably a Sunni businessman who was more interested in making money than championing the cause of Arab independence and agitating against Jewish settler colonialism.

To oust Assad, Washington turned to the Muslim Brotherhood, the same group it had used to destabilize Nasser's rule, and which had been waging an on-again-off-again jihad against Syria's Arab socialists since the 1960s.

The Muslim Brotherhood had played a lead role in drafting the Damascus Declaration in the mid-2000s, a manifesto demanding regime change. In 2007, the Ikhwan teamed up with a former Syrian vice-president to found the National Salvation Front. The front met frequently with the U.S. State Department and the U.S. National Security Council, as well as with the U.S. government-funded Middle East Partnership Initiative. The organization did openly what the CIA once did covertly, namely, funnel money and expertise to fifth columnists in countries whose governments Washington opposed.[100]

By 2009, just two years before the eruption of unrest throughout the Arab world, termed the Arab Spring, the Syrian Muslim Brotherhood denounced Assad's government as a foreign and hostile element in Syrian society that needed to be eliminated. According to the group's thinking, Assad, a follower of the heterodox Muslim Alawite sect, was a heretic. He was using Ba'athism as a cover to furtively advance a sectarian agenda to destroy Syria from within by oppressing 'true' (i.e., Sunni) Muslims. In the name of Islam, the heretical regime had to be overthrown.[101]

Violence would break out in Syria in the spring of 2011. A few months before, the scholar Liad Porat wrote a brief for the Crown Center for Middle East Studies, based at Brandeis University. "The movement's leaders," the scholar concluded, "continue to voice their hope for a civil revolt in Syria, wherein 'the Syrian people will perform its duty and liberate Syria from the tyrannical and corrupt regime.'" The Brotherhood stressed that it was engaged in a fight to the death with Assad's secular government.[102]

That the Syrian Muslim Brotherhood played a key role in the uprising was confirmed in 2012 by the U.S. Defense Intelligence Agency. A report from the agency said that the insurgency was sectarian and led by the Muslim Brotherhood and al-Qaeda in Iraq, the forerunner of Islamic State. The report added that the insurgents were supported by the West, Persian Gulf oil monarchies, and Turkey. The analysis correctly predicted the establishment of a "Salafist principality," an Islamic state, in Eastern Syria, noting that this was desired by the insurgency's foreign backers, who wanted to see the secular Arab nationalists isolated and cut-off from Iran.[103]

Israel had a role to play in the campaign to topple Bashar al-Assad's government, just as it had in efforts to topple his father's government. In the 1970s and early 1980s, Israel, along with Jordan, "actively supported the Syrian Muslim Brotherhood in a bloody civil war against the government of President Hafez Assad," recalls the journalist and author Robert Dreyfus. "Israeli- and Jordanian-sponsored" Islamist guerrillas "killed hundreds of Syrians, exploded car bombs, and assassinated Soviet diplomats and military personnel in Syrian cities."[104]

In the US-sponsored renewal of the Islamist insurgency from 2011 forward, the Saudis, Qataris, Jordanians, Turks, and Americans actively supported the jihadists. So too did Israel. Under a program called Operation Good Neighbor, the Israeli military provided anti-Arabist jihadists with "over 1524 tons of food, 250 tons of clothes, 947,520 liters of fuel, 21 generators, 24,900 palettes of medical equipment and medicine," on top of weapons, according to *The Jerusalem Post*.[105] *The Wall Street Journal* revealed that the Israeli army was "in regular communication with rebel groups and its assistance" included "undisclosed payments to commanders that" helped "pay salaries of fighters and buy ammunition and weapons."[106]

Israeli paramedics patrolled the border between Israeli-annexed Golan and Syria, treating Islamist guerrilla casualties, and arranging for serious cases to be transported to Israeli hospitals.[107] Approximately 4,000 Islamist guerrillas[108] were given medical treatment in Israel from 2013 to 2018.[109] Casualties, many of them al Qaeda fighters, were often taken through the Israeli lines for hospital treatment in Haifa.[110] All were returned to the battlefield after recovery.[111]

On top of engaging in indirect aggression against the Syrian government through its active support of Islamist insurgents, Israel also engaged in direct aggression. According to the head of the Israeli Air Force Air Division, Brigadier General Amnon Ein Dar, Israeli Defense Forces carried out thousands of bombing raids in Syria in 2017 alone.[112] Israeli war planes conducted strikes against warehouses and military bases,[113] defense industry facilities,[114] fuel depots, and other targets.[115]

The "Israeli military violated Syrian airspace more than 750 times in" a four-month period in 2017. Its aircraft spent more than "3,200 hours over the country. On average, more than six Israeli aircraft entered Syrian airspace each day in that period," reported the Nazareth-based journalist Jonathan Cook.[116]

Some in Syria joke: "How can you say that al Qaeda doesn't have an air force? They have the Israeli air force," Assad told *Foreign Affairs*. "They are supporting the rebels in Syria. It is very clear."[117] Importantly, Israel's direct aggression was coordinated with jihadist activity. "Whenever we make advances in some place," Assad said, the Israelis "make an attack in order to undermine the army."[118]

Robert Fisk observed that Israel only ever bombed the Syrian military and its allies, and never ISIS.[119] "If we have to choose between ISIS and Assad, we'll take ISIS," said Michael Oren, a prominent lawmaker from Israel's governing coalition and a former ambassador to Washington. "ISIS has flatbed trucks and machine guns. Assad represents the strategic arch from Tehran to Beirut, 130,000 rockets in the hands of Hezbollah, and the Iranian nuclear program."[120] Israel provided passive support for ISIS by refraining from bombing ISIS targets, and active support to al Qaeda fighters. The jihadists opposed Syria; they opposed Syria's main West Asian backer, Iran; and as guerrilla organizations, and not state militaries, they posed a less significant threat to Israel than did Syria. Hence, Israel favored Islamists over Assad.

Alon Pinkas, a former Israeli consul general in New York, likened the war between the jihadists and Syria's secular government to the Iraq-Iran war—one the West, and Israel, hoped would lead to the common ruin of both sides. "This is a playoff situation in which you need both teams to lose, but at least you don't want one to win — we'll settle for a tie," said Pinkas. "Let them both bleed, hemorrhage to death: that's the strategic thinking here. As long as this lingers, there's no real threat from Syria."[121]

When asked in 2017 by the Venezuelan-based Latin American television network, TeleSur, what role Israel was playing in the war against Syria, Assad replied:

> It is playing this role in different forms; first, by direct aggression, particularly by using warplanes, artillery, or missiles against Syrian Army positions. Second, it is supporting [Islamist insurgents] in two ways: first by providing direct support in the form of weapons, and second by providing logistic support, i.e. allowing them to conduct military exercises in the areas it controls. It also provides them with medical assistance in its hospitals.[122]

The renewal of the Islamist insurgency against Syria was orchestrated by the United States to weaken the Axis of Resistance to US hegemony in the Middle East. While the insurgency was revivified to serve US foreign policy goals, Israel was a major beneficiary. The war severely depleted the Syrian military, reducing its ability to act as a palladium against Zionist settler colonialism; it forced Damascus to surrender its chemical weapons-capability, a capability it had hoped would allow it to approach WMD parity with a nuclear-armed Israel; it diverted world attention from Israel's expanding colonization of Palestine; it provoked a schism between Hamas, which had been supported by Iran, and the Resistance Axis. Hamas, an offshoot of the Muslim Brotherhood, sided with the *Ikhwan's* insurgency in Syria.[123]

Israel's most significant contribution to the longstanding war on Arab socialism in Syria was to deny Damascus access to a nuclear deterrent that may have allowed it to stay the hand of US aggression. US forces arrogantly crossed the Iraqi border into Syria, without feeling the slightest compulsion to seek Syria's permission. The invasion was a flagrant violation of international law, comparable to the Nazi invasion of France. Eventually, US forces would occupy nearly one-third of Syrian territory, pronounce the occupation indefinite, and announce that they had no intention of ceding the captured territory to an Arab socialist government.[124] It's unlikely that the Pentagon would have been so bold had Damascus possessed an atomic saber. Israel ensured that it didn't and therefore facilitated Washington's malign behavior in the region.

When Israeli fighter jets secretly destroyed Syria's Al-Kubar reactor in 2007, Tel Aviv believed the reactor, built with the assistance of North Korea, was less than a year away from producing fissile material for an atomic bomb. To avoid war, Israel declined to take responsibility for the attack, allowing the Syrian government to pretend it never happened. With neither side acknowledging the Israeli aggression, Damascus could avoid public pressure to retaliate. Assad didn't want to go war with Israel. Syria—weaker than its neighbor—would almost inevitably suffer a humiliating defeat. Israel had lured Nasser into the 1967 war, and Assad intended to stay clear of the same trap. The Israelis undertook the attack with the full knowledge of the United States. In his 2010 memoir, *Decision Point*, George W. Bush recalled that the Israelis "wanted total secrecy." They "wanted to avoid anything that might back Syria in a corner and force Assad to retaliate."[125] Jonathan Cook points out that "Almost no one implicates the US in the Israeli attacks that wiped out Iraq and Syria's nuclear program. A nuclear-armed Iraq or Syria, however, would have deterred later US-backed moves at regime overthrow."[126]

CONCLUSION

Diversion

"Do the energy corporations fail to understand their interests, or are they part of the Lobby too?"

Noam Chomsky[1]

Just as some have theorized revolution as a Judeo-Bolshevik conspiracy, others have theorized US Middle East policy as a Judeo-Israeli conspiracy. In both cases, the observed instigators—of revolutions and of US policy—are said not to be the instigators at all; they are, instead, simply puppets. It is the Jews, pulling the strings in the background, who are to blame. If Lenin and Stalin were the gentile face of a Judeo-Bolshevik conspiracy to destroy Western civilization, then US presidents are marionettes manipulated by a Judeo-Israeli conspiracy to subvert US foreign policy.

At the heart of the Judeo-Israeli hijack view of US foreign policy is a basic misunderstanding of the interests of the people who are said to be misled by Machiavellian Jews operating in the shadows. US ideologues attributed Arab nationalist revolutions to a communist conspiracy originating in Moscow, denying that Arabs had legitimate grievances against their Western-imposed rulers and that revolution was the means of redress. The Arabs didn't need Moscow to drive them to revolution. The oppression inflicted by the despots imposed by colonial powers was all that was required.

Advocates of the view that Israel wields enormous influence over US Middle East policy cite as evidence US policy itself: what Washington does in the Middle East, they say, is injurious to the interests of the United

States. At the same time, it is helpful to Israel. Therefore, it must be true that Israel and the 'Jewish lobby' have hijacked US Middle East policy to obtain Israeli benefits at US expense. It would hold therefore that we shouldn't blame Washington for the frightful state of the Middle East; we should blame the self-declared Jewish state.

All of this, however, rests on a fundamental misunderstanding of whose interests US foreign policy serves. It is assumed that when decision-makers set policy that they are guided by the common interests of US citizens. The evidence, however, points in a different direction. Rather than taking the common interests of US citizens into account, policy-makers pay special attention to the needs of corporate America. US Middle East policy may be at odds with US interests, where US interests are equated to the common interests of Americans, but it is not at odds with corporate America's interests. What Washington does in the Middle East benefits US investors to a high degree. US Middle East policy has delivered enormous benefits to US oil companies, for which the Persian Gulf is a leading source of 'black gold.' US Middle East policy has also delivered enormous benefits to US arms manufacturers, who act as armorers to the Arab world's imposed leaders, and to US banks, in whose accounts the proceeds of Middle East oil sales are deposited.

At the end of World War II, US officials celebrated the Middle East as a 'stupendous source of strategic power' and an immense 'material prize.' Can we imagine investor-dominated Washington *not* pursuing a policy of imperial control of the region? Exponents of US Middle East policy as a Judeo-Israeli conspiracy have a naïve understanding of the forces that drive US foreign policy. The Israelis-have-hijacked-our-foreign-policy crowd have imbibed uncritically Washington's public relations spin about the United States intended to act as a force for good and stability in the Middle East, in pursuit of peace, harmony, and democracy, and on behalf of the common good of US citizens. It is not Israel that has made the Middle East a region of unremitting war; it is the mutual hostility of US investor interests and those of local forces of independence that have turned the region into a zone of unceasing conflict. These two forces are fighting over who will benefit from West Asia's petroleum resources—the local population, or investors in New York.

Those who believe that Israeli prime ministers dictate US Middle East policy, as evidenced by the reality that US policy in West Asia is against the common interests of Americans, err in defining US interests as the interests of US citizens in the main, rather than the interests of US citizens who, through their ownership and control of major economic assets, exert enormous influence over US public policy. The political scientists Martin Gilens and Benjamin I. Page spelled it out in their 2014 study of over 1,700 US policy issues: "[E]conomic elites and organized groups representing business interests have substantial impacts on government policy, while average citizens and mass-based interest groups have little or no independent influence."[2] A US Middle East policy that benefits average citizens and mass-based interest groups is of academic interest alone: it doesn't exist. It is a mistake, then, to assume that in the absence of a world without Israel that US Middle East policy would look different—that it would benefit average citizens and mass-based interest groups. It would still look the way it does today, because US Middle East policy is shaped by economic elites and organized groups representing US business interests, not Israel or American Jews acting on the self-appointed Jewish state's behalf.

The Judeo-Israeli conspiracy theory of US Middle East policy assumes that under normal circumstances US Middle East policy is formulated by decision-makers in the common interests of Americans. Upon examination, however, they discover, quite correctly, that the common interests of Americans are not served by US Middle East policy. From this they conclude that circumstances are not normal, and that some intervening force must have knocked US foreign policy off its normal course. But which force? Noting, again, quite correctly, that US policy benefits Israel, they conclude that Israel must be the agency that has caused US policy to divagate from its accustomed course of promoting the common interest of Americans. But is Israel the only beneficiary?

An alternative explanation holds that there is an additional, senior beneficiary whose interests define US Middle East policy, and that Israel only benefits incidentally inasmuch as its interests overlap those of the principal beneficiary. According to this explanation, it is not normal for decision-makers to formulate US Middle East policy in the common interests of Americans. Instead, decision-makers formulate policy for the Arab and Muslim worlds in the interests of the most influential sector of US society—the country's major investors. A US Middle East policy that represents the common interests of Americans may be the ideal, and it may be desirable, but it is hardly normal. Israel benefits from US Middle East policy because it defends and promotes corporate America's interests in the Middle East. The Jewish settler colonial state acts to suppress forces that insist that Arab and Persian oil must be used for the benefit of the region's inhabitants and not US investors. The common interests of Americans are not even a consideration.

Two of the principal proponents of the idea that Israel dominates the direction of US Middle East policy are the US political scientists, John Mearsheimer and Stephen Walt. Mearsheimer and Walt believe that Israel exercises outsize influence over US foreign policy through the "Israeli lobby," and especially the American Israel Public Affairs Committee, or AIPAC. The Committee was formed in 1951,[3] is aligned with Republicans and Christian evangelicals, and has 100,000 members. It has 18 offices, a staff of 300, a budget of $60 million, and an endowment of $140 million. It also has a strong relationship with the State Department and Pentagon and provides guidance to 31 pro-Israel political action committees, or PACs. The PACs give tens of million of dollars in campaign contributions to pro-Israel candidates.[4]

To be sure, AIPAC is a powerful lobby, but so too are "the American Association of Retired People, the National Rifle Association, the US Chamber of Commerce, and the American Petroleum Institute," as historian Arno J. Mayer has pointed out.[5] As powerful as AIPAC is, it is no match for the combined influence of corporate America and its financial arm, Wall Street—the economic elites and organized groups representing business interests of the Gilens and Page study. It would be absurd to believe that a lobby with a $60 million budget has an influence over US foreign policy that comes even close to the influence corporate America can—and does—bring to bear on Washington.

Mearsheimer and Walt believe that the United States "has a terrorism problem in good part because it is so closely allied with Israel, and not the other way around."[6] By implication, if Washington wasn't closely allied with Israel, it wouldn't have a terrorism problem. The duo point to Osama bin Laden as evidence. "There is no question," they write, "that many al-Qaida leaders, including Osama bin Laden, are motivated by Israel's presence in Jerusalem and the plight of the Palestinians." What they fail to mention is that there's no question that many al-Qaida leaders are also motivated by the US presence in the Persian Gulf, and Washington's use of quislings as instruments of indirect rule over the Middle East.

In 1998 bin Laden explained why the United States has a terrorism problem.

> The call to wage war against America was made because America [is] sending tens of thousands of its troops to [the Arabian peninsula], over and above its meddling in [Saudi] affairs and [Saudi] politics, and its support of the oppressive, corrupt and tyrannical regime that is in control. These are the reasons behind the singling out of America as a target.[7]

In May 2003, al Qaeda elaborated on why the United States has a terrorism problem:

> The Muslim countries today are colonized. Colonialism is either direct or veiled … masking colonialism … is exactly what happened in Afghanistan when the United States occupied that country and installed an Afghan agent, Hamid Karzai … there is no difference between the Karzai of Yemen, the Karzai of Pakistan, the Karzai of Jordan, the Karzai of Qatar, the Karzai of Kuwait, the Karzai of Egypt, and the long list of Karzai traitors ruling the Muslim countries.[8]

In other words, West Asia's leaders are quislings who veil the indirect rule of the United States.

Continuing its exegesis on the origins of the US terrorism problem, al Qaeda explained that:

> The ruler of a country is the one that has the authority in it … the real ruler [of Saudi Arabia] is the Crusader United States. The subservience of [local] rulers is no different from the subservience of the emirs or governors of provinces to the king or the president. The rule of the agent is the rule of the one that made him agent.[9]

The Islamist organization added that:

> It is important to know that the colonialist enemy might give up veiled colonialism and establish, through its armies, colonialism where there is little fear of resistance or the agent leadership could not achieve the interests of colonialism or had deviated—even in a small way—from its hegemony. For this reason, the United States chose to invade Iraq militarily, and might choose to invade any Muslim country near or far from Iraq at any time. [The United States] can occupy a country whenever it wants, and this is exactly what the United States is doing in Saudi Arabia.[10]

Pape observed that within "Saudi Arabia there is little debate over al Qaeda's objection to American forces in the region and over 95% of Saudi society reportedly agreed with Bin Laden on the matter."[11]

Israel didn't occupy the Persian Gulf militarily. It didn't invade Iraq. It doesn't control Saudi Arabia, Yemen, Pakistan, Afghanistan, Qatar, Kuwait and Egypt through a system of veiled colonialism. And yet the US occupation of the Persian Gulf, the invasion of Iraq, colonialism through the indirect rule of 'Karzais' is, according to al Qaeda, why the United States has a terrorism problem. Were Washington to disavow Israel, it would make no difference; US veiled colonialism would carry on.

Mearsheimer and Walt are blind to the way the United States is perceived in the Third World. They believe that only Israel has a maculated reputation among Arabs and Muslims, and that the US alliance with Israel sullies an otherwise sterling US reputation in the Third World. But far from seeing the United States as a shining star whose brilliance has been dimmed by association with Israel, the Third World sees the two countries as complementary and organically interconnected—as two faces of the same evil. Israel has become indistinguishable from "the Yankee in the eyes of the oppressed and tortured populaces of the teeming Third World,"[12] including the Arab section of it. "Israel is America and Europe combined in Palestine,"[13] was how Leila Khaled put it. In order to solve its terrorism problem, Washington would have to do far more than cancel its special relationship with Israel. It would have to turn away from imperialism—the real reason Islamists of the al Qaeda stripe have attacked US targets. But Mearsheimer and Walt fail to grasp that the United States is an imperialist power—and it is for this reason that they go wrong.

The two political scientists argue that 'rogue states' in the Middle East, by which they mean Islamic Iran, Arab socialist Iraq and Arab socialist Syria, "are not a dire threat to vital US interests," but are to Israel.[14] But once again they fail to define US interests. If the United States has constructed and defends a global system that is subordinate to the needs of US investors,[15] then rogue states are a threat because they challenge the global system, threatening to redirect their economies away from satisfying the demands of US investors to satisfying the material needs of local populations. We could argue that the two political scientists serve the useful purpose for the US political and economic elite of obscuring the role US foreign policy plays as an instrument of US investors by scapegoating Israel. And indeed, the US foreign policy critic Noam Chomsky has. He argued that the Mearsheimer-Walt thesis has "plenty of appeal" because "it leaves the US government untouched on its high pinnacle of nobility, 'Wilsonian idealism,' etc. merely in the grip of an all-powerful force that it cannot escape."[16]

Another argument invoked by those who theorize US Middle East policy as a Judeo-Israeli conspiracy is that in supporting Israel, the United States is backing a state whose values are inconsistent with US liberal democracy. Aspects "of Israeli democracy are at odds with core American values," Mearsheimer and Walt point out.[17] Israel discriminates on the basis of race, religion and ethnicity; it provides more rights to Jews than non-Jews. How could Washington support a state that rejects liberal democratic fundamentals? The explanation must be that the Israeli lobby has coerced Washington into backing Israel.

While it is true that Israel is a *Herrenvolk* democracy, or a democracy for the Jews and a Jewish state for the Arabs, it was not so long ago that the United States was also a *Herrenvolk* democracy, and an argument can be made that, in practice, it remains so today. This isn't to excuse Israel's *Herrenvolk* democracy, but to point to the Mearsheimer-Walt practice of seeing Israel as it is and the United States as it pretends to be. The duo might also be asked to explain the unacknowledged but altogether real US special relationship with Saudi Arabia, a state whose core values are ones that US politicians, editorial writers, and intellectuals would define as far more at odds with professed American values than any embraced by Israel. Were Mearsheimer and Walt consistent, they would have to argue that Washington's special relationship with Saudi Arabia has no connection to the profit-making interests of US oil companies, US arms manufacturers, and US banks, but that its origins can be found in a Saudi lobby that has hijacked US foreign policy. With its gargantuan oil wealth, Saudi Arabia is far better placed to influence US Middle East policy than is AIPAC with its $60 million per annum budget, surely a pittance against what the Saudi monarchy could muster.

Those who blame US Middle East policy on Israel, rather than corporate America, point to US military aid to the self-declared Jewish state as evidence for their hijack thesis. Israel receives more US military aid than any other country, and, they suggest, in mind-boggling amounts. Furthermore, the quantity of military aid that flows to Israel every year is said to be far in excess of the benefits returned to the United States. For example, Washington had to rely on its own military forces to invade and occupy Iraq, and to protect the Persian Gulf from the threat of Saddam fulfilling the Arabist promise of Arab oil for the Arabs. What good is it to spend billions of dollars on the Israeli military, if the United States has to do all the heavy lifting? Surely, this reveals that the Jews have coerced Washington into a profligate military aid program.

This argument suffers from a number of weaknesses. First, the amount of military aid Israel receives, while larger than that given to any other country, is not as large as some critics of the US-Israeli relationship suggest. Opponents of the special relationship often sum military aid to Israel over a long period to make it appear especially large. For example, we might be told that Israel received over $92 billion in US military aid to 2017, a seemingly staggering amount.[18] But the average yearly figure for US military aid to Israel over this period works out to a far more modest $1.34 billion. In 2018, Washington committed to giving Israel $38 billion in military aid over 10 years, in annual tranches of $3.8 billion.[19] To put the figure in perspective, the US National Defense Authorization Act approved US military spending of $716 billion in 2018. This means that in 2018, US military aid to Israel was only 1/188 as large as the Pentagon's budget.

What's more, it's not as if Israel is given US military aid to spend as it pleases. US aid to Israel is tied to US manufacturing interests; the Zionist state is obligated to spend the US subvention on US-made military gear. The $3.8 billion that Washington gives Israel every year is a $3.8 billion subsidy to US arms manufacturers. The funds flow directly from the US Treasury to the accounts receivable departments of Lockheed-Martin, Raytheon, Boeing, Northrop-Grumman, and other US armorers.

The annual cost to Washington of operating a single carrier strike group—an aircraft carrier, its air wing, its five combat support ships, one attack submarine, and 6,700 sailors—is approximately $3.3 billion, close to the level of annual US military aid to Israel.[20] Are the benefits Israel delivers to US investors in helping to suppress local forces that insist the Middle East's petroleum resources and associated shipping routes be used for the benefit of the local population—the Assads, the Saddams, the Iranians, Hezbollah—worth the annual cost of a single carrier strike group? The answer from the point of view of US businesses that profit from Arab oil and arms sales to the region's quisling leaders is obvious.

"Justifying the largest foreign-aid program in the history of the United States in terms of an American strategic investment has not been difficult for leaders on either side," observes Beit-Hallahmi. "Israeli leaders have rightly pointed out that the US is getting a real bargain; as Yaakov Meridor," then Israel's minister of economy pointed out: "Even if we consider only Israeli air power, we are a very cheap investment for the Americans. We have six hundred jet fighters, and to keep this number of planes, the United States would have need of a dozen aircraft carriers."[21]

The view was no less strongly shared on the US side. Asked in 1995 whether the United States should give aid to Israel, the chairman of the Senate Foreign Relations Committee, Jesse Helms, replied: "If Israel did not exist, what would U.S. defense costs in the Middle East be? Israel is at least the equivalent of a U.S. aircraft carrier in the Middle East. Without Israel promoting its and America's common interests, we would be badly off indeed."[22] Michael Oren, who served as Israel's ambassador to the US, claimed that Alexander Haig, Reagan's secretary of state, said that Israel is "the largest American aircraft carrier in the world that cannot be sunk, does not carry even one American soldier, and is located in a critical region for American national security."[23] *The Jerusalem Post* characterized US aid to Israel as "an investment in" a "superior Western military force that can operate at long range ... protecting America's interests in the region." This, by the way, accorded with the view of US president Barack Obama.[24] Meanwhile, Major General George Keegan, head of US Air Force Intelligence, estimated that it would cost US taxpayers $125 billion to maintain a military force in West Asia equal to Israel's. The special relationship between the United States and Israel, he concluded, was worth "five CIAs."[25] In the mid-1980s, Israel's prime minister Shimon Peres argued that Israel provides Washington an extension of US foreign policy at a lower expense than the United States could provide itself, an argument with which the Chair of the Senate Foreign Relations Committee, Richard Lugar, agreed.[26]

Israel is completely at the mercy of the United States for its existence. It must do Washington's bidding, or risk losing the special relationship that protects it. Without the shelter Washington provides, Israel would perish. While heavily armed with sophisticated weaponry, the settler colonial state is a small island of only eight million (of whom six million are settlers) in a sea of Arabs who regard the existence of the state as an abomination against the values of democracy, equality, and progress, and an affront to their national aspirations. The states that border Israel—Egypt,

Lebanon, Syria and Jordan—are home to over 130 million Arabs who wish the dissolution of Zionism as fervently as indigenous south Africans hoped for the end of apartheid. There are approximately 270 million Arabs further afield who wish the same, as well as 80 million Iranians, 70 million Turks, and countless other Muslims who are hostile to Israel, the last of the settler colonial states. Because Israel depends on Washington for survival it is highly motivated to align with US aims. There's little chance of Israel acting in ways that contradict the US investor interests that undergird US foreign policy. Israel's interests and those of US investors are coterminous; the two states are united by the reality that they share a common enemy—the people of the Middle East. Both Zionist Israel and Wall Street-driven America are hostile to the local forces of independence and national assertiveness that would, if they could, take their land, markets, labor, and natural resources into their own hands, and use them for their own benefit. In a democratic global order, local economies would be under local control.

But democracy is the last thing either Zionists or Wall Street want. What these allied forces desire is for the people of the Middle East to cede their interests and surrender their rights. Zionists want Arabs to accede to the theft of their land (what's formally called recognizing Israel's right to exist) and Wall Street wants them to accede to the theft of their markets, their labor, and above all, their oil (what's informally called accepting US 'leadership.')

At the heart of the unceasing wars on the Middle East reposes the question of who owns and controls Arab and Persian oil and the marine and overland routes to and from it—the natives, or the US government and the investors it represents? The Zionist answer has always been clear: Western political and economic interests must have supremacy in the Middle East. Israel began as a European colony, established anachronistically just as the great wave of decolonization was getting started. As the United States superseded Britain and France as the dominant imperialist power in the region, Israel transitioned from the formers' outpost of terror in the Arab world into a power projection platform for US investor interests. Throughout this transition Israel has remained interlocked with imperial power, unfailingly serving as the West's beachhead in the Middle East.

BIBLIOGRAPHY

Aburish, Said K. *A Brutal Friendship: The West and the Arab Elite*, (Victor Gollancz, 1997).

--*Saddam Hussein: The Politics of Revenge*, (Bloomsbury, 2001).

--*Nasser, The Last Arab: A Biography*, (St. Martin's Press, 2004).

--*The Rise, Corruption and Coming Fall of the House of Saud*, (Bloomsbury, 2005).

Barbusse, Henri. *Stalin: A New World Seen Through One Man*, (Read Books, 2011).

Beckert, Sven. *Empire of Cotton: A Global History*. (Vintage Books, 20014).

Beit-Hallahmi, Benjamin. *The Israeli Connection: Who Israel Arms and Why*, (Pantheon Books, 1987).

--*Original Sins: Reflections of the History of Zionism and Israel*, (Olive Branch Press, 1993).

Brzezinski, Zbigniew. *The Grand Chessboard: American Primacy and its Geostrategic Imperatives*, (Basic Books, 1997).

Cattan, Henry. *The Palestine Question*, (Croom Helm, 1988).

Carroll, Raymond. *Anwar Sadat*, (F. Watts, 1982).

Césaire, Aimé. *Discourse on Colonialism*, (Monthly Review Press, 2000).

Chomsky, Noam. *Fateful Triangle: The United States, Israel, and the Palestinians*, (Pluto Press, 1999).

--*Hegemony or Survival: America's Quest for Global Dominance*, (Henry Holt & Company, 2003).

--*How the World Works*, (Soft Skull Press, 2011).

Dreyfus, Robert. *Devil's Game: How the United States Helped Unleash Fundamentalist Islam*, Henry Holt & Company, 2005).

Ellis, John. *The Social History of the Machine Gun*, (Arno Press, 1981).

Finkelstein, Norman G. *The Holocaust Industry: Reflections on the Exploitation of Jewish Suffering*, (Verso, 2000).

Franklin, Bruce (Ed.). *The Essential Stalin: Major Theoretical Writings, 1905-1952*, (Doubleday Anchor, 1972).

Fromkin, David. *A Peace to End All Peace: The Fall of the Ottoman Empire and the Creation of the Modern World*, (Henry Holt & Company, 2009).

Fuller, Graham E. *A World Without Islam*, (Little, Brown & Company, 2010).

Gowans, Stephen. *Washington's Long War on Syria*, (Baraka Books, 2017).

--*Patriots, Traitors and Empires: The Story of Korea's Struggle for Freedom*, (Baraka Books, 2018).

Hadawi, Sami. *Bitter Harvest: A Modern History of Palestine*, (Scorpion Publishing, 1989).

Herzl, Theodor. *The Jewish State*, (Quid Pro Books, 2014).

--*Old New Land*, (Stellar Editions, 2016).

Hitler, Adolph. *Mein Kampf*, (Coda Books, 2011).

Khaled, Leila, (with George Hajjar). *My People Shall Live: The Autobiography of a Revolutionary*, (Hodder and Stoughton. 1973).

Kiernan, V. G. *America, The New imperialism: From White Settlement to World Hegemony*, (Verso, 2005).

Khalidi, Rashid. *The Iron Cage: The Story of the Palestinian Struggle for Statehood*, (Boston Press, 2007).

Koestler, Arthur. *Promise and Fulfillment: Palestine 1917-1949*, (Macmillan, 1949).

Lindqvist, Sven. *A History of Bombing*, (The New Press, 2000).

--*The Dead Do Not Die: Exterminate All The Brutes and Terra Nullius*, (The New Press, 2014).

Losurdo, Domenico. *War and Revolution: Rethinking the Twentieth Century*, (Verso, 2015).

--*Class Struggle: A Political and Philosophical History*, (Palgrave MacMillan, 2016).

Macdonald, James. *When Globalization Fails: The Rise and Fall of Pax Americana*, (Farrar, Straus and Giroux, 2015).

Marx, Karl and Friedrich Engels. *Communist Manifesto*. In (Leo Panitch and Colin Leys, Eds.). *The Communist Manifesto Now, The Socialist Register 1998*, (Monthly Review Press, 1998).

Marx, Karl. *Capital: A Critique of Political Economy, Volume One*, (Random House, 1977).

Mayer, Arno J. *The Furies: Violence and Terror in the French and Russian Revolutions*, (Princeton University Press, 2000).

--*Plowshares into Swords: From Zionism to Israel*, (Verso, 2008).

--*Why Did the Heavens Not Darken? The 'Final Solution' in History*, (Verso, 2012).

Nasser, Gamal Abdel. *The Philosophy of the Revolution*, (Mondale Press, 1955).

Olusoga, David and Casper W. Erichsen. *The Kaiser's Holocaust: Germany's Forgotten Genocide and the Colonial Roots of Nazism*, (Faber & Faber, 2010).

Osman, Tarek. *Egypt on the Brink*, (Yale University Press, 2010).

Polakow-Suransky, Sasha. *Unspoken Alliance: Israel's Secret Relationship with Apartheid South Africa*, (Vintage, 2011).

Pape, Robert A. *Dying to Win: The Structural Logic of Suicide Terrorism*, (Random House, 2006).

Pappe, Ilan. *The Ethnic Cleansing of Palestine*, (One World Publications, 2006).

Pauwels, Jacques R. *The Great Class War: 1914-1918*, (James Lorimer & Company, 2016).

Polk, William R. *Understanding Iraq*, (Harper Perennial, 2005).

--*Understanding Iran: Everything You Need to Know, From Persia to the Islamic Republic, From Cyrus to Ahmadinejad*, (Palgrave MacMillan, 2009).

Primakov, Yevgeny. *Russia and the Arabs: Behind the Scenes in the Middle East from the Cold War to the Present*, (Basic Books, 2009).

Rudeé, George. *Robespierre: Portrait of a Revolutionary Democrat*, (Viking Press, 1975).

Schneer, Jonathan. *The Balfour Declaration: The Origins of the Arab-Israel Conflict*, (Anchor Canada, 2010).

Shlaim, Avi. *The Iron Wall: Israel and the Arab World*, (W. W. Norton & Company, 2014).

Szymanski, Albert. *The Capitalist State and the Politics of Class*, (Winthrop Publishers, 1978).

Talbot, David. *The Devil's Chessboard: Allen Dulles, the CIA, and the Rise of America's Secret Government*, (Harper Collins, 2015).

Taylor, Alan. *Colonial America: A Very Short introduction*, (Oxford University Press, 2013).

Wheelock, Keith. *Nasser's New Egypt*, (Praeger, 1960).

Woodward, Bob. *Obama's Wars*, (Simon & Schuster, 2010).

--*Fear: Trump in the White House*, (Simon & Schuster, 2018).

Yaqub, Salim. *Containing Arab Nationalism: The Eisenhower Doctrine and the Middle East*, (University of North Caroline Press, 2004).

Notes

Introduction

1. Adam Shatz, "The sea is the same sea," *The London Review of Books*, (Vol. 40 No. 16 · 30 August 2018).
2. George Rudeé, *Robespierre: Portrait of a Revolutionary Democrat*, (Viking Press, 1975), 101.
3. Arno J. Mayer, *The Furies: Violence and Terror in the French and Russian Revolutions*, (Princeton University Press, 2000), 274-275.
4. Benjamin Beit-Hallahmi, *Original Sins: Reflections of the History of Zionism and Israel*, (Olive Branch Press, 1993), 113.
5. Ari Shavit, "Survival of the fittest," *Haaretz*, January 8, 2004.
6. Robert Fisk, "I asked Israel's only journalist in Palestine to show me something shocking—and this is what I saw," *The independent*, September 20, 2018.
7. Said K. Aburish, *Nasser, The Last Arab: A Biography*, (St. Martin's Press, 2004), 14.
8. William R. Polk, *Understanding Iraq*, (Harper Perennial, 2005), 127-128
9. Yaroslav Trofimov, "Israel's main concern in Syria: Iran, not ISIS," *The Wall Street Journal*, March 17, 2016.

Chapter One. Anti-Semitism

1. Theodor Herzl, *The Jewish State*, (Quid Pro Books, 2014), 12.
2. *Original Sins*, 63.
3. Eli Kavon, "Christian Zionism and the Balfour Declaration," *The Jerusalem Post*, October 21, 2017.
4. *Original Sins*, 39.
5. Domenico Losurdo, *Class Struggle: A Political and Philosophical History*, (Palgrave MacMillan, 2016), 104.
6. *Original Sins*, 64.
7. Ice, Thomas D., "William Blackstone and American Christian Zionism," (2009). Article Archives. Paper 56. https://digitalcommons.liberty.edu/cgi/viewcontent.cgi?article=1055&context=pretrib_arch
8. Ice

9. Arthur Koestler, *Promise and Fulfillment: Palestine 1917-1949*, (Macmillan, 1949), 3.

10. Noam Chomsky, "The imperial way: American decline in perspective, part 2," *tomdispatch.com*, February 15, 2012; Eli Kavon, "Christian Zionism and the Balfour Declaration," *The Jerusalem Post*, October 21, 2017.

11. "Who Was the Most pro-Jewish U.S. President? Woodrow Wilson, Obviously," Haaretz, September 25, 2013.

12. David Fromkin, *A Peace to End All Peace: The Fall of the Ottoman Empire and the Creation of the Modern World*, (Henry Holt & Company, 2009), 295.

13. J. L. Talmon, quoted in *Original Sins*, 64.

14. Domenico Losurdo, *War and Revolution: Rethinking the Twentieth Century* (Verso, 2015), 152.

15. Jacques R. Pauwels, *The Great Class War: 1914-1918*, (James Lorimer & Company, 2016), 89; *War and Revolution*, 152, 191.

16. *The Great Class War: 1914-1918*, 90.

17. *War and Revolution*, 195.

18. Arno J. Mayer, *The Furies: Violence and Terror in the French and Russian Revolutions*, (Princeton University Press, 2000), 268-269.

19. *The Great Class War: 1914-1918*, 89.

20. Arno J. Mayer, *Why Did the Heavens Not Darken? The 'Final Solution' in History*, (Verso, 2012), 5.

21. *War and Revolution*, 17.

22. Stefano G. Azzara, "Domenico Losurdo: Classical German philosophy, a critique of liberalism and 'critical Marxism'", http://domenicolosurdopresentazazing.blogspot.com, May 14, 2007.

23. *Original Sins*, 32.

24. *Original Sins*, 30-31.

25. *Original Sins*, 30.

26. *Original Sins*, 31.

27. *Original Sins*, 30.

28. *Original Sins*, 30-31.

29. *Original Sins*, 30-31.

30. *War and Revolution*, 178-179.

31. *A Peace to End All Peace*, 468-469.

32. *A Peace to End All Peace*, 468-469.

33. *A Peace to End All Peace*, 247.

34. *A Peace to End All Peace*, 198.

35. *A Peace to End All Peace*, 442-443.

36. David Talbot, *The Devil's Chessboard: Allen Dulles, the CIA, and the Rise of America's Secret Government*, (Harper Collins, 2015), 46.

37. *A Peace to End All Peace*, 466.

38. *A Peace to End All Peace*, 466-467.

39. *A Peace to End All Peace*, 469.

40. *A Peace to End All Peace*, 467.

41. *War and Revolution*, 152.

42. *Original Sins*, 39.

43. Domenico Losurdo, "Collapse of 'existing socialism' in Eastern Europe: Democratic revolution or restoration?" *Nature, Society, and Thought*, vol. 7, no. 2 (1994), 203-204.
44. *Original Sins,* 30.

Chapter Two. Zionism

1. *The Jewish State,* 9.
2. *The Jewish State,* 2.
3. *The Jewish State,* 2.
4. *The Jewish State,* 12.
5. *The Jewish State,* 3.
6. *The Jewish State,* 3.
7. *The Jewish State,* 16.
8. *The Jewish State,* 69.
9. Adolph Hitler, *Mein Kampf,* (Coda Books, 2011), 60.
10. *The Jewish State,* 61.
11. *The Jewish State,* 62.
12. *The Jewish State,* 62.
13. *Mein Kampf,* 71.
14. *Mein Kampf,* 75.
15. *Mein Kampf,* 121.
16. *Mein Kampf,* 154.
17. *Mein Kampf,* 61.
18. Theodor Herzl, *Old New Land,* (Stellar Editions, 2016), 77.
19. *Old New Land,* 53.
20. *The Jewish State,* 10.
21. *The Jewish State,* 19.
22. *The Jewish State,* 3.
23. *The Jewish State,* 9.
24. Old New Land, 114.
25. Old New Land, 122-123.
26. *The Jewish State,* 11.
27. *Old New Land,* 109.
28. *Old New Land,* 110.
29. *Old New Land,* 110.
30. *Old New Land,* 110.
31. "Three Visions for African Americans," The Constitutional Rights Foundation, http://www.crf-usa.org/brown-v-board-50th-anniversary/three-visions-for-african-americans.html)
32. Eric Foner, "Roots of Black Power," *The New York Times*, February 5, 1984.
33. *Old New Land,* 30.
34. *Old New Land,* 30.
35. *Old New Land,* 82.
36. *Old New Land,* 82.
37. *Old New Land,* 81.

38. *Old New Land*, 82.
39. *Old New Land*, 30.
40. *Old New Land*, 129.
41. *Old New Land*, 48.
42. *Old New Land*, 81.
43. *Old New Land*, 83.
44. *Mein Kampf*, 45.
45. Ari Shavit, "Survival of the fittest," *Haaretz*, January 8, 2004.
46. *The Jewish State*, 3.
47. *Mein Kampf*, 45.
48. *Mein Kampf*, 42.
49. *Mein Kampf*, 44.
50. *Mein Kampf*, 44.
51. *Mein Kampf*, 44.
52. *Mein Kampf*, 44.
53. *The Jewish State*, 6.
54. *The Jewish State*, 4.
55. *The Jewish State*, 4.
56. Quoted in Sven Lindqvist, *A History of Bombing*, (The New Press, 2000), 17.
57. *A History of Bombing*, 17.
58. PM of Israel Verified account @IsraeliPM Aug 29.
59. *Old New Land,* 46.
60. *The Jewish State*, 15.
61. *The Jewish State*, 12.
62. *The Jewish State*, 7.
63. *Old New Land*, 85.
64. Quoted in Losurdo, *Class Struggle*, 154.
65. *The Jewish State*, 20.
66. *The Jewish State*, 20.

Chapter Three. *Nakba*

1. Benjamin Beit-Hallahmi, *The Israeli Connection: Who Israel Arms and Why*, (Pantheon Books, 1987), 239
2. Sami Hadawi, *Bitter Harvest: Palestine 1914-1979*, (Caravan Books, 1983), 29.
3. Avi Shlaim, *The Iron Wall: Israel and the Arab World*, (W. W. Norton & Company, 2014), 3-4.
4. *Original Sins*, 78.
5. *The Iron Wall: Israel and the Arab World,* 4-5.
6. Imperialist powers as described by Linin, quoted in *Class Struggle*, 158.
7. David M. Halbfinger, "Balfour Declaration of support for Jewish homeland still divisive at 100," *The New York Times*, November 2, 2017.
8. *Promise and Fulfillment*, 3.
9. *Original Sins*, 66.
10. *A Peace to End All Peace,* 292.

11. *Original Sins*, 37.
12. *Original Sins*, 195.
13. *A Peace to End All Peace*, 292.
14. *A Peace to End All Peace*, 292.
15. *A Peace to End All Peace*, 292.
16. *Old New Land*, 28.
17. *Original Sins*, 59.
18. *Original Sins*, 59.
19. Jonathan Schneer, "The Balfour Declaration: A Hundred Years On," *Foreign Affairs*, November 2, 2017.
20. *The Iron Wall: Israel and the Arab World*, 11.
21. *The Iron Wall: Israel and the Arab World*, 11.
22. Vladimir Ze'ev Jabotinsky, *The Iron Wall*, November, 1923, http://www.marxists.de/middleast/ironwall/ironwall.htm
23. *The Iron Wall: Israel and the Arab World*, 16-17.
24. *The Iron Wall: Israel and the Arab World*, 19.
25. *The Iron Wall: Israel and the Arab World*, 19-20.
26. *The Iron Wall: Israel and the Arab World*, 19-20.
27. *The Iron Wall: Israel and the Arab World*, 22-23.
28. *Original Sins*, 72.
29. *Original Sins*, 81.
30. *The Israeli Connection*, 179.
31. *Original Sins*, 81.
32. *Nasser, The Last Arab*, 25.
33. *Nasser, The Last Arab*, 24- 25.
34. Said K. Aburish, *Saddam Hussein: The Politics of Revenge*, (Bloomsbury, 2001), 33.
35. Said K. Aburish, *A Brutal Friendship: The West and the Arab Elite*, (Victor Gollancz, 1997), 32, 163.
36. *A Brutal Friendship*, 96.
37. Ishaan Tharoor, "The dark side of Winston Churchill's legacy no one should forget," *The Washington Post*, February 3, 2015.
38. Tom Heyden, "The 10 greatest controversies of Winston Churchill's career," *BBC News Magazine*, January 26, 2015.
39. "Israel, Palestine and what a Curzon declaration might have looked like," *The Guardian*, October 13, 2017.
40. *The Israeli Connection*, 21.

Chapter Four. Imperialism

1. Graham E. Fuller, *A World Without Islam* (Little, Brown & Company, 2010), 252-253.
2. Martin Gilens and Benjamin I. Page, "Testing Theories of American Politics: Elites, Interest Groups, and Average Citizens," *Perspectives on Politics*, Fall 2014
3. Zbigniew Brzezinski, *The Grand Chessboard: American Primacy and its Geostrategic Imperatives*, (Basic Books, 1997), 40.

4. Alan Taylor, *Colonial America: A Very Short introduction*, (Oxford University Press, 2013), 122.

5. *Colonial America*, 123.

6. Quoted in Noam Chomsky, *Fateful Triangle: The United States, Israel, and the Palestinians*, (Pluto Press, 1999), 61.

7. Robert Dreyfus, "Next we take Iran," *Mother Jones*, July/August 2006.

8. Arno J. Mayer, *Plowshares into Swords: From Zionism to Israel*, (Verso, 2008), 5.

9. Patrick Cockburn, "How the disappearance of a journalist and a humiliating remark by Trump shows Saudi Arabia's weakness," *The Independent*, October 5, 2018.

10. Stephanie Yang and Amrith Ramkumar, "In oil's huge drop, all signs say made in the U.S.A.," *The Wall Street Journal*, November 23, 2018.

11. Noam Chomsky, "The imperial way: American decline in perspective, part 2," *tomdispatch.com*, February 15, 2012.

12. "Oil dependence and US foreign policy," *The Council on Foreign Relations*, https://www.cfr.org/timeline/oil-dependence-and-us-foreign-policy

13. "Where Does America Get Oil? You May Be Surprised," *NPR*, April 12, 2012.

14. Rick Perry, "The world can live without Iranian oil," *The Wall Street Journal*, November 4, 2018.

15. Sarah McFarlane, "Iran sanctions won't fuel oil prices for long," *The Wall Street Journal*, November 3, 2018.

16. Stephanie Yang and Amrith Ramkumar, "In oil's huge drop, all signs say made in the U.S.A.," *The Wall Street Journal*, November 23, 2018.

17. Robert Dreyfus, "The thirty-year itch," *Mother Jones*, March/April 2003.

18. Emre Peker, "Trump slams Germany over gas imports from Germany," *The Wall Street Journal*, July 11, 2018.

19. Bojan Pancevski and Emre Peker, "US opposition to pipeline hangs over meeting between Putin and Merkel," *The Wall Street Journal*, August 18, 2018.

20. Emre Peker, "Trump slams Germany over gas imports from Germany," *The Wall Street Journal*, July 11, 2018.

21. Bojan Pancevski, "Trump Presses Germany to Drop Russian Pipeline for Trade Deal," *The Wall Street Journal*, May 17, 2018.

22. Noam Chomsky, *How the World Works*, (Soft Skull Press, 2011, 24.

Chapter Five. Division

1. Leila Khaled (with George Hajjar), *My People Shall Live: The Autobiography of a Revolutionary*,(Hodder and Stoughton. 1973), 165-166.

2. *Nasser, The Last Arab*, 184.

3. *Saddam Hussein*, 58.

4. *Nasser, The Last Arab*, 143.

5. *Saddam Hussein*, 100.

6. *Saddam Hussein*, 272.

7. Steven Mufson, "Conflict in Libya: U.S. oil companies sit on sidelines as Gaddafi maintains hold," *The Washington Post*, June 10, 2011.

8. Robert Fisk, "9/11 remembered: Robert Fisk's close encounter with Osama bin Laden, the man who shook the world," *The Independent*, September 11, 2018.

9. Quoted in Tariq Ali, "Blinded by Israel, Visionless in Gaza," *Counterpunch*, July 23, 2014.

10. Quoted in Tariq Ali, "Blinded by Israel, Visionless in Gaza," *Counterpunch*, July 23, 2014.

11. *Saddam Hussein*, 33.

12. *Nasser, The Last Arab*, 173.

13. *Nasser, The Last Arab*, 93.

14. *Saddam Hussein*, 7.

15. *Saddam Hussein*, 25.

16. Majeed Gly, "A word from Mr. Kurd," *The Wall Street Journal*, October 1, 2018.

17. *A Brutal Friendship*, 16.

18. *The Israeli Connection*, 5.

19. *The Israeli Connection*, 8.

20. *My People Shall Live*, 44.

21. *Nasser, The Last Arab*, 247.

Chapter Six. Nasserism

1. *Original Sins*, 66.

2. Sven Lindqvist, *A History of Bombing*, (The New Press, 2000), 18.

3. *Nasser, The Last Arab*, 14.

4. *Nasser, The Last Arab*, 14.

5. Yevgeny Primakov, *Russia and the Arabs: Behind the Scenes in the Middle East from the Cold War to the Present*, (Basic Books, 2009), 4-5.

6. *Nasser, The Last Arab*, 36.

7. *Nasser, The Last Arab*, 8; Tarek Osman, *Egypt on the Brink*, (Yale University Press, 2010), 45.

8. Raymond Carroll, *Anwar Sadat*, (F. Watts, 1982), 38.

9. *Russia and the Arabs*, 83.

10. *Nasser, The Last Arab*, 132.

11. *Nasser, The Last Arab*, 109; *Plowshares into Swords*, 246.

12. *My People Shall Live*, 44.

13. Robert Fisk, "Old Crisis, New Lesson," *Counterpunch*, January 15, 2003.

14. *Nasser, The Last Arab*, 233.

15. *Nasser, The Last Arab*, 111.

16. *Plowshares into Swords*, 246.

17. *Nasser, The Last Arab*, 233.

18. Robert Fisk, "Old Crisis, New Lesson," *Counterpunch*, January 15, 2003.

19. *Nasser, The Last Arab*, 161.

20. *Nasser, The Last Arab*, 144.

21. *Nasser, The Last Arab*, 103.

22. *Nasser, The Last Arab*, 87.

23. *Nasser, The Last Arab*, 80.

24. *Nasser, The Last Arab*, 146.

25. *Nasser, The Last Arab*, 130.

26. *Nasser, The Last Arab*, 97.

27. *Nasser, The Last Arab*, 97.

28. *Nasser, The Last Arab*, 60.

29. *Nasser, The Last Arab*, 196.

30. *Nasser, The Last Arab*, 229.

31. *Nasser, The Last Arab*, 232.

32. *A Brutal Friendship*, 33.

33. *A Brutal Friendship*, 33.

34. *Nasser, The Last Arab*, 150.

35. *Nasser, The Last Arab*, 103.

36. Bob Woodward, *Obama's Wars*, (Simon & Schuster, 2010), 53.

37. *Nasser, The Last Arab*, 233.

38. *A Brutal Friendship*, 92.

39. *Nasser, The Last Arab*, 100.

40. Statement of the Proclamation of the Organization, May 28, 1964. https://web.archive.org/web/20111211172543/http://www.un.int/wcm/content/site/palestine/pid/12355

41. Gamal Abdel Nasser, *The Philosophy of the Revolution*, (Mondale Press, 1955), 69.

42. *Nasser, The Last Arab*, 233.

43. *Nasser, The Last Arab*, 88.

44. *Nasser, The Last Arab*, 81, 143.

45. *Nasser, The Last Arab*, 193.

46. *Nasser, The Last Arab*, 175.

47. *Saddam Hussein*, 41.

48. *My People Shall Live*, 56-57.

49. See *Class Struggle*.

50. *Class Struggle*, 19.

51. *Class Struggle*, 12.

52. *War and Revolution*, 291.

53. Domenico Losurdo: 'Liberalism, the most dogged enemy of freedom'," *Verso Books*, July 16, 2018.

54. *Nasser, The Last Arab*, 139-140.

55. *Nasser, The Last Arab*, 201.

56. *Nasser, The Last Arab*, 140.

57. Keith Wheelock, *Nasser's New Egypt*, (Praeger, 1960), 132.

58. *Nasser, The Last Arab*, 237.

59. *Nasser, The Last Arab*, 139.

60. *Nasser, The Last Arab*, 138.

61. *Russia and the Arabs*, 11.

62. *Russia and the Arabs*, 11.

63. *My People Shall Live*, 74.

64. *How the World Works*, 12.

65. *Nasser, The Last Arab*, 128.

66. *Nasser, The Last Arab*, 91.

67. *Nasser, The Last Arab*, 46, 50-51.

68. Robert Dreyfus, "Cold war, holy warrior," *Mother Jones*, January/February 2006.

69. *Nasser, The Last Arab*, 48, 89.

70. Robert Dreyfus, "Cold war, holy warrior," *Mother Jones*, January/February 2006.

71. Robert Dreyfus, "Cold war, holy warrior," *Mother Jones*, January/February 2006.

72. Robert Dreyfus, "Cold war, holy warrior," *Mother Jones*, January/February 2006.

73. *Nasser, The Last Arab*, 303.

74. Robert Dreyfus, "Cold war, holy warrior," *Mother Jones*, January/February 2006.

75. *Nasser, The Last Arab*, 264.

76. *Nasser, The Last Arab*, 128.

77. *Nasser, The Last Arab*, 198-199.

78. *Nasser, The Last Arab*, 256.

79. *Nasser, The Last Arab*, 316.

80. *The Israeli Connection*, 5-6.

81. *Plowshares into Swords*, 2.

82. Adam Shatz, "The sea is the same sea," *The London Review of Books*, Vol. 40 No. 16, 30 August 2018.

83. *The Israeli Connection*, 21.

84. *The Israeli Connection*, 5.

85. *Nasser, The Last Arab*, 72, 99.

Chapter Seven. *Naksa*

1. *Nasser, The Last Arab*, 250.

2. *The Devil's Chessboard*, 2.

3. *Plowshares into Swords*, 246.

4. V. G. Kiernan, *America, The New imperialism: From White Settlement to World Hegemony*, (Verso, 2005), 310.

5. *America, The New imperialism*, 310.

6. *Plowshares into Swords*, 246.

7. *Ibid*, 246.

8. *Fateful Triangle*, 65.

9. *Nasser, The Last Arab*, 94.

10. *Saddam Hussein*, 34.

11. *Nasser, The Last Arab*, 80.

12. *The Israeli Connection*, 5-6.

13. *Nasser, The Last Arab*, 111.

14. *Ibid*, 109.

15. *The Israeli Connection*, 190.

16. *Ibid*, 190.

17. *Ibid*, 190.

18. *Plowshares into Swords*, 80.

19. *Nasser, the Last Arab*, 109.

20. *Ibid*, 109.

21. *The Israeli Connection*, 5.

22. *Plowshares into Swords*, 248.

23. *Ibid, 147.*

24. *Nasser, The Last Arab,* 127.

25. Salim Yaqub, *Containing Arab Nationalism: The Eisenhower Doctrine and the Middle East,* (University of North Caroline Press, 2004), 1-2.

26. *The Israeli Connection,* 187.

27. *Russia and the Arabs,* 3.

28. National Security Strategy of the United States, White House, March, 1990, p. 13, http://nssarchive.us/NSSR/1990.pdf

29. *Nasser, The Last Arab,* 247.

30. *Ibid, 4.*

31. *Ibid, 316.*

32. *My People Shall Live,* 44.

33. *Nasser, The Last Arab,* 90.

34. *Ibid, 90.*

35. *Ibid, 168.*

36. *Ibid, 112.*

37. CNN, October 21, 1997, http://edition.cnn.com/WORLD/9710/21/mandela.trip/

38. Al Arabiya English, November 27, 2016.

39. "President of Venezuela Hugo Chavez: Israel Uses the Methods of Hitler, the U.S. Uses the Methods of Dracula. I'm a Nasserist who Has Crossed the Deserts, Ridden Camels, and Sung Along with the Bedouins. Al-Jazeera Plays a Role in Liberating the World," Middle East Media Research Institute TV Monitor Project, August 4, 2006, https://www.memri.org/tv/president-venezuela-hugo-chavez-israel-uses-methods-hitler-us-uses-methods-dracula-im-nasserist/transcript August 4, 2006.

40. *Nasser, The Last Arab,* 102.

41. *Ibid, 146.*

42. *Ibid, 247.*

43. *Ibid, 210.*

44. *Ibid, 257.*

45. *The Israeli Connection,* 18.

46. *Nasser, The Last Arab,* 251.

47. William J. Broad and David E. Sanger, "Last secret' of 1967 war: Israel's doomsday plan for nuclear display," *The New York Times,* June 3, 2017.

48. *The Israeli Connection,* 19.

49. *Nasser, The Last Arab,* 252.

50. *Ibid, 253.*

51. *Ibid, 253.*

52. *Ibid, 255.*

53. Khalid Amayreh, "The 1967-war revisited (Part I)," *The Palestinian Information Center,* June 6, 2009.

54. Khalid Amayreh, "The 1967-war revisited (Part I)," *The Palestinian Information Center,* June 6, 2009.

55. *Nasser, The Last Arab,* 255.

56. *Ibid, 258.*

57. *Ibid, 256.*

58. *Ibid, 260.*

59. *Ibid,* 260.
60. *Ibid,* 264.
61. *My People Shall Live,* 103.
62. "Strategy for the Liberation of Palestine", *Popular Front for the Liberation of Palestine,* February, 1969.
63. *Nasser, The Last Arab,* 247.
64. *Ibid,* 281.
65. *My People Shall Live,* 97.
66. *Nasser, The Last Arab,* 250.
67. *My People Shall Live,* 56.
68. *Nasser, The Last Arab,* 145.
69. *Ibid,* 276.
70. *Ibid,* 280.
71. *Ibid,* 292.
72. *The Israeli Connection,* 105.
73. *Ibid,* 160-161.
74. *Ibid,* 167.
75. *Hegemony or Survival,* 164-165.
76. *The Israeli Connection,* 5.
77. Abu-Manneh Bashir, "Israel in the US Empire," *Monthly Review,* March 1, 2007.
78. Noam Chomsky, "The imperial way: American decline in perspective, part 2," *tomdispatch.com,* February 15, 2012.
79. *Original Sins,* 67.
80. Virtual Jewish Library, https://www.jewishvirtuallibrary.org/total-u-s-foreign-aid-to-israel-1949-present .
81. Noam Chomsky, "The Israel Lobby?" *ZNet,* March 28, 2016.
82. *Saddam Hussein,* 90-91; Abu-Manneh Bashir, "Israel in the US Empire," *Monthly Review,* March 1, 2007.
83. *Hegemony or Survival,* 165.

Chapter Eight. Progress

1. In *Les Miserables,* Hugo wrote of the French Revolution, "From its cruelest blows there resulted a caress for the human race." Henri Barbusse, *Stalin: A New World Seen Through One Man,* (Read Books, 2011), 83.
2. *The Israeli Connection,* 199.
3. *The Israeli Connection,* 179.
4. Karl Marx. *Capital: A Critique of Political Economy.* Volume 1. Chapter 31.
5. Svend Beckert, "How the west got rich and modern capitalism was born," *PBS Newshour,* February 13, 2015.
6. Svend Beckert, "How the west got rich and modern capitalism was born," *PBS Newshour,* February 13, 2015.
7. Lenin's definition of imperialism, quoted in *Class Struggle,* 158.
8. *A Brutal Friendship,* 83.
9. *Hegemony or Survival,* 165-166.

10. *The Israeli Connection,* 6-7.
11. *Hegemony or Survival,* 166.
12. *A Brutal Friendship,* 84.
13. *A Brutal Friendship,* 83.
14. *Saddam Hussein,* 106.
15. *A Brutal Friendship,* 84.
16. Abu-Manneh Bashir, "Israel in the US Empire," *Monthly Review,* March 1, 2007.
17. Michael Peck, "The time America almost invaded OPEC," *The National interest,* April 10, 2014.
18. Henry Kissinger (Miles Ignotus), "Seizing Arab oil," *Harper's,* March 1975; Robert Dreyfus, "The thirty-year itch," *Mother Jones,* March/April 2003.
19. Walter Isaacson, "Madeleine's War," *Time,* May 17, 1999.

Chapter Nine. Saddam

1. *Saddam Hussein,* 100.
2. David N. Gibbs, "Afghanistan: The Soviet Invasion in Retrospect," *International Politics* 37.2 (2000): 241-242.
3. Christopher van Hollen, "Don't engulf the Gulf," *Foreign Affairs,* June 1, 1981.
4. *Fateful Triangle,* 63-64.
5. Bruce Franklin (Ed.), *The Essential Stalin: Major Theoretical Writings, 1905-1952,* (Doubleday Anchor, 1972), 3.
6. Tim Beal, "From the enthusiasm of Churchill to the manipulation of Trump: The covert dangers of chemical warfare," *Covert Action Magazine,* December 8, 2018.
7. *Saddam Hussein,* 96.
8. *Saddam Hussein,* 119.
9. *Saddam Hussein,* 92.
10. *Saddam Hussein,* 99.
11. *Saddam Hussein,* 100.
12. *Saddam Hussein,* 100.
13. *A Brutal Friendship,* 86-87.
14. *Saddam Hussein,* 106.
15. *Saddam Hussein,* 110.
16. *Saddam Hussein,* 111.
17. *Saddam Hussein,* 111.
18. *Saddam Hussein,* 114.
19. *Saddam Hussein,* 114.
20. *A Brutal Friendship,* 42.
21. *Saddam Hussein,* 182.
22. *Saddam Hussein,* 182.
23. *Saddam Hussein,* 117.
24. *Saddam Hussein,* 118-119.
25. *Saddam Hussein,* 119.
26. *Saddam Hussein,* 128.
27. *Saddam Hussein,* 129.

28. *Saddam Hussein,* 129-130.
29. *Saddam Hussein,* 132.
30. *Saddam Hussein,* 274.
31. John Ellis, *The Social History of the Machine Gun,* (Arno Press, 1981), 86.
32. Dave Lindorff , "McMaster of War," *LRB blog,* 19 February 2018.
33. National Security Strategy 2017.
34. *Original Sins,* 86.
35. *Original Sins,* 183.
36. Ethan Bronner, "Israel senses bluffing in Iran's threats of retaliation", *The New York Times,* January 26, 2012
37. *Saddam Hussein,* 140.
38. *Saddam Hussein,* 140.
39. *Saddam Hussein,* 187.
40. *Saddam Hussein,* 205.
41. Tom Mayer, "Zionism, Imperialism, and Socialism", *Monthly Review,* November 1, 2013.
42. *Saddam Hussein,* 147.

Chapter Ten. Syria

1. Daniel Pipes, "Palestine for the Syrians?" *Commentary,* December 1986.
2. Daniel Pipes, "Palestine for the Syrians?" *Commentary,* December 1986.
3. *A Brutal Friendship,* 28.
4. Daniel Pipes, "Palestine for the Syrians?" *Commentary,* December 1986.
5. Daniel Pipes, "Syria's imperial Dream: Foreign adventure shore up Assad's regime," *The New Republic,* June 9, 1986.
6. Daniel Pipes, "Palestine for the Syrians?" *Commentary,* December 1986.
7. Daniel Pipes, "Palestine for the Syrians?" *Commentary,* December 1986
8. Daniel Pipes, "Palestine for the Syrians?" *Commentary,* December 1986.
9. Daniel Pipes, "Palestine for the Syrians?" *Commentary,* December 1986.
10. Daniel Pipes, "Syria's imperial Dream: Foreign adventure shore up Assad's regime," *The New Republic,* June 9, 1986.
11. *A Brutal Friendship,* 176.
12. Daniel Pipes, "Palestine for the Syrians?" *Commentary,* December 1986.
13. *A Brutal Friendship,* 98.
14. Daniel Pipes, "Palestine for the Syrians?" *Commentary,* December 1986.
15. *A Brutal Friendship,* 28.
16. Daniel Pipes, "Syria's imperial Dream: Foreign adventure shore up Assad's regime," *The New Republic,* June 9, 1986.
17. *Nasser, The Last Arab,* 163.
18. Robert A. Pape, *Dying to Win: The Structural Logic of Suicide Terrorism,* (Random House, 2006), 156.
19. *The Israeli Connection,* 20.
20. *The Israeli Connection,* 19-20.
21. *The Israeli Connection,* 20.

22. *The Israeli Connection,* 21.

23. Robert Fisk, "I traced missile casings in Syria back to their original sellers, so it's time for the west to reveal who they sell arms to," *The Independent,* July 23, 2018.

24. *Dying to Win,* 131.

25. *Hegemony or Survival,* 166.

26. Abu-Manneh Bashir, "Israel in the US Empire," *Monthly Review,* March 1, 2007.

27. *Dying to Win,* 131.

28. *Dying to Win,* 131.

29. *Dying to Win,* 131-132.

30. *Dying to Win,* 31.

31. *Dying to Win,* 136.

32. *Dying to Win,* 137.

33. *Dying to Win,* 137.

34. *Dying to Win,* 136-137.

35. *Dying to Win,* 136-137.

36. Tomis Kapitan in Richard Fumerton and Diane Jeske, eds. "Can Terrorism be Justified?" *Readings in Political Philosophy* (Broadview Press, 2011), 1068-1087.

37. Tomis Kapitan in Richard Fumerton and Diane Jeske, eds. "Can Terrorism be Justified?" *Readings in Political Philosophy* (Broadview Press, 2011), 1068-1087.

38. Can Terrorism be Justified?

39. Adapting the words of Arno J. Mayer, *The Furies,* 118.

40. See Stephen Gowans, *Patriots, Traitors and Empires: The Story of Korea's Struggle for Freedom,* (Baraka Books, 2018), Chapter 14.

41. Barbara Crossette, "Iraq sanctions kill children, UN reports," *The New York Times,* December 1, 1996.

42. John Mueller and Karl Mueller, "Sanctions of Mass Destruction," *Foreign Affairs,* May/June 1999.

43. *Class Struggle,* 250.

44. Can Terrorism be Justified?

45. Can Terrorism be Justified?

46. *Dying to Win,* 132.

Chapter Eleven. Settlers

1. *The Israeli Connection,* 161.

2. Benjamin Beit-Hallahmi, "The Israel Connection," *The New York Review of Books,* November 19, 1987.

3. Quoted in Domenico Losurdo, "What is fundamentalism?" *Nature, Science, and Thought,* vol. 17, no. 1 (2004)

4. *War and Revolution,* 184.

5. Michael Taube, "'Little House' has been condemned," *The Wall Street Journal,* July 4, 2018.

6. Tom Heyden, "The 10 greatest controversies of Winston Churchill's career," *BBC News Magazine,* January 26, 2015.

7. Aimé Césaire, *Discourse on Colonialism,* (Monthly Review Press, 2000), 36.

8. The phrase: 'what was done in the heart of darkness Hitler did in the heart of Europe' is based on Sven Lindqvist, *The Dead Do Not Die: Exterminate All The Brutes and Terra Nullius, The New Press*, 2014, p. 178.

9. *War and Revolution*, 284.

10. *War and Revolution*, 286.

11. Jeffrey D. Sachs, "Ending America's war of choice in the Middle East," *Horizons: Journal of the Center for international Relations and Sustainable Development*, Spring, 2018.

12. Domenico Losurdo, "What is fundamentalism?" *Nature, Science, and Thought*, vol. 17, no. 1 (2004).

13. *The Israeli Connection*, 147.

14. *The Israeli Connection*, 161.

15. Quoted in *War and Revolution*, 235-236.

16. *War and Revolution*, 236-237.

17. *War and Revolution*, 263-264.

18. *The Israeli Connection*, 112.

19. *The Israeli Connection*, 160-161.

20. Gal Berkman, "Writer takes controversial look at Israel-South Africa ties," *Forward*, June 9, 2010.

21. *The Israeli Connection*, 147.

22. *The Israeli Connection*, 159.

23. Resolution 77 (XII) of the Organization of African Unity, adopted in 1975.

24. *The Israeli Connection*, 159.

25. Chris McGreal, "Revealed: how Israel offered to sell South Africa nuclear weapons," *The Guardian*, May 24, 2010.

26. *The Israeli Connection*, 166.

27. *The Israeli Connection*, 109.

28. *The Israeli Connection*, 118.

29. *The Israeli Connection*, 121.

30. *The Israeli Connection*, 121.

31. *The Israeli Connection*, 121.

32. *The Israeli Connection*, 130.

33. Chris McGreal, "Revealed: how Israel offered to sell South Africa nuclear weapons," *The Guardian*, May 24, 2010.

34. *The Israeli Connection*, 133.

35. Gal Berkman, "Writer takes controversial look at Israel-South Africa ties," *Forward*, June 9, 2010.

36. *The Israeli Connection*, 132.

37. *The Israeli Connection*, 132.

38. *The Israeli Connection*, 140.

39. *Original Sins*, 72.

40. *The Israeli Connection*, 140.

41. *The Israeli Connection*, 63.

Chapter Twelve. Iran

1. "President of Venezuela Hugo Chavez: Israel Uses the Methods of Hitler, the U.S. Uses the Methods of Dracula. I'm a Nasserist who Has Crossed the Deserts, Ridden Camels, and Sung Along with the Bedouins. Al-Jazeera Plays a Role in Liberating the World," Middle East Media Research Institute TV Monitor Project, August 4, 2006, https://www.memri.org/tv/president-venezuela-hugo-chavez-israel-uses-methods-hitler-us-uses-methods-dracula-im-nasserist/transcript August 4, 2006.
2. Thomas Erdbrink, "Iranians see little hope elections will alleviate economic strain," *The New York Times*, May 15, 2017.
3. William R. Polk, *Understanding Iran: Everything You Need to Know, From Persia to the Islamic Republic, From Cyrus to Ahmadinejad,* (Palgrave MacMillan), 2009, 212.
4. "Iranian car lines keep rolling despite sanctions" *Reuters*, June 29, 2011.
5. Asa Fitch and Jared Malsin, "Behind Iran's protests: A struggling economy despite sanctions relief," *The Wall Street Journal*, January 3, 2018.
6. "Discord is enemy's tool to dominate Muslim nations: Ayatollah Khamenei," *Khamanei.ir*, December 17, 2016.
7. "We are with every group that is steadfast on the path of Resistance: Ayatollah Khamenei," *Khamanei.ir*.
8. Howard Schneider, "Iran, Syria mock U.S. policy, Ahmadinejad speaks of Israel's 'annihilation'", *The Washington Post*, February 26, 2010.
9. Thomas Erdbrink, "Iranians once shrugged off Trump's bluster. Now they worried." *The New York Times*, February 9, 2017.
10. John McCain, "John McCain: I choose the Kurds," *The New York Times*, October 24, 2017.
11. *Saddam Hussein*, 2.
12. *Saddam Hussein*, 5-6.
13. *Saddam Hussein*, 27.
14. *Saddam Hussein*, 7.
15. *Saddam Hussein*, 163.
16. *Saddam Hussein*, 166.
17. *Saddam Hussein*, 166-167.
18. *Saddam Hussein*, 186.
19. *Saddam Hussein*, 191.
20. *Saddam Hussein*, 199.
21. *Saddam Hussein*, 183-184.
22. *Saddam Hussein*, 185.
23. *Saddam Hussein*, 210.
24. *Saddam Hussein*, 189.
25. *Saddam Hussein*, 204.
26. *Saddam Hussein*, 210.
27. *Saddam Hussein*, 245.
28. *Saddam Hussein*, 247.
29. *Saddam Hussein*, 221.
30. *Saddam Hussein*, 229.
31. *Saddam Hussein*, 252.

32. *Saddam Hussein*, 246.

33. *Saddam Hussein*, 204.

34. *Saddam Hussein*, 205.

35. *Saddam Hussein*, 199.

36. *Saddam Hussein*, 259.

37. *Saddam Hussein*, 252.

38. *Saddam Hussein*, 252.

39. *Saddam Hussein*, 260.

40. *Saddam Hussein*, 261.

41. *Saddam Hussein*, 269-270.

42. *Saddam Hussein*, 269-272.

43. *Saddam Hussein*, 278.

44. *Saddam Hussein*, 279.

45. *Saddam Hussein*, 281-282.

46. *Saddam Hussein*, 282.

47. Said K. Aburish, *The Rise, Corruption and Coming Fall of the House of Saud*, (Bloomsbury, 2005), 3.

48. *Saddam Hussein*, 290-291.

49. Robert Dreyfus, "The thirty-year itch," *Mother Jones*, March/April 2003.

50. *Dying to Win*, 124.

51. Robert Fisk, "9/11 remembered: Robert Fisk's close encounter with Osama bin Laden, the man who shook the world," *The Independent*, September 11, 2018.

52. *Dying to Win*, 114.

53. *Dying to Win*, 117.

54. Quoted in Jeffrey D. Sachs, "Ending America's war of choice in the Middle East," *Horizons: Journal of the Center for international Relations and Sustainable Development*, Spring, 2018.

55. *Fear*, 109.

56. Mohsen M. Milsani, "Tehran's Take: Understanding Iran's U.S. policy," *Foreign Affairs*, July/August 2009.

57. Thomas Erdbrink, "Hard-liners and reformers tapped Iranians' ire, both are protest targets." *The New York Times*, January 2, 2018.

58. Barbara Opall-Rome, "Israeli defense minister seeks defense budget boost," *Defense News*, November 22, 2017.

59. Nazila Fathi, "Wipe Israel 'off the map' Iranian says," *The New York Times*, October 27, 2005.

60. Glenn Kessler, "Did Ahmadinejad really say Israel should be 'wiped off the map'?" *The Washington Post*, October 6, 2011.

61. Glenn Kessler, "Did Ahmadinejad really say Israel should be 'wiped off the map'?" *The Washington Post*, October 6, 2011.

62. Isabel Kershner, "Israeli strike on Iran would be 'stupid,' ex-spy chief says", *The New York Times*, May 8, 2011.

63. Isabel Kershner, "Israelis fear fallout from Netanyahu's blunt comments," *The New York Times*, September 12, 2012.

64. Thomas Erdbrink and Jodi Rudoren, "U.N. nuclear monitor meets leading Iranians", *The New York Times*, May 21, 2012.

65. Joel Greenberg, "Benjamin Netanyahu invokes Holocaust in push against Iran", *The Washington Post*, February 29, 2012.

66. Joel Greenberg, "Benjamin Netanyahu invokes Holocaust in push against Iran", *The Washington Post*, February 29, 2012.

67. Barak Ravid "Mossad chief: Nuclear Iran not necessarily existential threat to Israel," *Haaretz*, December 29, 2011.

68. *Haaretz.com* (Israel), October 25, 2007; print edition October 26, cited in William Blum, The Anti-Empire Report, February 3, 2012.

69. Carol E. Lee and Jay Solomon, "U.S. considers new message on Iran", *The Wall Street Journal*, February 28, 2012.

70. *New York Times*, June 4, 2008, cited by Mazda Majidi, "What lies behind US policy toward Iran?" *Party for Socialism and Liberation*, June 12, 2008.

71. Guardian (UK), June 6, 2008 cited by Mazda Majidi, "What lies behind US policy toward Iran?" *Party for Socialism and Liberation*, June 12, 2008.

72. Helene Cooper, "Bush may end term with Iran issue unsettled," *The New York Times*, June 21, 2008.

73. Benny Morris, "Using Bombs to Stave Off War," *The New York Times*, July 18, 2008.

74. Mark Landler, "Iran policy now more in sync with Clinton's views," *The New York Times*, February 17, 2010.

75. Ethan Bronner, "Israel sense bluffing in Iran's threats of retaliation", *The New York Times*, January 26, 2012.

76. Ethan Bronner, "Israel sense bluffing in Iran's threats of retaliation", *The New York Times*, January 26, 2012.

77. Thom Shanker, "U.S. quietly supplies Israel with bunker-buster bombs", *The New York Times*, September 23, 2011.

78. Adam Entous and Julian E. Barnes, "Pentagon seeks mightier bomb vs. Iran", *The Wall Street Journal*, January 28, 2012.

79. Adam Entous and Julian E. Barnes, "Pentagon bulks up 'bunker buster' bomb to combat Iran", *The Wall Street Journal*, May 2, 2013.

80. David E. Sanger and Nicole Pelroth, "Iran is raising sophistication and frequency of cyberattacks, study says", *The New York Times*, April 15, 2015.

81. Michael R. Gordon, "Trump administration to close Palestine Liberation Organization office in Washington," *The Wall Street Journal*, September 10, 2018.

82. Mark Landler, "Trump's Twitter threat vs. Iran: Loud but hardly clear," *The New York Times*, July 23, 2018.

83. David E. Sanger and Gardiner Harris, "'America First' bears a new threat: military force," *The New York Times*, March 24, 2018.

84. John R. Bolton, "To stop Iran's bomb, bomb Iran," *The New York Times*, March 26, 2018.

85. Bob Woodward, *Fear: Trump in the White House*, (Simon & Schuster, 2018), 50.

86. *Fear*, 53.

87. Mark Perry, "James Mattis' 33-year grudge against Iran," *Politico*, December 4, 2016.

88. *Fear*, 83.

89. Mehdi Hasan, "Trump 'moderate' Defense Secretary has already brought us to the brink of war," *The Intercept*, March 1, 2017.

90. Scott Shane, "Adversaries of Iran said to be stepping up covert actions", *The New York Times*, January 11, 2012.

91. Artin Afkhami, "Tehran abuzz as book says Israel killed 5 scientists," *The New York Times*, July 11, 2012.

92. Ronen Bergman, "Israel's secret war with Iran," *The Wall Street Journal*, May 16, 2009.

93. Adam Entous and Danny Yadron, "U.S. spy net on Israel snares Congress," *The Wall Street Journal*, December 29, 2015.

94. William J. Broad, John Markoff and David E. Sanger, "Israel tests on worm called crucial in Iran nuclear delay", *The New York Times*, January 15, 2011.

95. Ellen Nakashima, Greg Miller and Julie Tate, "U.S., Israel developed Flame computer virus to slow Iranian nuclear efforts, officials say", *The Washington Post*, June 19, 2012.

96. *Nasser, The Last Arab*, 151.

97. *A Brutal Friendship*, 19.

98. *A Brutal Friendship*, 62.

99. *A Brutal Friendship*, 52.

100. Stephen Gowans, *Washington's Long War on Syria*, (Baraka Books, 2017), 98-99.

101. Stephen Gowans, *Washington's Long War on Syria*, (Baraka Books, 2017), 98-99.

102. Stephen Gowans, *Washington's Long War on Syria*, (Baraka Books, 2017), 98-99.

103. Stephen Gowans, *Washington's Long War on Syria*, (Baraka Books, 2017), 98-99.

104. Robert Dreyfus, "Political Islam vs. democracy," *Mother Jones*, November 29, 2005.

105. Anna Ahronheim, "IDF confirms: Israel provided light-weapons to Syrian rebels," *The Jerusalem Post*, September 4, 2018.

106. Rory Jones, Noam Raydan and Suha Ma'ayeh, "Israel gives secret aid to Syrian rebels," *The Wall Street Journal*, June 18, 2017; Mark MacKinnon, "Israel's mission creep in Syria raises nightmare scenario of wider war," *The Globe and Mail*, March 2, 2018.

107. Ashley Gallagher, "Some wounded Syrians seek treatment from Israeli hospitals", *Al Jazeera America*, March 18, 2014.

108. Isabel Kershner, "Israeli aid gives an unexpected 'glimmer of hope' for Syrians," *The New York Times*, July 20, 2017.

109. Mark MacKinnon, "Israel's mission creep in Syria raises nightmare scenario of wider war," *The Globe and Mail*, March 2, 2018.

110. Robert Fisk, "A view of the Syrian war from the Golan Heights," *The Independent*, November 4, 2016.

111. Mark MacKinnon, "Israel's mission creep in Syria raises nightmare scenario of wider war," *The Globe and Mail*, March 2, 2018.

112. David Morrison, "Israel complains about violation of its sovereignty while being a serial violator," *Open Democracy*, March 1, 2018; Gregory Shupak, "Painting an Israeli attack on Syria as Israeli 'retaliation'," *Fair.org*, February 21, 2018.

113. Ivan Nechepurenko, "Russia, Turkey and Iran propose conference on postwar Syria's future," *The New York Times*, November 22, 2017.

114. Anne Barnard, Michael R. Gordon and Jodi Rudoren, "Israel targeted Iranian missiles in Syria attack", *The New York Times*, May 4, 2013.

115. Sam Dagher, Nour Malas and Joshua Mitnick, "Strikes in Syria raise alarm", *The Wall Street Journal*, May 5, 2013.

116. Jonathan ., "The battle for Syria's skies will see a move from proxy clashes to direct ones," *The National*, April 29, 2018.

117. Yaroslav Trofimov, "Al Qaeda a lesser evil? Syria war pulls U.S., Israel apart," *The Wall Street Journal*, March 12, 2015.

118. "Syria's president speaks," *Foreign Affairs*, January 25, 2015.

119. Robert Fisk, "Donald Trump hasn't quite thought through his first foreign trip to Saudi Arabia, Israel and the Vatican," *The Independent*, May 6, 2017.

120. Yaroslav Trofimov, "Israel's Main Concern in Syria: Iran, not ISIS," *The Wall Street Journal*, March 17, 2016.

121. Jodi Rudoren, "Israel backs limited strike against Syria", *The New York Times*, September 5, 2013.

122. "President al-Assad to Telesur: Stopping outside support to terrorists and reconciliation among Syrians are means to restore security to Syria," *SANA*, April 27, 2017.

123. Yaroslav Trofimov, "Israel sees rising threat from Iran after ISIS," *The Wall Street Journal*, November 16, 2017.

124. Stephen Gowans, "Washington's Long War on Syria Isn't About to End: On the Contrary, the White House Has Approved Pentagon Plans for More Aggression," *what's left blog*, September 10, 2018; Stephen Gowans, "The (Largely Unrecognized) US Occupation of Syria," *what's left blog*, March 11, 2018.

125. Dov Lieber, "Israel says it destroyed Syrian nuclear reactor in 2007,' *The Wall Street Journal*, March 21, 2018.

126. Jonathan Cook, "US aid deal gives green light to Israel's erasure of Palestine," *counterpunch.org*, September 21, 2016.

Conclusion. Diversion

1. Noam Chomsky, "The Israel Lobby?" *ZNet*, March 28, 2006.

2. Martin Gilens and Benjamin I. Page, "Testing Theories of American Politics: Elites, Interest Groups, and Average Citizens," *Perspectives on Politics*, Fall 2014.

3. Julie Hirschfeld Davis, "Influential pro-Israel group suffers stinging political defeat," *The New York Times*, September 10, 2015.

4. Robert Dreyfus, "Is AIPAC still the chosen one?" *Mother Jones*, September/October, 2009.

5. *Plowshares into Swords*, 30.

6. John Mearsheimer and Stephen Walt, "The Israel Lobby," *London Review of Books*, March 23, 2006.

7. *Dying to Win*, 114.

8. *Dying to Win*, 118.

9. *Dying to Win*, 118.

10. *Dying to Win*, 118.

11. Robert A. Pape, "The strategic logic of suicide terrorism," *American Political Science Review*, (Vol. 97, No. 3, August 2003).

12. *The Israeli Connection*, 184.

13. *My People Shall Live*, 128.

14. John Mearsheimer and Stephen Walt, "The Israel Lobby," *London Review of Books*, March 23, 2006.

15. *How the World Works*, 21.

16. Noam Chomsky, "The Israel Lobby?" *ZNet*, March 28, 2016.

17. John Mearsheimer and Stephen Walt, "The Israel Lobby," *London Review of Books*, March 23, 2006.

18. https://www.jewishvirtuallibrary.org/total-u-s-foreign-aid-to-israel-1949-present.

19. Peter Baker and Julie Hirschfeld Davis, "U.S. finalizes deal to give Israel $38 billion in military aid," *The New York Times*, September 13, 2016.

20. Loren Thompson, "Why complaints over cost of new class of US aircraft carriers are off the mark," *Forbes.com*, March 24, 2016; George Will, "Is it time for the Navy to reassess the importance of the aircraft carrier?", *The National Review*, October 1, 2015.

21. *The Israeli Connection*, 195-196.

22. "Jesse Helms: Setting the Record Straight," *Middle East Quarterly*, (Volume 2: Number 1, 1995).

23. Jeffrey Goldberg, "Is Israel America's ultimate ally?" *The Atlantic*, April 26, 2011.

24. *The Israeli Connection*, 197.

25. *The Israeli Connection*, 198.

26. *The Israeli Connection*, 196-197.

Index

Abdulaziz Al Saud, King of Saudi
   Arabia, 65
Abdullah I, King of Jordan, 53, 86
Abu Izzidine, Nejla, 115
Abu-Manneh, Bashir, 156
Aburish, Said K.: on Arab defeat, 101; on
   division of Arab world, 76; on Hafez
   al-Assad, 200; on Jordan, 87; on
   Nasser, 80, 84–5, 96, 105, 114–15, 116,
   120; on Saddam Hussein, 144, 145; on
   US foreign policy, 187
Adams, John, 18
Adelson, Sheldon, 197
Afghanistan: Soviet invasion of, 73, 74,
   139–40
Aflaq, Michel, 144
Afrikaner colonial settlements, 168
Ahmadinejad, Mohamed, 182, 193, 194
Alawites, 29, 78–9
Albright, Madeleine, 137
Algeria: independence of, 106; Nasser's
   support of liberation of, 87–8
Amal Movement, 155, 161
Ambroise, Louis Gabriel, 21
American Israel Public Affairs
   Committee (AIPAC), 208, 211
American War of Independence, 169
Anglo-Persian Oil Company, 61
anti-colonial movement, 127–8
anti-Semitism, 10–11, 20–1, 27, 32–3, 39
apartheid, 171
Arab nationalism (Arabism), 70–1, 73,
   121

Arab oil embargo, 134, 135
Arab socialism, 90, 91–2, 93, 94, 111
Arab Spring, 201
Arab world: association with barbarian-
   ism, 37; division of, 14, 73–6, 77, 78,
   79, 89, 97; minorities in, 78–9;
   opposition to US domination, 72–3;
   political movements of, 70–1;
   population of, 74; Soviet Union and,
   66
Arafat, Yasser, 125, 152
al-Assad, Bashar, 16, 80, 94, 200, 201,
   202, 203
al-Assad, Hafez, 95, 151, 152, 153, 201
Axis of Resistance, 163, 199
Aziz, Tariq, 186

Ba'ath Socialist Party, 13–14, 22, 29, 64,
   185
Baghdad Pact, 103–4
Balfour, Arthur James, 19, 44, 45, 54, 81
Balfour Declaration, 19, 34, 44, 45, 46, 54
al-Banna, Hassan, 95, 96
Bannerman, Henry Campbell, 75
Barak, Ehud, 196
Beckert, Sven, 129
Begin, Menachem, 49, 119
Beit-Hallhami, Benjamin: on Israeli-
   Palestinian problem, 169; on Israel's
   foreign policy, 97; on Jewish
   nationality, 46; on Jewish radicalism,
   22, 23, 30; on kibbutz, 175; on
   recognition of Jewish state, 45; on

Kissinger Doctrine, 136; Manifest
Destiny, 63, 110; military capability
of, 147–8; Monroe Doctrine, 63, 110,
140; National Security Strategy, 148,
182–3; oil dependency of, 66, 67, 135;
pan-Arabist threat to, 74–5; political
regime of, 58; self-perception of,
167–8; settler colonialism of, 168;
state-directed terrorism of, 160, 161;
support of Muslim Brotherhood,
95–6; terrorism problem, 209–10
The Unspoken Alliance (Polakow-
Suransky), 171
US Middle East policy: beneficiaries of,
206–7, 207–8; corporate interests and,
69, 206–7, 211; Iran in, 192–3, 196–7,
198; Iraq in, 161; during Iraq-Iran
War, 186–7; Israel's role in, 210, 213;
Judeo-Israeli conspiracy theory of,
205–6, 207, 210, 211; oil as factor of,
68, 214; regional alliances, 73, 106–7;
Saudi Arabia in, 63, 64, 65, 211; Syria
in, 191, 203–4

Van Hollen, Christopher, 140

Walt, Stephen, 208, 210, 211
Weizman, Ezer, 133

Weizmann, Chaim, 44, 49, 106
Western military superiority, 147
Wilder, Laura Ingalls: *Little House on the
Prairie,* 165
Wilson, Woodrow, 19, 47
Winthrop, John, 167, 168
Wolfowitz, Paul, 190, 191
Woodward, Bob, 87
World Zionist Organization, 44

Yamit, colony of, 133
Yom Kippur War. See October War

Zeal for Zion (Goldman), 18
Zionism: as agent of Western imperialism, 41; anti-Semitism and, 32;
apartheid *vs.,* 171; Christian sympa-
thizers of, 17–20; as colonization
project, 12, 34, 36, 132; evolution of, 17;
international recognition of, 45; Jews'
attitude to, 39, 45–6; land question,
33–4, 43; origin of, 10–11, 31; as
pessimistic doctrine, 32–3; political,
10, 17, 19–20, 40, 43; as remedy against
revolutions, 40–1; Revisionist, 47; *vs.*
socialism, 11; sponsors of, 106–7; UN
condemnation of, 128

ALSO AVAILABLE FROM BARAKA BOOKS

Patriots, Traitors and Empires
The Story of Korea's Struggle for Freedom
Stephen Gowans

Washington's Long War on Syria
Stephen Gowans

Slouching Towards Sirte
NATO's War on Libya and Africa
Maximilian C. Forte

The Einstein File
The FBI's Secret War on the World's Most Famous Scientist
Fred Jerome (Forewords by Ajamu Baraka and David Suzuki)

Rwanda and the New Scramble for Africa
From Tragedy to Useful Imperial Fiction
Robin Philpot

Justice Belied
The Unbalanced Scales of International Criminal Justice
John Philpot & Sébastien Chartrand, Editors

Rebel Priest in the Time of Tyrants
Mission to Haiti, Ecuador and Chile
Claude Lacaille

A Distinct Alien Race
The Untold Story of Franco-Americans
Industrialization, Immigration, Religious Strife
David Vermette

Motherhood, The Mother of All Sexism
A Plea for Parental Equality
Marilyse Hamelin